THE UNIVERSITY OF WINCHESTER

Martial Rose Library
Tel: 01962 827306

To be returned on or before the day marked above, subject to recall.

D1470915

A CULTURAL HISTORY OF ANIMALS

GENERAL EDITORS: LINDA KALOF AND BRIGITTE RESL

Volume 1
A CULTURAL HISTORY OF ANIMALS IN ANTIQUITY
Edited by LINDA KALOF

Volume 2
A CULTURAL HISTORY OF ANIMALS IN THE MEDIEVAL AGE
Edited by BRIGITTE RESL

Volume 3
A CULTURAL HISTORY OF ANIMALS IN THE RENAISSANCE
Edited by BRUCE BOEHRER

Volume 4
A CULTURAL HISTORY OF ANIMALS IN THE AGE OF ENLIGHTENMENT
Edited by MATTHEW SENIOR

Volume 5
A CULTURAL HISTORY OF ANIMALS IN THE AGE OF EMPIRE
Edited by KATHLEEN KETE

Volume 6
A CULTURAL HISTORY OF ANIMALS IN THE MODERN AGE
Edited by RANDY MALAMUD

A CULTURAL HISTORY OF ANIMALS

IN THE MODERN AGE

Edited by Randy Malamud

Oxford • New York

For Nina, Jake, Ben, Twinkie, and Snidget

English edition
First published in 2007 by
Berg

Editorial offices:
First Floor, Angel Court, 81 St Clements Street, Oxford OX4 1AW, UK
175 Fifth Avenue, New York, NY 10010, USA

Paperback edition published in 2011
© Randy Malamud 2007, 2011

Berg is the imprint of Oxford International Publishers Ltd.

Library of Congress Cataloging-in-Publication Data

A cultural history of animals / edited by Linda Kalof and Brigitte Resl.
    p. cm.
  Includes bibliographical references and index.
  ISBN-13: 978-1-84520-496-9 (cloth)
  ISBN-10: 1-84520-496-4 (cloth)
  1. Animals and civilization. 2. Human-animal relationships—History. I. Kalof,
Linda. II. Pohl-Resl, Brigitte.

  QL85C85   2007
  590—dc22   2007031782

British Library Cataloguing-in-Publication Data

A catalogue record for this book is available from the British Library.

ISBN 978 1 84520 381 8 (volume 6, cloth)
      978 1 84788 822 8 (volume 6, paper)
      978 1 84520 496 9 (set, cloth)
      978 1 84788 823 5 (set, paper)

Typeset by Apex Publishing, LLC, Madison, WI

Printed in the United Kingdom by the MPG Books Group

www.bergpublishers.com

CONTENTS

ILLUSTRATIONS

CHAPTER 3

CHAPTER 4

CHAPTER 5

CHAPTER 6

CHAPTER 7

SERIES PREFACE

A Cultural History of Animals is a six-volume series reviewing the changing roles of animals in society and culture throughout history. Each volume follows the same basic structure, and begins with an outline account of the main characteristics of the roles of animals in the period under consideration. Following from that, specialists closely examine major aspects of the subject under seven key headings: symbolism, hunting, domestication, entertainment, science, philosophy, and art. The reader, therefore, has the choice between synchronic and diachronic approaches: A single volume can be read to obtain a thorough knowledge of the subject in a given period from a variety of perspectives, or one of the seven main aspects can be followed through time by reading the relevant chapters of all six volumes, thus providing a thematic understanding of changes and developments over the long term.

The six volumes divide the topic as follows:

Volume 1: A Cultural History of Animals in Antiquity (2500 BCE–1000 CE)

Volume 2: A Cultural History of Animals in the Medieval Age (1000–1400)

Volume 3: A Cultural History of Animals in the Renaissance (1400–1600)

Volume 4: A Cultural History of Animals in the Age of Enlightenment (1600–1800)

Volume 5: A Cultural History of Animals in the Age of Empire (1800–1920)

Volume 6: A Cultural History of Animals in the Modern Age (1920–2000)

General Editors, Linda Kalof and Brigitte Resl

Famous Animals in Modern Culture

RANDY MALAMUD

In the twentieth and twenty-first centuries, human culture has become more powerful—and thus, more dangerous to nonhuman animals—than ever before. The scope of modern society is global and instantaneous: ideas, beliefs, trends, and perversions are ubiquitously diffuse. The expansive reach of civilization's technological capabilities leads to global warming, habitat destruction, oil tanker spills, and radioactive and other toxic emissions. And such obvious (physical, chemical, spatial) threats to animals' well-being are accompanied by an array of less immediately apparent incursions into their lives.

Ecologically, a sophisticated international infrastructure facilitates the rampant gluttonous consumption of natural resources. Animals frequently figure as a resource—which is, of course, a cultural frame, and, from animals' point of view, as well as ecologists', a regrettable one. The consequence of constructing the animal-as-resource may literally involve eating, skinning, harvesting, or otherwise physically devouring the animal's body; but the construct may also denote a kind of cultural consumption—watching, framing, representing, characterizing, and reproducing the subject in a certain way—that may comparably devour animals.

Consider animals in our world: Pandas from China are airlifted to zoos in Atlanta and Washington; Chilean sea bass (actually from Antarctica) grace restaurants' tables in New York and London. Skins of baby seals killed in Newfoundland and newborn karakul lamb from Afghanistan are auctioned in Seattle, Toronto, Helsinki, and St. Petersburg, and the finished products are traded at fur fairs in Frankfurt, Hong Kong, Tokyo, and Montreal. South American chinchillas, African civets, and Amazonian parrots command exorbitant prices in the market for exotic pets. An African rhinoceros stars in a commercial for Dodge Durango, and a Bengal tiger in an ad for Dillard's department store.

Amid these and a thousand other postmodern dislocations, the idea of an animal's habitat threatens to become irrelevant, except as a historical curiosity. An animal's cultural context supplants its natural context. Contemporary culture resituates animals by positing that they belong anywhere, which is to say, they belong nowhere. They go where people put them ("go" not in the sense of having any agency or active volition in the process: but as one might say, a lamp "goes" nicely with a particular style of drapery—as an accoutrement, a prop). In "Why Look at Animals?" John Berger writes of the "reduction of the animal."[1]

Today, an animal's cultural image seems to be profoundly malleable, almost infinitely versatile; and this bodes ill because the absence of a fixed, meaningful identity facilitates its dizzying transformation into whatever its culturally imperialistic human fabricators want it to be. In the early nineteenth century, with the invention of zoos, people began taking animals from where they belong and resituating them where they do not belong, but where it is more convenient for people to experience them. In the modern age, cultural habits have reiterated this displacement: overwriting the authentic, natural animal with a script that amuses or benefits or otherwise satisfies our cultural cravings. An animal's existence today—its appearance, its life, its relation to people—is heavily attenuated by the frames imposed upon it and the tableaux arranged inside these frames. My task herein is to deconstruct the frames and problematize the tableaux (the canvases, the stages, the texts) inside those frames where these animals have been placed (painted, written, construed, arranged, stuffed, chained, trained, dissected, imagined) with an iron-fisted sense of entitlement and control on the part of the cultural hegemons, that is, us.

Every element of our biosphere is susceptible to the whims and prejudices of human culture. It is a challenging time to be a nonhuman animal, buffeted amid the frenzy of human existence. It would be comforting to think—as some have propounded—that anguished environmentalists like me are oversensitive Chicken Littles: that animals are mostly oblivious to our cultures; that the so-called wild will survive as it always has; that forest clearings, ozone depletions, extinctions, and the like are insignificant blips, and only self-flattering narcissism makes people presume that animals are affected by our cultural habits and practices. In *The Skeptical Environmentalist*,[2] Bjorn Lomborg rebuts widely argued beliefs that the global environment is progressively getting worse; he would have us believe that "the dogs go on with their doggy life"[3] much as they have ever done.

To some degree, for some animals, it may be true that our presence is benign: but it would be irresponsible to assume that, in large part, animals are immune from our cultural processes. Animals are intensely present in our cultural imagination—"Animals are good to think," as Claude Lévi-Strauss put it[4] (think about; think with; think through), and we have lately being thinking them voraciously. And one might suppose that thinking them voraciously is less immediately harmful to them than, say, eating or hunting or vivisecting them voraciously, but I suggest that it is not because the way people *think* animals dramatically affects their fate in our world: the conceptions and prejudices that filter through our cultural experience become hard facts, actions, behaviors, that literally and bodily involve animals.

Animals are thickly enmeshed in human culture simply because people are so interested in them. We use them in a range of ways—some benevolent, some silly, some violent—in the service of our own cultural drives, desires, fantasies, and obsessions. Usually people are heedless of the animal's integrity, the animal's rights, in these interactions: we see animals as ours by right (Genesis 1:26 assigns us this power) to use as we deem fit in our dominion over them.

When a person and a nonhuman animal encounter each other, the animal generally ends up somehow the worse for this meeting. This book foregrounds the animal as it meanders through human culture—or, to put it another way, as we lasso it into our culture. The writers whose essays follow attempt to grant value to the animal's perspective, the animal's consciousness, as we examine what people have done with them, and how, and why. In virtually every account of cultural representations that this book explores, one should note, the animals did not choose to participate. This is not to say that our relationship to them is always necessarily one of exploitation and domination, but one must always be attuned to that possibility. And just as the animals' consciousness and volition has been generally absent—overlooked, suppressed—on their side of these interactions, on the other side, the human side, an ethical dimension is infrequently addressed.

A dazzling panoply of animals surrounds us in our world: animals we fondle, and animals we hunt; animals who are movie stars, and animals who are porn stars; animals who are isolated (from other animals) in elaborate cultural frames, and animals living in compounds like puppy mills or factory farms or research labs, whose numbers are so vast and whose lives are so desolate as to overwhelm our sensibilities: animals we tune out, erase, rather than confront the moral problem they represent; animals we fetishize (exotic animals, expensive animals, illicit animals, charismatic animals); animals we subject to ridicule (tigers jumping through hoops; spectacles in zoos; subjects of "stupid pet tricks," a regular feature on late-night television entertainment); animals momentarily in vogue (emperor penguins, after a striking documentary; panda bears, amid political jousting; akita dogs, commercially overbred), and animals who float through the ether of television and the Internet; animals who are inappropriately transplanted into an ecosystem and run wild, or cause other ecological havoc, and animals who are refugees from habitats that people have polluted or confiscated.

If we try to think about these animals outside the proscribed subservient two-dimensional role to which they are almost always relegated in our culture, we may arrive at some interesting and insightful realizations about ourselves and about how much we don't know about animals; how much is obscured, spoiled, when people inscribe animals as subordinate elements of an anthropocentric narrative.

An Englishman, a Frenchman, a German, and a Jew are asked to write an essay about an elephant. The Englishman writes about "The Elephant and the British Empire." The Frenchman writes about "The Love Life of the Elephant." The German writes a large pedantic treatise on "The Toenail of the Elephant." And the Jew writes on "The Elephant and the Jewish Problem." Is it possible for people to imagine elephants beyond ourselves as elephant-imaginers? How can we get beyond our own problems and contemplate theirs?

Anthrozoology looks at animals, and at the people looking at animals. While it addresses the overlapping area, the intersection in a Venn diagram where the circles represent "people" and "animals," that area is not necessarily a common ground or a meeting place. In the anthrozoological text, animals tend to become distorted and people tend to become ecologically imperious. This text is not pervasively informed by ecological considerations or by a sane ethos of symbiosis. Its tropes may evoke a carnival barker—"Dancing bears! Counting horses!"—more than any scientific or rationalistic voice. The discourse of ecology is present but overshadowed by the discourses of commerce and imperialism: yes, certainly, it is generally known (thanks to Peter Singer's *Animal Liberation*[5]) that the chickens in factory farms are miserable, and the runoff from agribusiness pollutes our water tables, but the bottom line is cheap plentiful meat for us until you pry this drumstick out of my cold dead hands. The contemporary cultural history of animals shows that people do what we want with them, and we are lately coming up with cleverer ways of doing more and more things with them. We are a selfish species, and we are skillful, and ethically habituated, in the mechanics of ecological abrogation. We take what we want.

Anthrozoology is predicated upon our cultural location and our cultural habits and biases, and to the extent that it is implicated in these things, the anthrozoologist runs the risk (to mix a natural metaphor) of failing to see the forest for the trees: failing to see the animals, the entirety and the ecological complexity of their forested world, for all the cultural trees that distract us. But to the extent that anthrozoology can fight culture with culture and challenge the hegemonies that have relegated animals to cultural commodities and currencies that serve as fodder for our own anthropocentric carnival, the discourse promises a sharper and more enlightened look at the animals that live around us.

Keenly informed by cultural studies, this new field has the potential to transcend the pervasive speciesism in our world. Interdisciplinary in orientation, anthrozoology rescues animals from their pinned, fixed harnesses in any single discipline: they are no longer just the horse on the canvas, or the philosophical absence of a soul, or the zoological specimen to be dissected and taxonomized, or the caged experiment to be psychologically compared to man, the measure of all things. They are, instead, polymorphous and polyvalent. As disciplines such as philosophy, anthropology, landscape architecture, geography, literature, art, sociology, and the history of science are added to the mix that informs human–animal studies, animals can begin, in our intellectual estimation, to inhabit the world with a sense of place, spirit, mind, art, society, and all the other things that each of these intellectual traditions, individually, had denied the subordinate species.

Cultural studies at once expands and subverts our sense of a text, which promises beneficial opportunities for animals to escape from the textual constraints that have afflicted them historically. The stories of horses and fish and bugs that have been told invoke a limited scope of narratives, in which the animals are marginalized characters. With cultural studies promising to engage the world as text, and to read this text deconstructively, we may hope that in the future animals will fare better in our cultural imagination than they have done in the past.

How does an animal become famous? The answer, simply, is that people make it famous: fame—like so many other human constructs that animals bear the burden of carrying—is something that we impose, in accord with our cultural logic, prejudices, and whims. A person makes an animal famous by looking at it and then culturally developing that gaze in some way. The imposition of fame is likely to be motivated by some sort of human profit, though it is certainly conceivable that the condition of fame may be more altruistic in intent. Such is the case, for instance, with the photography of Britta Jaschinski, whose work is featured on the cover of this book and also in chapter 6 (Figures 6.2 and 6.4).

The animals Jaschinski selects to photograph acquire the fame of being seen and contemplated by a wide viewership, but it is an audience that is more likely than most to leverage the animals' fame into empathetic understanding and critical (if not subversive) cultural deliberation. The animals in her images are not glamorized or airbrushed; they are not ripe for fetishistic exploitation. Indeed, they actively resist such implication in conventional culture: they are often, it seems, pensively sad, which is not a situation that normally appeals to audiences for famous animals. Jaschinski's images force us to think in ways that uncomfortably, and sometimes brutally, interrogate our perspective as viewers, as people. Many of the images are somehow difficult to see, which contrasts with the conventional expectation that an animal subject should be easy to grasp. An otherworldly darkness permeates her work, a troubling philosophical depth that touches both the animal inside the frame and the human spectator who is outside looking at the creature. A sense of uncertainty resonates in her photography—uncertainty about the animal's context, the animal's sentience, the animal's feelings; this sense of the unknown, however aesthetically rich and provocative it is, resists the human audience's habitual expectations of omniscient control and insight with regard to animals.

This animal on the cover, a polar bear, was in captivity in a New York zoo at the moment this photograph was taken.[6] In many of Jaschinski's zoo photographs, the apparatus of captivity prominently frames the image (via the cages, the unnatural habitat, the weirdly intrusive perspective into which she places the viewer with respect to the animals, and the dreary, deadened milieu that her photography embodies technically). In this photograph, however, although we know that the polar bear is a zoo exhibit, the image itself gives away very few indications of this: it is possible (for us—is it also possible for the bear, I wonder?) to pretend, for a moment, that the bear is free.

The play of light gives the animal a keen glow, augmented by the almost magical bubbles emanating from its body. The form of the animal is sleek and seductive: the bear seems at the same time to be moving and still (which, of course, is inherently the case in the trope of photography: action and stasis coexist). The bubbles suggest the animal's keen hydrodynamic efficiency. The arms and legs give a sense of propulsion, yet they are at the same time relaxed. The bear is suspended, floating in the water, as if at rest, yet at the same time is obviously capable of large, powerful movement. It is calm, yet at the same time, it is a bear, and thus, dangerous. Its fur looks dry, though it is obviously wet. It is captive, and yet perhaps also, metaphysically, somewhat free. (Do we grant the bear a metaphysical consciousness? I do.) The photograph is living proof that the bear has internalized the contradictions of its existence, that it retains a nobility of spirit amid its depravity of circumstance. I believe (and I think Jaschinski believes) that it is wrong for us to see the bear in the way we are seeing it, in a zoo, or in a photograph of a zoo, and yet it is at the same time mesmerizing. Is the bear as fascinated by me, by us, its spectators, as we are of him? What does he think of us? We cannot know. The energy that Jaschinski's image conveys is at the same time profound and profane. The longer we regard this bear, if we learn anything, if we know anything, it is how much we *cannot* know.

A tremendously small proportion of all the animals in our world are famous. I begin my survey with two well-known animals: one vilified and one celebrated. Topsy was featured in a technological crusade, famous for having been killed in Thomas Edison's 1903 short film *Electrocuting an Elephant*. A circus elephant at Coney Island, Topsy had killed three people (including someone who had tried to feed her a lit cigarette), for which she was sentenced to death. After she refused to eat a cyanide-laced carrot, Edison suggested frying her: he had been publicly electrocuting cats and dogs with AC power because he wanted to discredit that type of current and advance his claim that DC was more effective and less dangerous. The scene opens with a keeper leading Topsy to her execution. Copper electrodes are attached to her feet, and 6,600 volts of electricity are turned on. Topsy becomes rigid, waves her trunk, and falls forward to the ground dead amid a cloud of smoke. Edison showed his film around the country in his campaign against alternating current. (It suggests one more line for the old joke: The inventor writes about "The Elephant and the History of Electricity.")

Rin-Tin-Tin, star of cinema, television, and radio from the 1920s to the 1950s, had a happier experience on film than Topsy. The first animal superstar of the modern age, he was actually not just one animal, but a series of several German shepherds. The original dog was found in a bombed-out dog kennel in France near the end of World War I. Film mogul Darryl F. Zanuck saw him performing at a dog show—reportedly, he could leap fourteen feet into the air—and decided that he could be a star. The dog dined each day on choice tenderloin steak prepared by a private chef. At the peak of his career with Warner Brothers he received ten thousand fan letters a week and was considered to be one of Hollywood's top stars. Legend has it that he died in the arms of actress Jean Harlow; he has a star on the Hollywood Walk of Fame.

Topsy and Rin-Tin-Tin may be taken as opposite ends of a continuum that measures an audience's relative admiration or disdain for famous animals: our proclivity to treat them like gods or to destroy them in the pursuit of our own enterprises. Yet as disparate as their lives were, they had a common experience in terms of being enmeshed in human culture: a lot of people watched them. They were assigned roles, and these roles became their lives. The ways in which they were treated had nothing to do with their desires or their natures: people did with them whatever they wanted to do, and the animals passively experienced the fame or infamy that people imposed upon them. They played their parts, happy, sad, or indifferent, pampered with haute cuisine or collapsing in a cloud of dust, amid the bizarrely unnatural narratives in which they were inscribed.

The nature of a select few animals' fame suggests something about the animal as individual, which is a rare occurrence: in most other ways, while animals may have a range of prominent functions in human culture, that prominence plays out in a way that is depersonalized (deanimalized) and in which the individual animal's integrity is effaced. Think of pigs who give their valves for heart operations, or dogs who sniff out bombs. These animals don't become famous heroes. Fame is granted to so few animals—when it happens, what does it show about our relations with them, and with the multitudes of animals who can never make such an impression upon the human consciousness?

Many of the famous animals in modern culture are fictitious caricatures: Bugs Bunny, Mickey Mouse, Donald Duck, Porky Pig, and so forth. They talk, they walk upright, and they engage in activities that are recognizably human, as opposed to authentically animal. Often they are depicted wearing some clothes, though not a full outfit: a sports coat, perhaps, but no pants; a tie, but no shirt. They are supposed to be regarded, this would suggest, as somewhat human—capable of donning some, but not all, of the accoutrements that real human beings wear. Perhaps the suggestion is that they aspire to natural, fully clothed humanity, but, being merely animal, cannot completely pull off the performance. The profusion of animal characters marketed to young children pretty much disappears as they move into young adulthood, suggesting that animals are at the bottom of the scale, fitting for youngsters until their minds mature beyond this and they are ready for higher-level narratives about real people. Animal stories are just the warm-up act.

Alongside these cartoon animals, there are a gaggle of famous show-biz animals in the mold of Rin-Tin-Tin, who have a slightly higher degree of reality than their animated counterparts: animals like Flipper, Lassie, Mr. Ed the talking horse, Francis the talking mule, Babe the talking pig—media stars, whose perverse existence, like that of cartoon animals, is shaped by the expectations and fantasies of the people who surround them. The subject of animals and language (their own language, and the possibility of a common language that would facilitate interspecies communication) could generate an extensive, fascinating anthrozoological deliberation. In the case of these famous talking animals, though, there is a striking absence of such interrogation. The animals just talk, and the people just watch.

Famous animals in visual culture may suffer brutally. Damien Hirst, an acclaimed British artist, rose to prominence by creating museum tableaux featuring dead animals. His installations depict, for example, a shark in formaldehyde, a pig sawn in half, and a rotting cow's head being eaten by live flies. Nathalia Edenmont, a Russian artist, also kills animals—mice, cats—to create displays that include their preserved heads. Eduardo Kac generates his art by genetically mutating rabbits so that they glow luminescently. Pinar Yolacan photographs old women dressed in blouses that she has sewn made out of the inner organs of chickens. Such desecrations of animals in contemporary art grow out of the science, or fashion, or culture, of taxidermy: killing animals, then stuffing them so as to preserve their forms as an eternal monument to our mastery over them; removing them from wherever they live, in the forest or ocean, and domesticating them in death, framing them in living rooms or art galleries or curiosity shops. Taxidermy, and this taxidermical art, both literally and figuratively sucks out their guts, their life, while keeping them perversely and paradoxically lifelike. The animals have suffered in the process of constructing these artifacts, and they suffer again, metaphysically, as the artwork—the representations of their corpses, their suffering—testifies eternally to what people can do to animals. Although these animals are famous—widely seen and discussed—they are at the same time anonymous: we don't really know anything about who they are.

Some animals' fame derives from their roles in enterprises that are deemed vital to human society. In 1957, a dog named Laika became the first living creature sent into outer space, in Sputnik 2. She was a stray dog, probably a mix of husky and terrier, who had been found wandering the streets of Moscow. The point of sending an animal up in a rocket was to show that a living creature could survive the launch and the weightlessness of outer space and to provide information on how living organisms react to space environments. She was the proverbial guinea pig. For decades, Soviet authorities had maintained that Laika lived for a week on the rocket ship, but more recently they admitted that she died, from stress and overheating, just a few hours after the flight was launched.

In the space race that became a major political and cultural battleground between the United States and the Soviet Union, Laika was a pawn. She became a hero—monuments to her were erected across the Soviet Union—but from her own point of view, she was a victim, a slave. What must it have been like for her to have experienced what she did? And if she truly was such a famous, heroic animal, why was the reality of her flight so different from the fallacious stories that the Soviets propagated about her? Her experience must have been fascinating, and horrific; but it was, of course, not the story that people wrapped around her. Science, we are told, is supposed to be predicated on the truth. The exploration of space is arguably the most enormous scientific endeavor of the twentieth century, and yet the story of the animal most famously involved in it is false. The gap between the story of the Sputnik mission as proclaimed to the world and Laika's actual experience, which dribbled out as a footnote decades after the event, indicates how little animals really matter in the story of human progress. People regularly and unthinkingly inscribe our stories over animals' own experiences. Animals are convenient vehicles for human narratives; their own stories, if they are even known at all, are irrelevant.

Another scientifically famous animal was Dolly, a Scottish sheep, the first mammal to have been successfully cloned from an adult cell. She lived from

1997 to 2003 and was named for Dolly Parton, because the cloned cell was a mammary cell and Dolly Parton has famously large breasts. Semiotically, then, Dolly's name is inflected by the cultural spirit (sexism in the case of Ms. Parton, speciesism in the case of the sheep) that inclines men to ogle rather than to look honestly at something. In the case of male lechers, and I think in the case of the cultural reception of Dolly the sheep as well, such leering obscures the real nature of the body that is being ogled. In different ways, both Dollies are objectified bodily forms that serve a purpose for a lustful, desirous audience, a purpose that overwrites their lives just as the Soviet mythographers overwrote Laika's life. A female bosom is a fecund canvas for the creation of male fantasies; abnormally large breasts practically invite the male gaze to run wild in the bosomy fields of imagination. And if we clone a sheep to graze in this field, well, it's all of a kind.

When Dolly developed a debilitating form of arthritis at an unusually early age, some scientists speculated that the cloning may have resulted in premature aging: her parent was six years old when the genetic material was taken from her, so Dolly may have had a genetic age of six years at her birth. Dolly's existence inflamed ethical controversies about cloning: our limited understanding of the applied genetics suggests, some believed, that scientists should not attempt to control so many genes at once. The untested process of cloning, many feared, whether animal, plant, or human, opened up a Pandora's box of so many potentially ignorant or nefarious ways of tampering with nature and the possibility of wreaking havoc on the equilibriums of our ecosystems. Like Laika, Dolly was a pioneer. Her sponsors celebrated her, as Laika's did, as the figurehead of a brave new world (promising medical breakthroughs via genetic engineering; preserving near-extinct species; advancing reproductive technology for the infertile; bringing back to life replicas of beloved Fluffies and Fidos). Others saw her as a hapless victim of hubristic human meddling in a sci-fi tableau where she was the fodder for our fantasies, but her actual identity was overwritten by these fantasies, by the narrative scientists invented with no less gusto than their inventions of the genetic technology itself.

Laika's remains are in the spectral dust orbiting the cosmos; Dolly's, stuffed, may be seen in Edinburgh's Royal Museum.

The likeness of Balto, a husky, stands in a statue in New York's Central Park (and the body itself is displayed in the Cleveland Museum of Natural History), while the image of Elsa, an African lion, is forever preserved in celluloid. These two famous animals met happier cultural fates than Laika and Dolly: their legacies embody at least a somewhat more positive, respectful sense of their characters.

Balto was the lead dog on the final leg of a 1925 serum run to Nome, Alaska, carrying diphtheria antitoxin from Anchorage. (The annual Iditarod dog sled race commemorates that run.) A deadly diphtheria epidemic was threatening to hit Nome's young people, and the only serum that could halt the outbreak was in Anchorage, a thousand miles away. The medicine could not be flown in because the only local planes had been dismantled for the winter, so officials decided to bring in the medicine by sled dog. More than twenty mushers took part, facing a blizzard with temperatures of –50°C. News coverage of the trip was worldwide.

After a week-long run, the Norwegian Gunnar Kaasen drove his team, led by Balto, into Nome. Balto and Kaasen became celebrities, though more than a dozen mushers and their teams participated. The dogs toured the United States until their fame waned, at which time the team was sold to a vaudeville organizer. When Cleveland residents raised $2,000 to purchase the animals from this sideshow, Balto and six companions were given a permanent home at the city zoo in 1927, where they received a hero's welcome. After Balto's death in 1933, at the age of eleven, he was taxidermized. (Alaskan schoolchildren have recently been lobbying to have his stuffed body returned to their state.) Although his name and his story are famous, still, his fame is a consequence of his service to people. And Balto's reward for his heroism was being relegated to a sideshow, then a zoo, before being mounted and put on display. It seems impossible for an animal, however famous, to avoid concomitant conditions of ignominy, or to parley that fame into something that might be meaningful and fulfilling on his own terms.

Elsa, an African lion, became famous in books and film: her story was told in Joy Adamson's trilogy *Born Free, Living Free,* and *Forever Free* (1960–1962), the first two of which were made into highly popular films (1966, 1972). The Adamsons found Elsa when Joy's husband, George, a game warden in Kenya, shot a lion who attacked him; the lion had three cubs: two were sent to zoos, and the Adamsons kept Elsa, deciding when she was three years old to teach her to live in the wild. Elsa was at first unable to prosper on the reserves where the Adamsons brought her but eventually managed to join with the other lions and adapt to her new life. She mated and had three cubs; the Adamsons kept tabs on her well-being and, after her death, kept contact with her cubs for a while.

Adamson's work touched a chord: she made people care about wild animals. She crafted an engaging narrative around the life of an animal, which is a hard thing to do. She made people aware of environmental challenges to wildlife habitats and to animals (though certainly to some extent Joy and her husband, who killed Elsa's mother, were part of the problem as well as part of the solution).

The movie's theme song was a paean to freedom: "Born free, as free as the wind blows / As free as the grass grows / Born free to follow your heart." It popularized the idea that animals, like people, cherish their freedom, and that their lives may be worth living under felicitous circumstances but not under constraint. Certainly there is rampant anthropomorphism in the story and the song, but this was apparently necessary to bring an ecologically attuned consciousness about the importance of an animal's freedom to a wide cultural audience. "Born Free" is one of the most famous contemporary cultural narratives about animals and their lives and their relations with people. Its style is a forerunner of a spate of documentaries that bring people direct visual experiences of what we might call real nature. The Adamsons were very intrusive in the lives of their animal friends, however well intentioned, and their experience raises concerns about whether human interaction with animals is inherently meddlesome and what our motivations are for connecting with animals. Still, overall, Elsa was arguably one of the most famous animals whom people saw in a relatively authentic way: through Adamson's depiction of the details of Elsa's development and her struggle to live in the wild, people got to know much more about her, than, say, Laika. And she lived out her life without having been captured or objectified, as Balto was. Elsa paved the way for a more intimate cultural relationship between people and animals, inspiring at least a dawning realization of the fact that animals might have desires and value in their own lives that are independent of people's relationship to them.

In these postmodern times, we might expect that the cyberculture would generate some digital approximation of taxidermy; Oolong, a rabbit, exemplifies the new electronic version of fetishizing the animal form. (A brief digression on animals' names: Oolong is inexplicably, irrelevantly, named after a variety of tea. Laika, Balto, and so forth: these are all, of course, names imposed upon animals by people, wholly meaningless to the animal subjects. I use these names as a necessary convenience, though they are simply one more layer in the human cultural overlay of these animals who are so enmeshed in human culture and language that their real identities are inaccessible. Trent Reznor, the front man of the band Nine Inch Nails, named his cat Fuckchop. Mark Twain had cats he called Beelzebub and Satan. President Franklin D. Roosevelt had a dog named President, and General George Patton had a dog named William the Conqueror. Frequently, people give animals strange and stupid names, and we should think about why we do this, what it signifies, and what might be a way to find better names, better ways to identify and address our animal companions.)

Oolong became a famous animal when Japanese photographer Hironori Akutagawa created a Web site[7] featuring hundreds of photographs of the rabbit balancing things on his head, an activity he calls Head Performance. (See Figure 0.1.) These objects include tea cups, an apple, an orange, a carrot, a piece of dried seaweed, a sesame bun, a book, a compact disc, a teakettle, a lit candle, a camera lens, a sprig of an evergreen, even a rabbit skull: things random

FIGURE 0.1: Oolong the rabbit is famous for such photographs, ubiquitously found across the Internet, of things on his head. Photo by Hironori Akutagawa.

and meaningless. The most famous of these photographs depicts Oolong balancing a pancake on his head, bearing the caption "I have no idea what you're talking about ... so here's a bunny with a pancake on its head." The site caught the attention of the media, including the *New York Times,* and became a widespread Internet meme. Oolong died on January 7, 2003; Akutagawa's photographs of the rabbit's last moments appear on his Web site.

What does this mean? What is the nature of Oolong's so-called fame? Countless thousands of people, probably millions, have seen Oolong's image and know who he is: what is the import, the currency, of this attention? Do they really know him? How do they know him? What do they know of him?

People like to look at animals and like to make animals do weird things. Elephants are made to paint pictures (with paintbrushes taped to their trunks), chickens are made to play the piano, monkeys are made to do acrobatics and parachute jumps. In the age of mechanical reproduction, people like to reproduce animals a great deal. This may be regarded as an abrogation of the animals' fecundity, especially with regard to rabbits (whose reproductive prowess is a central aspect of their cultural reputation): a kind of semiotic theft. What often happens when people engage animals is that we identify, and then steal, their spirits—their authenticity, their traits, their very animality. In Asia, poachers harvest the penises of tigers to make potions that (supposedly) prolong and intensify men's sexual pleasure and virility: thus, we have taken the animal's power, its sexuality, its reproductive potency (which is like stealing from not just the one animal, but all his progeny as well, which, because he has lost his penis, will not come to be: we have abrogated the fecundity and virility that we have denied the animal). People club baby seals, take their beautiful coats from them, sew them together, and wear them: so then *we* have the pelts, the beauty, instead of the seals. It is schadenfreude: we take pleasure from the deprivation of others.

In the case of Oolong, too, the viewer has something that the subject no longer has: what this is, precisely, is complicated and elusive, but also important. A rabbit, or any animal, has as its natural birthright a kind of integrity, a control over itself that involves a certain relationship to its environment—its nest, burrow, or hive; its tree or field—and an imagistic authenticity. There are certain ways that the image of a rabbit (and of course, the rabbit itself, as well, but I am concerned at the moment with images) can naturally be, and other ways that are artificial. To the extent that the image retains the authenticity of the rabbit's context, background, and frame, the subject preserves a good deal of control (at least, semiotic control: which is *not* nothing) over its life, its well-being, its habitat, and its existence. The abrogation of this authenticity of representation—a consummate example of which would be a representation of the animal with a pancake on its head—indicates the loss of the animal's natural and ecological harmony.

And what has the human viewer gained in this transaction? He has gained the power to displace the animal from its ecological well-being, and implicitly, thus, he has colonized for his own use the ecological space from which the rabbit has been evicted. There is thus more space—physical and geographical space, natural space, imaginative space—that the human being himself may inhabit: space where the person no longer has to compete with the animal for occupancy. It is irrelevant whether or not we actually need this space, or whether we can even use it: it is not necessarily the case that we have used up all of our ecological space, but it is simply a cultural fetish that we want more of it anyhow.

We want to expand—it is our manifest destiny; we want to have control, dominion, over as much space as possible. By displacing the rabbit from its nature, and from nature per se, we have gained at least the potential to subsume the resulting vacancy. By stripping the animal of its bodily control, of its natural dignity, we have gained the potential to arrogate to ourselves that much more of what we perceive as the zero-sum cache of biological and eco-logical control and dignity. The less the animals have, the more we might have. This mode of representing animals is a process of taking from them and adding to our own cultural store, our inventory.

Fame is itself a trope of displacement. Most animals are not famous. When we isolate and celebrate a single rabbit or dog as a famous animal, we relegate the rest to a heightened obscurity. Certainly most animals would prefer to be obscure. But the human cultural prejudice is that fame is good: fame is a sign of success and power, and so the hordes of anonymous animals confirm their own cultural insignificance. The famous animal is always singular, individual, while, as Deleuze and Guattari write in *A Thousand Plateaus,* the real animal is always multiple: part of a pack.[8] The cultural construct of fame strips the animal of his or her peers, his or her society, as it sets the animal who happens to become famous apart from the others.

Another popular Internet site that reproduces displaced animals is called The Infinite Cat project.[9] ("Infinite" is ironic: while there are indeed quite a large number of cats here, each one is keenly isolated—*finite*—in its Internet frame. It is the infinitude of animals that intimidates people; to avoid feel-ing overwhelmed by them, we divide and conquer.) Creator Mark Stanfill explains:

> It all began innocently enough when a user on an Apple help web site posted a picture of his cat, Frankie, contemplating the beauty of a flower. Shortly afterwards another user posted a picture of his cat bristling at the image of Frankie on the monitor. I decided this was too much fun and advanced the concept as The Infinite Cat Project which is, simply, cats regarding cats regarding cats in an electronic milieu. If you like this web site then thank your lucky stars that the world is populated with cats, Macs, and people with wayyyy too much time on their hands.

The site features thousands of images of cats: a cat looking at a cat on a computer screen who is looking at a cat on a computer screen who is looking at a cat on a computer screen, and so forth. (See Figure 0.2.) Again, we are tap-ping into the perceived fecundity, the infinitude, of the animal kingdom—cats are everywhere, right? Anyone can get one, free, anytime, anywhere: *Cats free to good home.* Except here, their infinitude is framed by, and subordinated to, our technology, and our fetishistic love for them. We make them look at each other through our technological lens. If it is the bane of our lives that we are tied to our computers (rather than, as Freud argues in *Civilization and Its Discontents,* running free and exuberantly through the forests and urinating on campfires), then we drag these cats down with us. The photos are funny, in

FIGURE 0.2: Boris watching Baby watching Nina watching Widget watching Cloudy watching Ada watching Sammie watching Bo watching Cojo watching Boomerang watching Pfefferminze watching Titch watching Kuplung at infinitecat.com. Credit: Mike Stanfill, creator, Infinite Cat Project; photography by Paul Copeland.

that the cats are looking at computer screens, and we know that they don't really want to do this, don't have to do this, to look at other members of their species, except, in fact, now they *do* have to do this, because we are making them. Everyone (even other animals) has to look at animals the way *we* look at them, as mediated by our technological and cognitive frames: and this is what infinitecat.com does. It is the logical culmination of what Edison did when he represented Topsy in the medium of film confronting, head-on, the technology of electricity: the force of the electrical image here isn't as manifestly lethal to these cats as it was to Topsy, but it is still dangerous.

Animal Planet, a cable television network, illustrates another type of frame for fame, organizing animals' lives into a series of half-hour blocks that parallel (through the programmers' contrivance) the cultural paradigms of our own existence. Consider the following program notes:

- *Animal Cops:* When a much loved pet is savaged by another dog, the Animal Cops are brought in to investigate and emotions run high in the courtroom.
- *Planet's Funniest Animals:* Take a peek into the hilarious lives of the world's most talented and entertaining individuals—animals! It's like having a million crazy pets right in your own living room—only you don't get as much hair on your couch.

- *Emergency Vets:* An English springer spaniel ingested a quart of safflower oil and a pen.
- *Crocodile Hunter:* "Have a go at these little beauties! I've put together a compilation of some bites, scrapes, belts, bashes, drops, punches, head butts, cuts, breaks, and smashes we've collected on camera."
- *Animal Miracles:* The tie between man and dog is tested when the dog falls into a river; a dolphin inspires a disabled child; a dog reveals a talent for sensing heart attacks; a guide dog risks his life to save his owner.
- *Pet Psychic:* Can humans actually communicate with animals? Can we know what animals are feeling? Sonya Fitzpatrick, a modern day Dr. Doolittle, thinks so. The Animal Planet's Pet Psychic believes they communicate with pictures and feelings that they send telepathically to each other and to her.
- *Ultimate Zoo:* There's a new African Savannah in Canada! Hippos are thriving in Missouri! Giant Pandas are in Atlanta! Follow Animal Planet's exploration of the most advanced zoo exhibits in the world. Watch as architects, zoo keepers, and vets recreate their habitats.[10]

(I would respond that there is *not* actually an African savannah in Canada, and hippos are *not* really thriving in Missouri ...)

How strange all this is: how artificially animals are made to fit into our world—they have cops, doctors, psychics, and so forth, just like us!—and how much of their authenticity, their nature, is stripped from them as we remove them from their own world. "It's like having a million crazy pets right in your own living room—only you don't get as much hair on your couch," promise the producers of *Planet's Funniest Animals*. Well, what's so funny about them? Are we laughing with them or at them? (Three guesses.) Why would anyone want to have a million crazy pets in his own living room? We wouldn't, really, but audiences crave this sense of animal infinitude: the viewer is like a king with a whole court, a whole planet, full of jesters: if there are a million of them, maybe one will really be funny. And there's no hair on the couch—yes, animals are a pain, aren't they, when we bring them into our lives, our frames, our rooms. Remember, they didn't *ask* to be here; hair on the ground wasn't a problem when they lived in nature. As we exploit them, still we complain about how troublesome the ingrates are!

Cats looking at cats, rabbits balancing pancakes: it is (or is supposed to be) funny (odd, unexpected) to people, and the animal subject is apparently oblivious. The animal is a prop, the sideshow star who is completely unaware of how funny he is, and that makes it even funnier. The animal is trained—most rabbits won't do "head performance"—but this one can do something delicate, deliberate, and completely pointless. This is important. We can, of course, train animals to do some things that at least are arguably useful (to us)—guide dogs for the blind, police horses—but it is also important for people to train animals to do things that are meaningless, simply because we can: because this testifies to our absolute cultural power over them, to make them do whatever we want, whether there is a reason for it or not. And so Akutagawa made Oolong sit there, under a pancake or a glove, day after day, and took picture after picture, which he broadcast to the world, to show Oolong's (and by extrapolation, potentially, any animal's) subjugation, humiliation. Day after day, it remains—what? Funny? Compelling? Sadistic? Bizarre?

Akutagawa exemplifies an obnoxious cultural habit: people put things on animals. Burdens: something is on top of animals, and the animals are underneath, subaltern. It may be a person atop a horse, or an elephant, or a camel, riding the animal, racing the animal, or it may be a harness, or a pancake, a weird semiotic evocation of a human, of the human. But essentially, something nonanimal, something not of the animal, something irrelevant to the animal, is made to be, and is thus represented, surmounting the animal.

In this cultural history of animals, there's a lot missing: a *natural* history of animals; animals when we're not seeing them, not petting them, not dressing them up and making them jump through the proverbial hoops. As we examine animals in culture, we must remember that this is part, but only part, of what and who these animals are. In other circumstances, probably happier circumstances for them, animals have greater self-determination and a more natural existence. We are interested in animals, by and large, in terms of what they can do for us—how they can please, or amuse, or satiate us—and so their own freedom and integrity are diametrically opposed to our ability to do with them what we will.

Animals in the news exemplify another kind of fame: transitory media attention. Some animals, to paraphrase Andy Warhol, will be famous for fifteen minutes. The biggest news stories are about threats (or perceived threats) that animals pose to people: swine flu, avian flu, killer African bees, mad cow disease, the possible origin of AIDS in monkeys. These stories portray animals as the dangerous other—though a more rational analysis shows that the real problem is not the animal itself, but rather, the human–animal interaction. One might argue that the real problem is people (who grind up animals to feed to other animals, for instance, generating what we dub mad cows), but much of this is projected onto the animals.

Commonly, ironically, when people address the threats to human beings that anthrozoological relations engender, attempts to confront and solve the problem may only worsen it. In 2005, for example, a program was begun to vaccinate billions of chickens in China as a barrier to avian flu, but some observers suggested that the people tramping from farm to farm to deliver the vaccinations actually increased the risk of spreading the disease. We always think we're in control and know what to do to fix the problem; our track record shows that this is wishful thinking. The fear that emanates from our relationship with animals (sometimes warranted, sometimes hysterical) suggests a guilty awareness that we have done considerable harm to other species, and ultimately we will get what we deserve.

In addition to the major animal-threat stories, news media are full of bizarre, troubling, and often insane stories about animals. Here is a representative sampling:

GUILTY: MAN TAPES FRIEND WHO DIED HAVING SEX WITH HORSE
Man Died of Perforated Colon

SEATTLE—A man who was videotaping a friend having sex with a horse when the friend died pleaded guilty earlier this week to trespassing at the Enumclaw, Wash., farm. The 54-year-old man was given a suspended jail sentence and fined $778. The man told police he and others often sneaked onto a neighbor's farm to have sex with animals. Kenneth Pinyan suffered a perforated colon July 2 and died from his injury. The King County prosecutor's office said no animal cruelty charges were filed because there was no evidence of injury to the horse.[11]

One reads this story with a mixture of disgust and fascination; I cannot wholly suppress my lurid desire to figure out more about this sex act, to visualize it, to try to imagine how it could happen, and how Mr. Pinyan conceptualized his relationship with this horse. How do people come up with such things? And why was his friend videotaping it? What are we looking at? Is there no limit to how voyeuristically perverse anthrozoological relations can get? Apparently not. Pornographic images of bestiality abound on the Web. Yes, apparently, people have always had their way with sheep and horses: but now, there are hundreds of Web sites promoting this. What does this mean? Presumably, there's a market for it. Is there more bestiality now than before the advent of the Internet?

HUNDREDS CELEBRATE GIANT PANDA WEDDING
Zoo Hopes Animals Will Mate

CHIANG MAI, Thailand—Hundreds turned out to celebrate the wedding of two giant pandas at a Thailand zoo Wednesday. Officials are planning to have the two pandas, Chuang Chuang and his female partner, Lin Hui, start mating. But the zoo wanted them to be married first. To celebrate the day, two mascots dressed as pandas and took the vows on behalf of the bears. Thailand has rented the two pandas from China for 10 years and hopes the pair will be able to produce offspring.[12]

Is this the flip side of the horse-copulating story? Did zoo officials wanted to make an honest panda out of Lin Hui? Why do people impose our habits, our cultural rituals, on animals? Why is it popular, and newsworthy, to impose irrelevant human institutions upon animals? Should we expect that someday *all* animals will be encouraged to get married before having sex?

EMILY THE STOWAWAY CAT TRAVELS HOME TO THE U.S. FROM PARIS IN STYLE

MILWAUKEE—Emily the cat is back—after flying home in the lap of luxury. The curious cat who wound up traveling to France in a cargo container touched down at the Milwaukee airport on Thursday, greeted by her family and a horde of reporters. A Continental cargo agent handed her over to cat's owners. Emily meowed and pawed at reporters' microphones as the family answered questions. "She'll be held onto a lot all the way home. And then when we get home, too, she'll be cuddled a lot," Donny McElhiney said. Her sumptuous return in business class on a Continental Airlines flight was a sharp contrast from her trip to France, where she was found thin and thirsty but still alive. "She seems a little calmer than she was before, just a little quieter, a little, maybe, wiser," said Lesley McElhiney, 32. Emily vanished from her Appleton home in late September. She apparently wandered into a nearby paper company's distribution centre and crawled into a container of paper bales. The container went by truck to Chicago and by ship to Belgium before the cat was found Oct. 24 at a laminating company in Nancy, France. Workers there used her tags to phone her veterinarian, who called the owners. Continental offered to fly the cat home from Paris after Emily's tale spread around the world and she cleared a one-month quarantine. "This was such a marvellous story, that we wanted to add something to it," Continental spokesman Philippe Fleury told AP Television News at Charles de Gaulle airport. After one Continental employee escorted Emily from Paris to Newark, N.J., cargo agent Gaylia McLeod accompanied the cat aboard a 50-seater from Newark to Milwaukee. "I know it's close to the holidays," a tearful McLeod said. "I'm happy to be a part of reuniting Emily with her family." On her flight home, Emily passed up a menu of peppered salmon filet and "opted for her French cat food" and some water, an airline spokeswoman said.[13]

We see here an illustration of how animals get sucked into globalism—global commerce, communication, public relations. It is common, as we survey a range of famous animals, for people to make a tremendous fuss about one animal, an individual animal, a token star, who is thus alienated from every other animal. We see the powerful sentimental pull of animals: the airline employee using the cat as a prop in her holiday story. We see the proliferation of animal stereotypes, here, the curious cat who made her way from Wisconsin to Europe. How much of this has to do with the animal, and how much with our own human constructions? Sure, cats are curious, some more than others. I believe that sharks are curious too. And moths. But I guess we have room for only one curious animal in our bestiary of metaphors, and cat, like curious, begins with c, so, *quod erat demonstrandum.*

A recent news story that seems more promising in terms of people's relationship with animals was headlined "It's Sensitive. Really. The Storied Narwhal Begins to Yield the Secrets of Its Tusk."[14] (See Figure 0.3.) The function of the narwhal's tusk, which can be as long as nine feet, has long been a mystery. Scientists have made the "startling discovery" that the tusk—actually a tooth—"forms a sensory organ of exceptional size and sensitivity" that "lets the animal measure minute changes in water temperature, pressure and makeup." An electron microscope revealed the subtleties of dental anatomy inherent in

FIGURE 0.3: The narwhals' intriguing tusks have stimulated the human imagination for centuries. Image by Kristin Laidre, at Noaa.gov.

the tusk, which contains ten million nerve endings that give the whale unique insights into its environment.

People are learning, piecemeal, finally, how amazing animals are. The narwhal, a rare whale native to the Arctic Ocean, had a storied cultural history because of its tusk, which had been thought to serve the function, possibly, of breaking ice, spearing fish, transmitting sound, poking the seabed for food, wooing females, defending babies, and establishing dominance in social hierarchies, among other things. People thought many things about what these tusks were for, and they were all wrong. Now, finally, we know what they are. (Maybe.) In the past, these tusks had been "sold as unicorn horns ... often for many times their weight in gold since they were said to possess magic powers. In the 16th century, Queen Elizabeth received a tusk valued at £10,000—the cost of a castle. Austrian lore holds that Kaiser Karl the Fifth paid off a large national debt with two tusks. In Vienna, the Hapsburgs had one made into a scepter heavy with diamonds, rubies, sapphires and emeralds."

The cultural currency—the iconography, the mythology—of something like the narwhal's tusk is powerful. And then we learn the truth, which doesn't really undercut the accretion of myths and guesses people had about the animal in the first place. Discovering things like this about animals may inspire people more generally to learn from animals: lessons (about biology, physics, nautical science, and many other things) that they can teach us, which can enrich our own lives and experiences without overwriting theirs. This is the sort of thing we might try harder to look for when we look at animals: trying to discover and appreciate the essence of who they are, and *how* they are.

Human myths, guesses, and fantasies about the narwhal are good things, I believe, at least until the point where those fantasies inspire people to start harvesting them for their tusks and fetishizing them, taking them off of the animals, and trying to abrogate the animals' magic for ourselves. Encrusting the tusk with jewels and making it into a scepter does *not* show an authentic sense of the animal's essence; rather, it shows what we can do to the animal, what we can take away from it. The Hapsburg scepter illustrates both the fascinating pull of animals' power, and at the same time, our proclivity to profane it, to overlay our own cultural value systems upon the artifacts of animals (which are, obviously, no longer the actual animals themselves: those creatures are long vanished, a waste product of the bounty we reap). Underlying an icon like this scepter, one can see a degree of the wonder people possess for animals, but loaded thickly on top of that is our tendency to colonize for humanity the essences of animals. And that is dangerously disrespectful for animals, as well as deceitful for us: people act as if we are honoring animals, but we are really desecrating them. Ecologically, it is a symptom of our heedless imperial harvesting of any and all baubles of nature that leaves the ecosystem as a whole poorer and more fragile. Why, I wonder, can we not admire the narwhal's tusk *on the narwhal?* Some people have been able to do this, and some have not. Perhaps the current news about narwhals makes us more prone to do so: I idealistically hope that more knowledge will lead to saner ethics, and now that we understand what the tusk actually does (and realize that detached from the animal and decoupaged with gems, it can no longer do this), we may be more inclined to leave it where it belongs.

In the modern era, we are seeing animals with new eyes. In the aftermath of the Enlightenment and the Industrial Revolution, the age of empire and the world wars, our anthropocentric praxis is starting to show cracks. We have created a cosmology that shamelessly celebrates our importance in the universe; we have reified human progress (framed in terms of commerce, Baconian science, expansion, and consumption) as the consummate expression of our meaning in the ecosphere. And still the planet is not at peace, but in a state of turmoil, and the environment is unstable, and the animals are manifestly displeased with us.

So we begin to interrogate our unexamined presuppositions about our relation to other species. There are more things on heaven and earth ... Some characterize our era as posthuman, which means, perhaps, that we are becoming aware of having overvalued our significance; our skimpy consciousness of other animals is retrograde. The others are more important, ecologically and spiritually, than we have acknowledged. They are more independent than we have allowed them to be, and more sentient that we ever imagined.

The other animals have voices that we strained to ignore, relegating them to catchall pretty terms such as *birdsong*, words like *meow*, but never dreaming that these were languages full of experiences and imaginations as vital as our own. All the things we have thought about animals are lately revisited as constructs that have sustained our own hegemony. The horse upon which a heroic general rides in eternally bronzed conquest; the cartoon coyote who collapses for the thousandth time as an anvil falls humorously on his stupid coyote head; the funniest home videos of cats crashing into glass doors and slip-sliding across the room on banana peels; the commodified dots of color swimming around in pet superstore tanks, in clear, pointless water, moving nowhere except in front of our eyes. The national symbols: the bald eagle, the proud buffalo. The metaphors: the wily fox, the curious cat, the dumb bunny, the proud lion. The stuffed animals in museums, and, rattier, in garage sales. The very words: ratty; catty; batty. What *is* it like to be a bat? (Thomas Nagel, famously, asked this philosophical question in 1974;[15] nobody has really bothered answering it.)

These highly acculturated animals I have presented are mere tokens, a few scattered evocations, of the hordes of animals that we shuffle through our cultural circuses. I wonder, what do they think of all this? What would they be doing if we had left them alone? How can we see, through them, in spite of them, beyond them, to the real animals that are all but obscure from the vantage point we have created?

Deleuze and Guattari's formulation of "becoming-animal" (which Ralph Acampora discusses in chapter 6) represents an ideal for the ecological and cultural prosperity of animals. It is a trope that envisions animals dynamically. In *A Thousand Plateaus,* Deleuze and Guattari describe a consciousness that challenges the conventional segregation between human and animal sentience. It invokes a fluidity between and among species, a permeability that eschews the boundaries between human and nonhuman. While their discussion begins by discussing the prevalence of interspecies transformations and metamorphoses in the genre of myth, they assert that the transformations they envision are not merely metaphor: "Becomings-animal are neither dreams nor phantasies. They are perfectly real."[16]

Deleuze and Guattari privilege action and intensity over mere form. *Becoming-animal* is about the whole animal and its life, rather than its iconically reductive cultural representation. "The wolf is not fundamentally a characteristic or a certain number of characteristics," they write, "it is a wolfing. The louse is a lousing, and so on."[17] Steve Baker explains Deleuze and Guattari's "suspicion that in handling animal form, [most conventional] artists are merely *imitating* the animal from a safe distance. Mere imitation has nothing to do with the intense and thorough-going experience of becoming-animal."[18] Becoming-animal describes an apotheosis, an epistemological epiphany about the nature of life, experience, and identity, that both human and nonhuman animals may experience; human beings are, of course, already animal, technically, but Deleuze and Guattari would have us interrogate and learn from the ground up our inherent animality.

An animal trope, lines of flight, describes the becoming-animal's transcendence of its two-dimensional subjectivity: these are the paths along which people must learn to see animals and to follow them. The lines of flight highlight the animals' mobility and agency; they are paths of escape from the captivity and inertia that plagues them in so many of their modern cultural incarnations.

Becoming-animal is an escape from human cultural constructions of the animal. The attack of Montecore during Siegfried & Roy's Las Vegas circus extravaganza offers an illustration. In 2003, the tiger lunged at his trainer, Roy Horn, during the act and dragged him offstage (most of the audience thought that the mauling was all part of the show), crushing his trachea and leaving deep puncture wounds on the back of his head; his heart stopped for a minute and he was resuscitated, but the entertainer was left partially paralyzed and lost control of his speech. Comedian Chris Rock offered this commentary on the attack: "Everybody's mad at the tiger. 'Oh, the tiger went crazy.' No, he didn't. That tiger went *tiger*. You know when that tiger was crazy? When he was riding on a little bike with a Hitler helmet on. That's when the tiger was thinking, 'I can't wait to bite somebody.'"[19] Rock illustrates a textbook example of the liberatory power of becoming-animal when he says, "That tiger went *tiger.*" It seems pretty clear to me, though Roy himself has remained in denial about this, that the tiger probably hated being (as the animals are billed on the marquee) a White Tiger of Nevada and performing twice a night on the strip, and this was how he manifested his feelings. It might seem inhuman (a word that probably needs to be revisited as we reevaluate the nature of humanism) to say this, but I believe that it is fitting to cheer the tiger who becomes a tiger: the animal who fights back against his cultural oppressors, as Montecore did.

The chimps in Will Self's *Great Apes*,[20] the pigeons in Patrick Neate's *The London Pigeon Wars*,[21] the richly fascinating idiosyncratic animal characters in José Emilio Pacheco's poetry collection *An Ark for the Next Millennium*,[22] are becoming-animals. The canvases of Olly & Suzi, in which the animals join together with the artists to mark the artwork, depict becoming-animals, as does the photography of Britta Jaschinski[23] in which the animals subversively resist the frames, the focus, the lighting, the cages that people have imposed upon them for so long, and appear instead with forms, appearances, and contexts that are so radically different from the simple creatures we are used to looking at that they are sometimes hardly recognizable.

There are also failed (stultified, perverted) becomings: Dracula exemplifies a bad becoming-bat, too heavily overwritten with Bram Stoker's and the audience's xenophobia and sexual anxieties. In H. G. Wells's *The Island of Dr. Moreau*, Moreau's beast folk, like Dracula's vampire, bring readers tantalizingly close to the human–animal boundary, which aids our understanding of becoming-animals: we have traditionally sublimated the closeness of this species divide, and we should venture closer. But as in *Dracula*, the antagonist's sociopathic insanity degrades the potential of Wells's text as a manifestation of becoming-animal. Rainer Maria Rilke's "The Panther" (1907) epitomizes the failure of the inchoate becoming-animal in the early modern age: poet and audience poignantly recognize this animal's intensity, and his soul, but remain powerless within the text to celebrate this or to ameliorate the animal's constraint. There are no lines of flight here (the panther is trapped in a cage at the zoo); there is no panthering. There is no emotion possible other than pathos.

Animals caught in the Internet become *something*, but they are not becoming-animals. The new media pixilated creatures like Oolong and the infinite kitties become *meme*—reproduced, but not fecund; not empowered—just more efficiently a subject of fetishistic voyeurism. While Deleuze and Guattari write that the becoming-animal is multiple, the multiplicity of the cybercultural animal is mere volume: mass of kilobytes, without meaningful content. The multiplicity of the animal is a necessary but not sufficient condition for becoming-animal.

The Web sites and animal channels are merely new and glitzy frames that encompass, restrictively, the same old animals inside. To see the *new* animal on the frontier, we must revisit and reform our own received ideas and habits; our new understanding of the narwhal's tusk stands as an example of our receptivity to the becoming-animal.

Many contemporary cultural accounts of animals, and even some that broach a transcendence of anthropocentric speciesism and that we might consider as incarnations of becoming-animal, involve a degree of fear. *Dracula* exemplifies the trope for this: van Helsing's fear of Dracula's bite (after the Transylvanian count has become-animal) that ruins the victim. Think also of Hitchcock's fearful titular creatures in *The Birds;* the rats in *Willard;* the fly in *The Fly;* the gorilla in *King Kong.* These films point to our subconscious fears about animals who turn on us, who hate us, and who attack us. We are afraid of a lot of animals: mosquitoes who carry West Nile virus, sharks who eat us when we are on vacation, pit bulls, deer ticks, bears, bats, spiders, rats, killer bees, mad cows, and on and on.

These fears could lead to improved relationships with animals. In *Heart of Darkness,* the text's primordial fear—"the horror, the horror"—signified the death knell of Eurocentric global exploitation, and forced readers to confront the power of the subaltern Africans (and the ethical abominations to which they had been subjected) who had been tamed, stylized, and marginalized, throughout the imperial enterprise. So too, our acknowledgment of animal fears can empower us to recognize and internalize the reality that there is actually something to be scared of (*contrapasso:* we have done poorly by the animals, and we may expect our acts to redound back upon us); and further, to accept the power of animals, all the different kinds of powers they have that we have suppressed. Given the subordinate fixities with which we have tried to construct animals in our world, it is indeed terrifying to imagine the chains, the bars, straining and breaking under the pressure exerted by the captive, the wronged prisoner. The good news is that we should not expect them, by and large, to be vengeful in the mode of Montecore (he was an isolated and exceptionally tormented victim: an individual, not a pack tiger): when they get out (when we let them out) of their cages, their frames, we may indeed hope that the packs of dogs go on with their doggy life.

The fearsome animals, as we deconstruct our fears, can be vehicles for our awareness of becoming-animal: we realize that we are of them, that—as Stoker's Englishmen with their ideas of racial supremacy were so loathe to accept—our fluids mix with theirs. And a scary scenario becomes a teachable moment in a larger ecosensibiltiy: we are all part of the same biosphere. We are all in this together. As Barry Commoner says: Everything is connected to everything else. Nature knows best.[24]

CHAPTER ONE

The Cosmic Spider and Her Worldwide Web

Sacred and Symbolic Animals in the Era of Change

BORIA SAX

Six to seven ravens are kept in the Tower of London at all times under the charge of the Yeoman Ravenmaster. They are given the run of the grounds, but their wings are trimmed on one side to prevent them from flying very far. Official publications of the tower, as well as many popular and scholarly works, say that the ravens have been there since archaic times, attracted by the prospect of feeding on human flesh after executions. They were domesticated under Charles II in the middle to late seventeenth century, when the king heard a prophecy that Great Britain would fall if the ravens left the tower. The birds of doom are usually photographed around a plaque commemorating the scaffold where prisoners in the tower were executed, which appears almost like a pagan altar for human sacrifices. (See Figure 1.1.)

In researching the ravens around the start of the twenty-first century, I discovered that they had been brought to the tower only in the last decades of the 1800s, while the legend that Great Britain would fall if the ravens left the tower dates only from the end of World War II.[1] In a severe crisis, people often turn spontaneously to archaic beliefs and practices. A bit like the Hebrews who worshipped the golden calf, Londoners during the Blitz turned to the ravens as avatars of fate. The black birds were associated with the corvid deity Bran,

FIGURE 1.1: A raven at the Tower of London looks on as a man reads to a little girl. Photo by Boria Sax.

whose head, according to medieval Welsh manuscripts, is buried in the tower. Men and women of contemporary times have not by any means lost their capacity for creating myths.[2]

Across the world from London, rites to animal gods have also been revived by another highly sophisticated society. In medical laboratories of South Korea, researchers in suits and ties hold religious services to placate the spirits of the mice, guinea pigs, rabbits and other animals that have been killed in laboratory experiments. Sacrifices such as anchovies, peanuts, and various fruits are left before a pagoda; sticks of incense and candles are lit, and prayers are offered to the animal spirits. The ceremonies are derived from ancient shamanistic and Buddhist traditions, which hold that the angry spirits of the departed animals might be reincarnated to extract vengeance in another life. According to some accounts, at one time laboratory machines were mysteriously breaking down, while lab personnel had strange diseases and nightmares. The problems ceased in the early 1980s, when the government began to sponsor ceremonies of conciliation.[3]

Today, the story of Wu-Kung, the monkey who became a Bodhisattva, rivals those of Kwan-Yin and the Buddha himself in popularity. The deities Hanuman, with the head of a monkey, and Ganesha, with the head of an elephant, may be arguably the two most beloved figures in the Hindu pantheon today.

FIGURE 1.2: Traditional representation of Ganesha, the elephant-headed god of wisdom and one of the most popular deities in the Hindu pantheon, riding up a rat.

(See Figure 1.2.) Many Hindu temples honor monkeys or even rats, which are fed by visitors and allowed to roam freely on the grounds. Cows are allowed to walk unhindered in the streets of predominantly Hindu cities, honored as nurturers that provide milk and are never butchered for food.

The religions of Native Americans have always remained largely theriomorphic—deities are thought of as having the forms of animals—even when, as with the Yaqui Indians, they are given a Catholic veneer. The Hopi, for example, still look to Spider Woman for guidance, while tribes of the western coast of North America continue to honor Raven. Many folk religions such as Santeria and Voodoo ceremoniously sacrifice animals. That practice sounds barbaric to many people and simply cruel to others, but it does accord animals a special status—as intermediaries between human beings and God.

Animal deities have often been revived, particularly in historical periods of dramatic change. There was a theriomorphic revival in the Renaissance as animals, particularly those of the Zodiac, became the center of many esoteric and alchemical practices. There have also been numerous minor revivals of this in folk rituals, among unconventional religious groups, and in esoteric observances, which are frequently practiced covertly to avoid persecution.

THE RETURN OF THE ANIMAL GODS

His outstretched arms reached from one end of the sky to the other. His body was covered with wings; fire shot from his eyes, and from the limbs sprang a hundred heads of dragons.[4] This was the monster Typhon, son of Mother Earth and the pit of Chaos,[5] who championed the titans in their war against the gods. He terrified the deities, who fled to Egypt and hid in the form of animals; Hermes, messenger of the gods, became an ibis; Artemis, goddess of the moon, became a cat; and Apollo, god of the sun, became a crow. Pan, a forest deity with the horns and legs of a goat, tried to change into a fish, but he was too terrified to complete the transformation. He remained with the tail of a fish and the head of a goat. Finally, Zeus, god of the sky, struck Typhon with thunder bolts, so the deities could safely assume human form and return home. Today, the monster Typhon lies imprisoned in Sicily beneath Mount Aetna, though he is still powerful enough to send out and torrents of flame and steams of molten rock.

The legend of the transformation of the gods into animals was first mentioned in a fragment by the poet Pindar in the fifth century, later elaborated by many Greek and Latin authors.[6] It explained why the deities of the Egyptians were so often portrayed in the form, or at least with the heads, of animals. The Greeks and Romans imagined their deities as idealized human beings, the titans as part human and part snake. The gods represented civilization; the titans were elemental forces of nature. By their victory in the war, the gods prepared the world for the coming of men and women.

But traditions, going back to very ancient times and continuing through the Renaissance until the present, have made Egypt the home of civilization. Educated Greeks and Romans may have seen the transformation of the gods into animals as a reversion to their original form. Theriomorphic deities did precede anthropomorphic ones, and the cave paintings center far more on animals, especially large mammals of great strength or speed, than on human beings. The earliest shrines, at Çatal Hüyük and elsewhere, are dedicated to animals such as the bull. Anthropomorphic deities do not begin to emerge until civilizations emerged in the early cities of Mesopotamia and, later, of Greece.

The story of the Greek deities assuming animal form to hide tells of a profound religious and ethnographic phenomenon. Veneration of animals remains submerged in human culture and can easily reemerge in time of crisis. The Greco-Roman gods were constantly accompanied by mascots, which represent their original form. Zeus was accompanied by an eagle, and he became an eagle to abduct Ganymede. Athena was accompanied by an owl, Artemis by a deer, and Hera by a cow. The Israelites returned to worship of a golden calf, the Apis bull, during a period of great hardship in their exodus from Egypt (Exo-

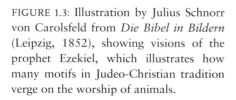

FIGURE 1.3: Illustration by Julius Schnorr von Carolsfeld from *Die Bibel in Bildern* (Leipzig, 1852), showing visions of the prophet Ezekiel, which illustrates how many motifs in Judeo-Christian tradition verge on the worship of animals.

dus 32:1–24). Moses crushed that insurrection, but the leader of the Israelites himself introduced a practice that at least verges closely on animal worship. When his people were subjected to a plague of serpents, Moses ordered a large bronze serpent erected, and those who looked upon it were protected from death (Numbers 21:6–9).

There was a partial revival of theriomorphic practices at the end of the Roman Empire, as the demise of the anthropomorphic Greco-Roman gods allowed more archaic practices to surface, often in the framework of Christianity. If one puts aside the ponderings of theologians and considers Christianity as a folk religion, with its legends of saints and wonder tales, it may well be closer than the paganism of the Greek and Roman elites to the natural world. Christ himself is often represented by the lamb, a favorite food animal of the Near East. Saint Mark is represented by a lion, and Saint Luke is an ox. The cults of saints, which are often thinly disguised pagan deities, also frequently feature animals. Saint Anthony preached to the fish, and Saint Francis was accompanied by a wolf and preached to birds. In a few cases, animals have been declared saints and their deeds have even become sites of pilgrimages. Thus the French Saint Guinefort is a dog and the Irish Saint Liban is a mermaid. The dove or pigeon remains in Christianity as a representation of the Holy Spirit. Theologians may insist that dove is just an arbitrary symbol, but then why are other symbols for the Holy Spirit almost never used? (See Figure 1.3.)

TOTEMISM

Something close to veneration is implicit in the very concept of an *animal*. It is very difficult to say what an animal is, but, on an experiential level, it is a lot easier to say what an animal is not; it is not, or not quite, a human being, not one of us. Biologists may now classify human beings as animals, but that is a technical definition that has not quickly changed the way we think. When we take one, say, a pet dog, into the human society, it ceases to seem entirely an animal but becomes almost human. According to the theologian Rudolf Otto, the foundation of religion is the experience of the *mysterium tremendum* or the "wholly other"—that which is entirely apart from ordinary experience and speech.[7] By defining ourselves as human beings, largely in opposition to animals, we envelop them in this mystery. As long as we can even speak of animals in this sense, they will continue to have a religious fascination.

Our attitudes toward animals blend envy, pity, scorn, and veneration in ways that are very difficult to explain. By any conventional measure of human welfare, life of animals in the wild would be completely intolerable. Very few animals even reach maturity. Less than one of a dozen rabbits will live to reproduce, and it will take hundreds of tadpoles to produce a single frog. No wild animal ever dies what we sometimes call a natural death. They must perpetually contend with the prospect of starvation, debilitating disease, and predators. Offspring of large predators such as lions and bears may even be devoured by their own fathers. In addition, many animals must face what appears to us to be either isolation or ferocious social pressures. And yet, the lives of wild animals often appear paradisial to us. They are lived with an immediacy and directness that often appears to more than compensate for all of the terrors. Animals, with their secret wisdom, can appear to transcend our grandest hopes and deepest fears.

Every animal is a repository of human traditions that date back far earlier than any living language or any city.[8] Songbirds remain the best symbols of conjugal love, while dogs continue to represent fidelity. Other animals such as crows or deer have symbolism that is far more complex and ambivalent, yet perhaps even more intense. The iconic power of animals makes them into a symbolic language in which we can most vividly express our hopes, fears, and values. As animals become ever more remote from our lives and are increasingly driven to extinction, those values may be imperiled as well. To put it another way, animals, with their links to the past and to the natural world, are guardians of cultural heritage going back several millennia.

The best term for our religious and cultural bonding with animals is probably totemism, which comes from an Ojibwa Indian word meaning "blood relative." The term first appeared around the end of the eighteenth century, and it was popularized in the Victorian era by anthropological folklorists such as Edwin Sidney Hartland, Edward Burnet Tylor, Andrew Lang, and Sir James George Frazer. They viewed totemism as an early stage in progress of humankind from savagery to civilization, based on the belief of tribal descent from an ancestor that mated with an animal. Most Victorians viewed such so-called primitive systems of belief with a combination of amused contempt and fascination, rarely doubting that these were based on simple credulity and doomed to extinction by the logic of history. Nevertheless, the Victorians loved to recount the exotic practices of savages, and the fascination extended to remnants of totemism in the modern world. Frazer, for all his scholarly dignity, took a childish delight in exposing the totemic roots of the Christian Eucharist and its association with cannibalism.[9]

The Victorian world, even more than our own, was pervaded by nostalgia for a mythical past, sometimes identified with childhood, sometimes with ancient civilizations or primitive peoples. Like the ancient Romans before them, the British in the Victorian era were absorbing the religious practices of the kingdoms they had conquered. The British Empire was driven not only by desire for wealth and power but also by a sort of religious quest analogous to the Crusades. The hold of Christianity on the imaginations of the British citizens was eroding, and poets such as Arnold and Tennyson were obsessed with the longing for, and precarious nature of, religious faith. The Victorians were forever searching for traditions that might rejuvenate Christianity or perhaps even, for the less conventionally devout, replace it entirely. They sought these as scholars, looking into ever more remote periods of the past, or as adventurers, going to either obscure villages or distant lands.

The Victorian tradition culminated with Frazer's *The Golden Bough*, first published in 1897, where a grand exploration of primitive cultures across many centuries and throughout the world. Frazier had begun as a scholar of ancient Greece and Rome, but his attempt to explain classical mythology had drawn him back further in the past to totemic religions. The effect of his work, surely not entirely unintended, was to spread nostalgia for mythologies of the archaic times. He deeply influenced such modern writers as W. B. Yeats, T. S. Eliot, James Joyce, and Robert Graves, none of whom had much confidence, or even much interest, in human progress.

In the early 1960s, the French anthropologist Claude Lévi-Strauss published *Le totemism aujourd'hui* (translated into English as *Totemism*), an attack on Victorian theories of mythology. The entire concept of totemism, he argued, had been based a superficial reading of mythologies. Anthropologists had often misunderstood metaphorical statements about kinship with animals as actual genealogies. Furthermore, anthropologists had confused the totemic animals of tribes with the guardian spirits of individuals. There had, in fact, never been any universal system of totemic belief. The societies that had been lumped together as primitive were in fact extremely diverse.

When Lévi-Strauss published his books on totemism in the early 1960s, Britain and France had, except for a few vestiges, surrendered their colonial empires. Furthermore, the traumas of the early to middle twentieth century—which had brought two world wars, the Gulag, the Holocaust, and the use of atomic weapons against a civilian population—had severely shaken any confidence in the superiority of so-called civilized culture and, for that matter, of human superiority over animals. Compared to Frazer and his contemporaries, Lévi-Strauss was under little pressure to uphold colonial ideologies, most notably the idea that western Europeans had a mission to civilize the rest of the world.

Like Frazier before him, Lévi-Strauss was far more nostalgic for early mythologies than he cared to admit. His work helped to free primitive cultures from the stigmas of violence, sexual abandon, and stupidity, while leaving the poetic qualities that had drawn people to them unchallenged. Shortly after writing *Le totemism aujourd'hui*, Claude Lévi-Strauss himself decided to revive the concept of totemism in *La Pensée sauvage* (1964, translated into English as *The Savage Mind*), a book that is sometimes considered the first work of anthrozoology. Totemism was, according to Lévi-Strauss, still meaningful, not as a set of beliefs but rather as a way of thinking. Primitive peoples named tribal units after animals or plants simply because diversity of species provided the most dramatic model for systems of classification. They organized the world, including human society, through analogies and associations drawn from the nature, which is almost the same thing as saying that these people lived in a zoocentric world.

Today, the word *totemism* is used broadly to describe the full range of practices, beliefs, and attitudes that are not centered on humanity. It is important to remember that totemism has never been a movement, or even a broad coalition, whether social, religious, or political. It is a way of relating to the world and can be seen from the ideas of Nazis such as Heinrich Himmler to socialists such as Barbara Ehrenreich, from conservative fundamentalists such as the snake handlers of the Bible Belt to neo-pagans such as Starhawk.

The contemporary world embodies vestiges of totemic practices inherited from archaic times such as naming sports teams after animals or depicting them on coins as emblems of a country. A glance at the new age or metaphysical section in any large bookshop will show a wide range of books on totemism with titles like *Animal-Speak: The Spiritual & Magical Powers of Creatures Great & Small* and *The Witch's Familiar: Spiritual Partnerships for Successful Magic*. Popular magazines of many varieties are full of articles about totems, as used in therapies, enchantments, strategies for professional success, and so on. It is true that the use in contemporary totemism of animals, while magical, is often completely utilitarian, designed to bring professional or personal accomplishment. But even in that respect, people today are not very different from their remote ancestors at the dawn of civilization.

The numinous quality of animals has, in many respects, actually increased in the twentieth century, as so many species have been driven to extinction. Their mystery has deepened as daily contact with animals has declined. Endangered animals, especially large predators, have acquired the status of martyrs. Wolves, for example, are constantly celebrated on posters, t-shirts, and jewelry.

THE MECHANICAL ANIMAL

In the course of civilization, machines have gradually taken over the functions of animals. Oxen are no longer used for plowing or to turn millstones. Horses are also rarely harnessed to a plow except in the poorest agricultural areas, and they are rarely used for transportation. Dogs no longer turn spits and are even becoming unusual as guardians of homes. Animal skins as clothing have been in great part replaced by plastics and synthetic fibers. In a very few instances, new uses have been found for animals, for example as guide dogs at the end of World War I, or, more recently, as drug and bomb sniffers. Even more dramatically, animals are now used to test medicines on a scale that would have been unimaginable before the modern period. But nearly everybody today deals constantly with machines in daily life and rarely, perhaps never, with animals.

In the human psyche as well, the role of animals has been partially taken over by mechanical devices. The fear of predators must have been overpowering for men and women a few millennia ago, since, even though most large predators have been driven to extinction or confined to zoos and parks, it remains powerful today. Hell is still imagined as an enormous mouth, and demons continue to be depicted with the teeth of animal predators. Many popular movies such as *Jaws, Jurassic Park,* and *Anaconda* are based on our horror of carnivorous animals today, and pursuit by beasts is a common motif in the dreams of normal people and the delusions of the psychotic. Men and women describe all manner of traumatic experiences from robbery to rape using the metaphor of predation. Sociobiologists have attempted to explain this fear of predators, which is out of proportion to any danger, as a biological inheritance from very archaic times.[10] The terror evoked by mechanical devices, while perhaps less immediate, can be just as visceral.

Much as people of the Stone Age feared being eaten by predators, those today fear being replaced by machines. Not only animals but many people as well have lost their jobs to machines. In the Industrial Era, this was largely a problem for factory workers, but now even teachers and nurses fear being rendered obsolete by automation. In many cases, employees can be retrained with no great difficulty, but the visceral fears go beyond inconvenience or loss of income. For many people, it can be one's purpose, one's place in the cosmos that is in question. At least since Mary Shelley wrote *Frankenstein* and E. T. A. Hoffmann wrote *The Sandman* in the early nineteenth century, writers have worried that human beings might be rendered obsolete by our creations.

One way in which animals have never, and perhaps cannot be, replaced by machines is as food, which has a special sort of intimacy. It suggests nurturing, even a shared identity with animals, something that is commemorated in ceremonies such as the Christian Eucharist. This is why people will not eat animals that they find repugnant. The ancient Egyptians, Hebrews, and Muslims have traditionally refused to eat the pig, an animal they usually despised, while most people today will not eat rats and insects for the same reason. The custom, today rarely still observed, of saying grace before a meal derives ultimately from the appeal of a hunter for pardon from the animal that he has killed. It is true that people often mistreat food animals, particularly in our compartmentalized society. The meat we buy in the supermarket is butchered to a point where it no longer even resembles any animal, limiting both our gratitude and our distress. But the act of eating meat, even in our secularized society, remains overlaid with complex meanings, shown by the great attention that we pay to the places and circumstances under which we eat.

In general, deities have been conceived in increasingly less theriomorphic form as technologies become more elaborate and people drift further from the natural world. Today, most people rarely even see animals apart from pets, common birds, and perhaps an occasional rodent. As animals are domesticated, driven to extinction, or replaced in our lives by machines, their physical abilities no longer inspire the same awe. Nevertheless, animals, particularly large predators, have not lost their iconic power, which is exploited everywhere from heraldry to advertisements.

At the dawn of the modern era, the philosopher René Descartes theorized that animals were machines while human beings had a soul and free will, but debates about his theory are anachronistic because we have come to think of machines in very different terms. For Descartes and his contemporaries, the paradigmatic machine was the watch—characterized by jerky motion, hypnotic repetition, perfectibility, and absolute subordination to the agenda of its owner.[11] Throughout most of the Industrial Era, the eighteenth through early twentieth centuries, philosophers constantly imagined the deity as a divine watchmaker. The paradigmatic machine of today is the computer, which can be as unpredictable as any mad genius in a laboratory.

Whatever their abilities, computers, unlike animals, are not profoundly integrated into the human imagination. Even the most beautifully designed Web sites have a flatness about them; everything they show appears transitory and insubstantial. In the realm of computers, the sacred hardly seems to exist as a category. Who ever heard of a sacred Web site, a sacred e-mail, or a sacred computer program? But taken as a whole, the vastness of the information on the Internet evokes something like religious awe. Since we cannot express this awe in the usual language of computers, we turn, like apostate Hebrews, to traditional symbols, most often those of animals. Among the most ubiquitous, for example, is the spider that is at least implicitly connoted in the World Wide Web, a figure recalling a vast number of deities from Spider Woman of the Hopi Indians and Anansi of northwest Africa to the Egyptian Neith and the Greco-Roman fates.

THE ENVIRONMENT: WHAT'S LEFT?

Today, we are accustomed to thinking of environmentalism as a movement of the Left, but that was far from the case when it began at around the middle of the nineteenth century. Much of the impetus for the movement came from the German Wihelm Heinrich Riehl, who laid the foundations for European conservatism in the middle of the nineteenth century. Riehl believed that government should be based not on abstract principles, such as those proclaimed by the French and American revolutions, but on organic traditions that had developed over millennia. The state was an organic creation, in which each class, like the organs of the body, had a distinct function. He imagined a harmonious society in which lords and peasants, joined by bonds of duty and mutual affection, would work toward a greater good, embodied in the landscapes that were their heritage.[12]

Riehl and his followers sometimes spoke of the social order as a sort of supraindividual organism, of which all trades, classes, and individuals form a part. The idea had some precedent in Christianity, where partaking of the Eucharist unites people in the single body of Christ. It had even older roots in mystical Judeo-Christian and Islamic traditions, according to which the original Adam, before Eve was created from his rib, contained all of humankind. Many defenders of the feudal order, however, thought of a supraindividual in terms of pagan traditions, perpetuated by aristocratic houses through heraldic signs, in which the collective self of the people would be represented by an animal, often a large predator, such as the bear or wolf.

For the European Left, the idea of protecting the natural world was still too closely associated with the forest laws of the middle ages. Hunting of the stag, for example, had been reserved for kings and princes, who often went about it with the solemnity of a totem sacrifice. Peasants who might shoot at deer that were devouring their fields were punished with utmost brutality. The deer represented royalty, whereas the forests seemed a vestige of the feudal order. The resentment often extended to forests themselves, which were still viewed as a royal domain.[13]

The conservatives in the tradition of Riehl were a mostly a nostalgic lot, delighting in pageantry and lamenting a doomed way of life. But around the end of the nineteenth century, biological theorists such as Ernst Haeckel, who coined the term *ecology*, combined the organic model of human society with Social Darwinism to produce a far more militant ideology. For the Fascists of

Mussolini's Italy and the Nazis of Hitler's Germany, the state was itself a living thing, to which individuals must be absolutely subordinate, much as organs are subordinate to the body. It was, furthermore, a predator, devouring and digesting other countries like beasts of prey attacking herds.

Hitler and the Nazis had a totemic identification with wolves, and, shortly after they came to power, Nazi Germany became the first modern country to place the wolf among protected species. Hitler referred to the SS as "a pack of wolves," was known as Little Wolf, and gave his various headquarters names like Wolf's Gulch and Wolf's Lair. Hermann Göring, one of his most trusted ministers, described the Nazi deputies in the Reichstag as "wolves among the sheep." The German shepherd had been created in the early twentieth century by the militantly nationalistic breeder Max von Stephanitz; he claimed it was a recreation of the "primeval German dog," which, unlike other dogs, was derived entirely from the wolf. This theory was widely disseminated by Konrad Z. Lorenz, a member of the Nazi party and its chief ideologist on issues relating to animals, both during and after the Nazi period. Walter Darré, the Nazi Minister of Agriculture, by contrast promoted the pig as the central animal of the Aryan race.[14]

In North America, which had never known the brutalities of medieval forest law, the protection of nature had a different status. The pristine landscapes of North America had been a source of pride since the earliest settlements. They had long been taken for granted as a sort of divine inheritance, but around the start of the twentieth century people were becoming increasingly aware that the forests and grasslands that once covered North America were rapidly being depleted. President Theodore Roosevelt, an avid outdoorsman and amateur naturalist, created the first national parks in the United States, in which vast tracts of land were protected. He thought, however, of those lands mostly in utilitarian terms, as a place of beauty and recreation. Large predators such as the wolf and mountain lion, in part because of their association with the aristocratic order of the Old World, were ruthlessly hunted to near extinction.[15]

A sense that not only the American landscapes themselves but also animals, including predators, might be sacred goes back to Henry David Thoreau and John Muir, but it became a guiding force in the environmental movement through the work of Aldo Leopold. In an essay entitled "Thinking like a Mountain," from his 1949 book *The Sand County Almanac*, Leopold expressed this in what has become by far the most famous passage in American environmental literature:

When our rifles were empty, the old wolf was down, and a pup was dragging a leg into impassable slide-rocks. We reached the old wolf in time to watch a fierce green fire dying in her eyes. I realized then, and have known ever since, that there was something new to me in those eyes—something known only to her and to the mountain. I was young then, and full of trigger-itch; I thought that because fewer wolves meant more deer, that no wolves would mean hunters' paradise. But after seeing the green fire die, I sensed that neither the wolf nor the mountain agreed with such a view.[16]

From this point on, ecology in the United States has inclined toward a totemic, even pagan, perspective on animals.

During and after World War II, although many activists continued to work quietly for conservation, the environmental movement was depoliticized and went into eclipse in the United States, in part because of its association with the Fascist and Nazi movements. The intelligentsia tended to consider rural people to be backward and narrow minded. Those who worried about landscapes were suspected of being indulgent, while those who worked for the welfare of animals lay under suspicion of being sentimental. Writers celebrated the energy and vitality of big cities, with their jazz, high fashion, theatre, and avant gardes. This did not change much even with the initial upheavals of the late 1960s. The early hippies made pilgrimages to urban centers such as Haight-Ashbury in San Francisco and Greenwich Village in New York, perhaps stopping briefly in rural areas on the way.

Then, around the start of the 1970s, rural issues, previously identified most with the political Right, were discovered by the Left. The first Earth Day was celebrated with great fanfare in 1970. About a decade later, the animal rights movement was revived by Henry Spira, Peter Singer, and Tom Regan. Both movements shared a renewed emphasis on animals, but there were profound differences between them.

The environmental movements focused on species, whereas the animal rights movement centered on animals as individuals. The animal rights movement, though it often made rhetorical appeals to the ideal of equality, used humanity as the standard against which all animals were to be measured. It endeavored only to extend some of the protections and rights accorded to people to a least a few other species. In contrast, the environmental movement took a totemic view of animals and endeavored to protect their habitats. The advocates of animal rights emphasized the way in which certain animals such as chimpanzees or dogs resemble people, while environmental activists emphasized the ways in which animals are different from humankind.

The activism of the late 1960s and early 1970s gradually gave way to a more reflective period, in which many thinkers tried to synthesize the disparate ideals that had driven the protests of the past decade or so. As the 1960s had spawned a vast diversity of movements, the following decades generated or revived theories and critical approaches, many of which were centered on the natural world. These included, for example, ecofeminism, deep ecology ecopsychology, Gaia theory, and ecocriticism. These intellectual approaches were neither unified nor monolithic, but, in general, they attempted to restore a sense of the sacredness of the natural world, partly in the hope that this would lead people to spontaneously protect animals and the environment.[17]

As the twentieth century drew to a close, Paul Shepard published *The Others: How Animals Made Us Human,* the first and most influential manifesto of contemporary totemism. It is a book in the Victorian tradition, ranging over many cultures and eras with vast but unsystematic learning. Shepard argues that virtually all human activities originally were conceived in imitation of animals. These include technologies, such as pointed implements, which are derived from horns and beaks. They include the arts, such as dance, which often imitates the movements of animals. They include modes of government, which are derived from the observation of animal behavior. As human beings lose contact with the natural world, all of our institutions are severed from their foundation and lose their meaning. The sacrament of Shepard's totemic religion is the hunt, and he forever castigates the sentimentality of urban dwellers that object to it. In the end, he leaves us with little more than nostalgia for a past that, however bloody, is inspiring, and with the quixotic nobility of a crusade to bring it back.

At about that time, I founded Nature in Legend and Story (NILAS), an organization dedicated to what we call totemic literature. According to our mission statement, "We view literature and the arts as inheritors of the tradition of old mythologies, which were less concerned with interpersonal relationships than with the orientation of the human race with respect to other beings." The most thorough exploration of this philosophy is in the anthology entitled *What Are Animals to Us?*, a collection of papers from the 2003 NILAS conference, edited by David Aftandilian.[18]

Most of us who participated in some way in these movements of the middle to later twentieth century sometimes felt exhilaration at the dramatic upheavals. Bob Dylan's song "The Times They are A-Changin'" became an anthem of the 1960s and 1970s. *Revolutionary* and *subversive* were favorite words, used for a vast range of purposes from starting riots to selling toothpaste. But today the changes of that era seem no more than a prelude to, even a distraction from, far greater transformations that were to come.

NEW ANIMALS FOR A NEW MILLENNIUM

Two years before the start of the new millennium, Elizabeth de Fontenay published *Le silence des bêtes: La philosophie à l'épreuve de l'animalité* (The silence of beasts: Animals in philosophy and experience), probably the most extensive survey of animals in philosophy that has been written. Her opening passage states: "It is very probably that the last decade of this millennium will remain known as the inauguration of the era of cloning. So perhaps we are living at the last time when it will be possible, without sounding overly strange, to undertake a meditation on animals, as they have been traditionally conceived, imagined and desired in the Occident" (my translation). Fontenay may have exaggerated the immediate impact of cloning, but that is only one of the dramatic changes in biotechnology, technology, and human thought that are taking place as we enter a new millennium. It is rapidly becoming impossible to discuss the cultural and ethical issues raised by animals without reference to computers and to biotechnology.

Since the start of the twenty-first century, no writer will ever again be able to take for granted the natural divisions of animals into species or even natural processes such as reproduction. Since Victorian times, many people have held that Darwin's theory of evolution challenges our notions of human distinctness. True enough, but that is hardly even the beginning of the intellectual challenges that we face in the new millennium. Organ transplants such as giving the heart of baboon to a human baby also blur the division between animals and human beings. Some researchers have suggests implanting embryos of chimpanzees into human women, while one biotech company has transplanted human DNA into the egg of a cow.[19]

But the distinctions among other species, both animal and plant, is also becoming increasingly porous. Scientists have, by tinkering with the genetic code, produced a combination of a sheep and goat known as a "geep." Scientists have also performed experiments such as inserting the gene of a firefly into a tobacco plant to produce a plant with leaves that glow and inserting genes from a flounder into a tomato plant to increase resistance to frost. From the standpoint of science and industry, all living things often seem to be little more than temporary carriers of information inscribed in the genetic code, which can be endlessly edited and recombined,[20] a bit like Web pages hosted on a server. Many cultural critics are used to opposing human pride to the interests of animals and the environment, yet this vision undermines both at once. It diminishes individuals and reduces species to insignificance, though the idea does have a certain grandeur. The double helix of DNA, in consequence, is known as the cosmic serpent, named after the most primeval of animal deities.

Perhaps most dramatically, computer technology now blurs the boundaries between mind and matter, between objects and living things. Technicians have managed to create computers that can surpass human beings in many complex mental processes, such as playing chess. Computer simulations have become celebrities, and they now routinely act alongside human beings in movies. But just because human beings make computers does not mean that we understand them. Even experts need to take the rational nature of computers largely on faith, since no single individual is able to understand more than a few facets of their construction. For all the precision of their internal components, computers are very quirky, and using them is often very intuitive. Computers designed to play chess may have phenomenal calculating ability, yet they are prone to occasionally make obvious blunders, the sort that, when made by a human chess master, would be ascribed to carelessness or fatigue.

As Sherry Turkle has pointed out in *Life on the Screen: Identity in the Age of the Internet*, the difference between cybertechnology and the human mind has seemed less pronounced since a revolution in computer technology that began around the early 1990s. Computer programming has been profoundly influenced by biology, most specifically by evolutionary theory.[21] The emphasis in design and use of computers is now less on their ability to follow elaborate directions than to learn like living things, from experience. Computers are now used less for calculation than for simulation. Just as with medicine, experts in computer technology concentrate mostly on finding out *what* works without being greatly concerned about the *how*. Unable to claim special status on the basis of their intellects, human beings now even have difficulty making a romantic claim to divine irrationality.

Today, however, mechanical devices from cell phones to prosthetic limbs are so integrated into our routines that many of us can hardly imagine life without them. Furthermore, our days are elaborately scheduled, in ways that were inconceivable before the development of accurate timepieces. We increasingly envy the freedom and spontaneity of animals in the wild, which appear to come and go as they please, even if they are in perpetual danger. Animals often begin to appear, in a traditional sense, more human than human beings.

As the basic categories with which people have divided up the world become indistinct, language itself, the great pride of humanity, is failing. We face the most radical challenge to our traditional hierarchal divisions of the world since these were first systematically articulated by Aristotle. The breakdown of our linguistic categories, in turn, forces us to confront directly the mysteries of our world. We can no longer simply delegate philosophy to academic specialists or religion to theologians. For that matter, we cannot even leave animals to the zoologists. No authority can now shield us from primordial experiences such as confrontation with creatures that are profoundly different from ourselves.

The social, cultural, and philosophical issues raised by animals, while never simple, have grown vastly more complicated within the past few decades. It is now difficult to even formulate, let alone address, these concerns in abstract terms, and so philosophy is giving way to storytelling as a preferred mode of intellectual exploration. What is a human being? What is an animal? Who knows? But we do not really need answers in order to tell a good story. Telling of stories is, as it has been since Neolithic people gathered around a fire, a means of organizing experience, and we can still turn to it when abstractions fail.

HIGH-TECH MAGIC

During the Industrial Age, people constantly complained about the disenchantment of the world. Keats wrote in "Lamia:"

> Philosophy will clip an Angel's wings,
> Conquer all mysteries by rule and line,
> Empty the haunted air, and gnomed mine—
> Unweave a rainbow.

Nobody writes that way about the science of today. No cosmology has ever been more extravagant than that of contemporary physics, with its multiple dimensions, alternate universes, and cosmic strings. The air is haunted as perhaps never before, filled with electronic messages we decipher and countless others that we do not. If the spiritual problems of the Industrial Age were regimentation and alienation, those of the contemporary world are chaos and insecurity. If the old sciences were generally reductive, suggesting that things were less than they appeared, the theory of emergence reveals them as far more than their component parts.[22]

The world we confront may be confusing and uncertain, at times even terrifying, but it is vibrant and alive. Research shows increasingly that animals are far more than incomplete human beings. We know that bats, for example, navigate with great precision by radar. Elephants communicate over long distances by calls with frequencies too low to be detected by the human ear, while bees can see colors in the ultraviolet portion of the spectrum inaccessible to human eyes. Sharks can find prey by means of magnetic fields, which are generated by electric currents inside the body. Who knows what other senses animals may have, which humans either lack entirely or possess, at most, in a far more rudimentary form?

While raising the status of animals, such discoveries also challenge thoughtlessly anthropomorphic views of them. We know only that they much perceive the world in radically different ways than our own. This difference must surely extend to such basic parameters of our existence as time, space, death, life, pain, delight, hope, and fear. The task of empathizing with animals challenges, and perhaps liberates, the human imagination. In many respects, the culture of postindustrial society resembles the magical world of medieval epics more than it does naturalistic novels. We are closer to *Beowulf* than, for example, to

Dickens. The rupture with the culture of industrial society may allow earlier cultural forms, including totemism, to reemerge.

DOES POSTHUMAN MEAN POSTANIMAL?

Challenges to anthropocentric philosophy have often been made in the name of environmentalism, of animal rights, of new age religion or, simply, of scientific research. Still, a little probing generally shows that these challenges are themselves usually based on highly anthropocentric premises. Almost all philosophies of animal rights judge animals according to their similarity to human beings, while environmental philosophies accord human beings primary responsibility for the condition of the world. Throughout the 1970s and 1980s, the slogan of environmentalists was, "Save the earth." As for science, it is entirely oriented around extending the comprehension, and often the welfare, of humanity.

An anthropocentric view of the universe is now so deeply integrated into virtually all of our traditions that it is truly difficult to even imagine discarding it. But frequent attacks on anthropocentric philosophy, from Leopold to Singer, show, even if philosophers seldom probe their full implications, that we are not satisfied with the apparent dominion of humankind. If indeed we—and, of course "we" means *homo sapiens*—do eventually move away from an anthropocentric view of the universe, it will probably not be through a movement but rather a broad trend that embraces all sectors of society.

According to the Italian Roberto Marchesini, anthropocentric perspective is based on what he called the "myth of incompleteness," the idea that human beings have been, by comparison with other creatures, insufficiently endowed by nature and require culture to become complete. Humans, Marchesini argues, are gifted with robust senses, excellent balance, and fine muscular coordination that may be unique among large animals. Humans are as complete as other creatures, or at least could be if they allowed themselves to.

Far from making human beings whole, culture is, and has always been, the source of our incompleteness. It is what drives us constantly to affiliate with other things, whether plants, animals, machines, or ideas, in the hope that these will make us whole. The hope is perpetually disappointed, as every affiliation creates a perceived need for new ones. To give one modest but typical example, antibiotics may protect our sources of food, yet they cause diseases to mutate, necessitating new, ever stronger antibiotics and other medicines. And even if we accept that medical intervention is driven by necessity, the same cannot be said for many of our other affiliations, for example, with abstract philosophies or pets. Though Marchesini does not go into this, the myth of incompleteness, where human beings are exalted by their tragic destiny, seems to mark a transition from theriomorphic to anthropomorphic religion. Even in justifying human dominance, it preserves an admiration, even awe, for animals, which live in a completeness and a harmony about which we can only dream.

The earliest explicit articulation of the myth of incompleteness is found the myth of Prometheus, first told in *Works and Days* by the Greek Hesiod around the middle of the eighth century BCE. The trickster Prometheus had induced Zeus to accept the poorer part of a sacrifice, the gristle and bone, leaving almost all of the meat to people. Zeus also punished mankind by withholding fire, but Prometheus stole fire and brought it to men in a reed of fennel. Zeus chained Prometheus to a rock in the Caucus Mountains, where an eagle gnawed on his liver every day until finally he was released by Heracles. Zeus punished mankind by creating the first woman, Pandora, whom he gave to Epimetheus, the foolish brother of Prometheus, in marriage. Then as a wedding gift, he gave a box containing all of the evils in the world. Moved by curiosity, Pandora opened the present, releasing strife, famine, and every other ill. For Hesiod, Prometheus was simply a perverse trickster, but for later Greeks such as Aeschylus he became a tragic hero and a benefactor of humanity. The fire stolen by Prometheus represents culture, needed by human beings as compensation for their lack of natural gifts; the box of Pandora represents the perils of human life in alienation from the natural world.

In the new millennium, human beings have become in many ways more powerful than ever before, able to reattach severed limbs and to send satellites into space. And yet human beings are simultaneously further than ever from the ideal of autonomy. We are able to do virtually nothing entirely on our own but require the assistance of biotechnological, mechanical, and intellectual devices. Our bodies are centers of so much aggressive intervention, everything from facial creams and deodorant to gene therapy and plastic surgery, that our bodies may hardly seem to *belong to* us, still less to *be* us, any more. The solution for Marchesini is to abandon the illusion of human autonomy, accepting external contributions to human identity.[23] Human identity has traditionally been defined largely in opposition to animals, but now they must become part of us Though Marchesini does not explicitly make the connection, this is what we traditionally think of as totemism.

It is not clear that a breakdown of the division between the realms of humans and nature is desirable, since that could, for example, place in jeopardy our ideals of human rights. Something of the sort already happened in Nazi Germany, where a blurring of the boundary between animals and humans enabled the regime to breed, herd, and slaughter people like livestock.[24] At the same time, a breakdown could remove the remaining restraints on intervention in the natural world.[25]

On the other hand, it is by no means clear that articulating the ideals of human rights has advanced their substance. John Locke, the philosopher who articulated the modern notion of human rights in the eighteenth century, invested in the slave trade. The modern era that brought the dissemination of the ideal has also seen the expansion of chattel slavery, the Gulag, the Holocaust, and other perhaps unprecedented crimes against humanity. Similarly, the spread of environmentalist ideals has accompanied the devastation of the natural world.

The desire for union with nature has run through our culture since the start of civilization. It is expressed in countless stories throughout the world of animal brides, representing the natural world, that marry a man and live in an intense but precarious harmony until the husband makes a tragic mistake.[26] The yearning for this union is older, and probably more profound, than even our traditions of human rights or the foundations of environmentalism.

HUMANS AND NATURE IN THE
TWENTY-FIRST CENTURY

Predicting the future, even in general terms, is never much more than an intellectual game, since trends, no matter how ancient or how recent, can reverse themselves almost instantly. Only time will tell whether the boundary between human beings and nature will, as Marchesini has predicted, disappear, but the line is more flexible and more robust than perhaps he acknowledges. The boundary has constantly shifted over the millennia, as mermaids, angels, apes, Indians, fairies, women, dogs, and other beings seemingly crossed that border, living now with us and now with animals on the other side. Perhaps we shall decide that powerful computers and large mammals are civilized, whereas reptiles and insects are not. It is easy to think up any number of ways the world may be divided in two categories. Those in the human realm have always gazed across that invisible line, with a combination of fear, scorn, reverence, and awe. We have loved nature, just as we love animals, deeply and sincerely, but we have constantly destroyed it nevertheless. This is commemorated in many of our oldest myths.

When the Babylonian goddess Tiamat was slain by the god Marduk, the gods made the earth from her body. In the Greek tradition, Tiamat became Gaia, or Mother Earth; in the Hebrew tradition she became the sea monster Leviathan, a creature so large that the entire earth can rest easily on one of his fins. The waters of the Jordan cannot quench Leviathan's thirst and his breath makes the oceans seethe and boil. (See Figure 1.4.)

Tradition tells that when the creation of the world was completed, there were two leviathans, a male and a female. God realized that, should they reproduce, the creatures would in time destroy the world. He killed one leviathan, and, so the remaining monster would not become lonely, God now plays with the monster during the last hours of each day.

When the end of the world approaches, God will kill the remaining leviathan as well. The just will dine in a tent made of the monster's skin,[27] but, as

FIGURE 1.4: A relief from the Temple of Enurta at Nimrud, Assyria, which may represent an androgynous form of the goddess Tiamat.

Shakespeare has reminded us in *Macbeth*, prophecies are not always what they seem. Perhaps this one means that Leviathan will swallow men and women. The men and women will be in a tent if Leviathan is dead and in a belly if the monster is alive. Yet perhaps even the distinction between life and death is far more complicated than many of us had thought. Who shall have triumphed in the end? The people or Leviathan? Humanity or Nature?

It may be that, back within the womb of Tiamat, man and nature will again be one.

CHAPTER TWO

An Anthropological Examination of Hunting

Ethnography and Sensation

GARRY MARVIN

Early in the morning a farmer, dressed in dull green and brown work clothes, a dog at his side, leaves his house and walks quietly along a hedgerow toward a wood. At the edge of the wood he takes two cartridges from his pocket and puts them into his shotgun. He removes the safety catch. With the gun ready he continues slowly and quietly along the edge of the wood—an unobtrusive presence in the landscape. All of his senses alert, his eyes scan the near distance. He is not interested in the occasional pheasant that flaps out of the trees and into the field, nor the rabbits feeding along the hedgerows. His aim, if his aim is true, is to shoot one of the local foxes that might turn their attention to his poultry or lambs.

There is intense activity by midmorning in a grassed paddock in front of a farmhouse. Dozens of people, dressed in highly polished boots, cream jodhpurs, red or black coats, and velvet-covered hats, are mounted on immaculately groomed horses. It is a convivial social gathering. Each of them takes a drink offered on trays by members of the farmer's family and move on to greet and chat with friends. At the edge of the assembling riders is a man dressed in formal riding attire with a red jacket;[1] around his horse are a score or so of increasingly restless hounds. Although he talks with those who greet him, his attention is on the hounds, and he occasionally raises his voice to one that attempts to slip away from the pack. Mixing with this group of riders are men, women, and children, dressed in everyday country clothing, who pat the hounds, stroke horses while talking with the riders, share a drink, and joke with other people on foot. The man with the hounds raises his horn to his lips and blows. The hounds move off excitedly, the crowd parts to let him through. The riders will follow when he is at some distance from them, and those on foot follow on behind. A foxhunt has begun.

In a sense each of these practices are foxhunts—in each there is an attempt to find and kill foxes—but the similarity ends at this very basic level. Although both take place in the spaces of the English countryside, and both center on interactions between humans and animals, the nature of these interactions are differently configured and differently performed. The first example is a private, individual, everyday working practice and unmarked; the second is a public, communal, and highly elaborated event. Nobody attends to watch the farmer in his attempt to kill foxes whereas on any hunting day large numbers of people, on foot and on horseback, will gather to follow the activities of the huntsman[2] and his hounds as they attempt to bring about the death of a fox. The over-elaboration of means compared with ends, the order and structure of the event, the formal rules of procedure and engagement, the extensive but unwritten rules of etiquette, the importance attached to dress codes, the complex descriptive vocabulary, the forms of address between participants, the sounds provided by the huntsman's horn and the baying of the hounds, and the cultural elaboration of all of the animals involved might suggest to an outsider seeking to understand foxhunting that this is a highly complex ritual, ceremonial, performative event. The farmer out with his gun is an unadorned practice; it has a simplicity, an immediacy, and a utilitarian quality compared with the mounted foxhunt that is marked by excess and intensification. It is this excess and the complex proce-dures to achieve what could be achieved in much simpler and perhaps more im-mediate ways—a dead fox—that suggest that foxhunting can be interpreted as a cultural performance and a performance of a different order from the farmer with his gun.

My central concern in this chapter is to explore some of the performative and expressive elements of foxhunting.[3] Such a performative approach attends to the complexity of the event as it is enacted in the spaces of the countryside, but it is an approach that must be adopted with care. Those who participate in foxhunting do not consciously set out to create a cultural performance and they certainly do not, in my experience, ever consciously think of the event, in its totality, as a performance. They certainly make judgements in terms of the qualities of performance, or capabilities, of certain participants within the event, but such judgments are connected with the immediacy of the event as it is being created around them and by them, rather than a distanced reflec-tion on its meaning. Edward Schiefflen has commented that in recent years anthropologists interested in cultural performances, however they are defined, have increasingly moved from studying them as systems of representations (symbolic transformations, cultural texts) to looking at them as processes of practice and performance. In part this reflects a growing dissatisfaction with purely symbolic approaches to understanding material like rituals, which seem to be curiously robbed of life and power when distanced in discussions concerned largely with meaning. *Performance* deals more with actions than text: with habits of the body more than structures of symbols, with illocutionary rather than propositional force, with the social construction of reality rather than its representation.[4]

Meanings can certainly be imposed on the event or drawn out of it but my concern here is to explore the life and power of foxhunting through a consideration of the elements and activities out of which it is composed, how it achieves its aims, how the participants, both human and animal, are involved in its construction and enactment, and what cultural sense it has for them: in total, how the performance works.

Presence is fundamental for the foxhunt. Whereas the farmer with his gun attempts to be a nonpresence, the Hunt openly and deliberately announces itself in the countryside. Through its processes it engages and connects human and animal bodies, generates excitement and emotion, both mental and visceral, and dramatically enacts a set of relationships with the natural world.

It is necessary at the outset to offer a short description of some of the key elements of what actually occurs in a hunt. A significant point to emphasize here is that, unlike the case of the farmer out with his gun, the human participants in foxhunting are not directly hunting their prey. They do not themselves attempt to find, pursue, and kill foxes; this is done by the hounds, their agents.

When the huntsman arrives at the place, perhaps a small wood or hedgerow, where he intends to begin the day's hunting, he will use his horn and his voice to encourage the hounds to begin searching for the scent of a fox. In this form of hunting the hounds do not look for a fox using their eyes. These are scent hounds rather than gaze hounds. At this point they might catch the strong scent of a fox that has been recently disturbed by their arrival or they might catch the faint and evaporating scent of a fox that passed that way some time before. If there is any scent at all, those hounds that pick up on it will begin to whimper excitedly; a sound that draws other members of the pack to them. They will move off in the direction of the scent and, if it becomes more definite, the whimpering and squeaking becomes a more convincing baying. The huntsman will make sure that all the pack is engaged and he will gallop after them. Once the hounds and huntsman have been given enough distance, so that there is no danger that they will be interfered with, the field master[5] will lead the mounted riders after them. If the hounds maintain contact with the scent of the fleeing fox, the countryside begins to resonate with the baying of the hounds, the encouraging horn calls of the huntsman and the sounds of horses galloping across the landscape. The Hunt is in full cry. Such intensity might be built up over many, fast-paced miles or it might last only a few minutes. The hounds can, at any moment, lose the scent. Scent can evaporate quickly so that the hounds are left with nothing to follow; their cries cease and their fast, directed run subsides and finally comes to a halt.

A fox that is aware of the danger behind it may become evasive, change the direction of its flight, cross and recross its path, apparently attempting to disguise its scent by running through livestock or along a stream or road. It may seek the safety of terrain where it is difficult for hounds to follow. If the hounds cannot reconnect with the scent then the huntsman will gather them around him, move to another potential site, and begin the process over again in the hope of picking up the scent of another fox. If, however, the hounds are able to hold onto the scent they will begin to gain ground on the fox and begin to outpace it. At a certain moment they will lift their heads to see their prey and, surging forward, increase their speed to catch and kill the fox on the move. The huntsman and the following riders will arrive to see a swirling mass of hounds tearing at a dead fox. The huntsman will blow The Kill on his horn. The Hunt has come to a successful conclusion. After a pause, to allow the horses, hounds, and riders to regain their breaths, the huntsman will lead them off to begin again.[6]

This short description does not adequately capture the dramatic ebbs and flows of the event, the pulsing between activity and excitement and waiting and stillness, the successes, false starts, and failures, the surprising turns in the relationships between the hounds and the fox, the personal dramas of and dangers for the riders as they succeed or fail in jumping hedges, gates, ditches, and streams, or in staying on their horses at the gallop to keep up with the Hunt. What it does point to are the highly complex relationships among humans, hounds, horses, foxes, and the countryside that are integral to, and constitutive of, foxhunting. Foxhunting is present in the countryside in very different ways from everyday practices of fox killing. In foxhunting humans and hounds do not attempt to engage with foxes directly, quietly, efficiently, and unobtrusively. They announce their presence in the countryside and draw attention to themselves both visibly and audibly, and they expect the encounter with the fox to be convoluted, difficult, and challenging. The rules of hunting both allow the fox the possibility of escape and restrict the possibilities of its capture and thus they open a space for an encounter of a different order.

Based on an original perceived need to control a rural pest, participants in foxhunting have, over the last two hundred years, transposed fox killing from the mundane into another register and have created what is arguably the most complex performative event in the English countryside. Central to this chapter is a concern to attend to the ways in which foxhunting is present in the spaces of this countryside and how the nature and structuring of its presence can be interpreted as constituting a set of performances in and with the natural world. To continue this exploration it is necessary to consider the spaces in which foxhunting is enacted.

At the national level the countryside is framed for foxhunting. England is divided into named Hunt countries by the Masters of Foxhounds Association.[7] These are constituted as territories over which the Hunt, registered to each so-called country, has the right to operate, and Hunts may not, except in exceptional circumstances, hunt foxes in the territory of adjacent Hunts.

Those who go foxhunting do not, in the main, travel to different parts of the country to hunt. They become members or supporters of the Hunt in area in which they live,[8] and such membership might have been continuous in families for generations. Hunt members are immensely committed to their Hunt and express a deep sense of belonging to a particular Hunt country. It is a countryside of which they have a close and intimate knowledge because of their hunting experiences. It is not a countryside they visit, but one they are of and to which they belong. Going hunting does not involve an outward movement to elsewhere but rather an inward movement toward the spaces and places that the participants see, experience, and often inhabit on a familiar, daily basis. On a hunting day, however, the inward movement, the movement toward a more immediate connectedness, results in the heightening and intensification of being in the countryside. The very landscapes and that which they contain are transformed into a performance space for the day. But that transformation, although new, fresh, and full of immediate potential on each hunting day also has a long history that gives it a powerful depth and resonance for those who have regularly hunted across it. As I have argued elsewhere, for the participants, hunting converts the countryside into another space:

> a sacred space of deep emotional significance and social and cultural resonance. This is not a mere landscape of more or less beauty; it consists, as Michael Mayerfield Bell has commented, of "sites of story and memory."[9] The performance of hunting—often continued for hundreds of years—in this space imbues it with a set of sensual and experiential qualities that become enriched with each hunting event. The memories are of what has or has not happened there before; the present excitement is one of potential, what might occur and what experience it will generate.[10]

It is highly significant that foxhunting is staged and enacted within the spaces of the worked, agricultural, countryside. Although mounted Hunts will enter landscapes of wild countryside—for example, moorland and forest (depending very much on the location of the particular Hunt)—in the main it takes place across grasslands and cultivated fields, along hedgerows and through small woods. These are spaces of human activity rather than of untouched

wilderness. The significance of this is to be found in the attitudes to and perceptions of the central character—the fox. One of the central reasons given for
hunting foxes is that they are considered or perceived to be rural pests by many
farmers and by those who hunt: intrusive and destructive animals that prey on
poultry, lambs, and other livestock. The fox has been the focus of their attention and concern in the countryside for centuries because, instead of being a
wild animal that directs its attention to other wild animals as a source of food,
it is thought to intrude improperly into human affairs in its search for food.
As such, it is seen as a trespasser and poacher that leaves the wild places and
enters fields and farmyards to steal and kill. For those who hunt, the fox is a
creature that disturbs the proper rural order in terms of the relationships between humans and the animals they raise for their purposes. In part, foxhunting is an attempt to bring this order back into balance through pursuing and
killing foxes, and to do so it is necessarily conducted in the lived space of this
central animal and of those people who are most concerned with it.

The landscapes of the countryside are not merely a stage or a setting for the
event but rather they are essentially constitutive of foxhunting. They demand
a knowledge and awareness of them and an immersion into them for hunting
to take place and to be successful. The animals, configured as performers (as
shown in the following section), respond to and interact with all the elements
that make up the richly textured physicality of the countryside. The nature of
the terrain itself, the places for hiding or of exposure, the wind, rain, and sunshine, and the presence of other animals, buildings, paths, and roadways are all
responded to and used by the fox in its attempt to escape the attention of the
hounds. For all the participants, both human and animal, there is an intense,
immediate, and visceral engagement with the natural world during hunting.
All of them sense, feel, and respond to the weather conditions; all watch the
countryside for signs of significance; all hear the sounds of the countryside and
react to them in different ways; all are aware of the presence of others. Hounds
draw the scent of foxes into their bodies while ignoring other scents that as-
sault them. Humans can sometimes pick up the faint trace of fox scent but they
are certainly aware of the smells of the countryside and the rich animal odors
of hounds and horses as they come close. Riders have their bodies closely and
sometime precariously connected with their horses and must be alert to anything that might disturb that equilibrium.

During its enactment foxhunting demands and creates a sustained awareness, responsiveness, sensuousness, and thoughtfulness about the countryside
and the lives it contains. The event is shot through with the everyday concerns
of the working countryside, but it also bursts through this everyday life. Radi-
ating out from the participants is a space that becomes, through the desires,
demands, and practices of hunting itself, a space in which everything is im-
bued with, and takes on, a greater significance, in which the experience of the

ordinary is magnified, heightened, and intensified. None of the participants, neither human nor animal, can participate unless they are alert and responsive to the totality of the countryside. On a nonhunting day the movement of a flock of sheep, the barking of farm dogs, the wind direction, the rising or falling temperature, the density of undergrowth in a wood, or the height of a particular crop may not be things that people pay attention to, but they become immensely significant on a hunting day because they are all elements that might indicate where a fox has gone or where one might be found.

The overarching theme here is that foxhunting reconfigures the countryside as a challenging space, and it is the variety and intensity of these different challenges that constitute part of the multifaceted enjoyment of hunting. In an important sense the countryside is not a setting for foxhunting and certainly neither an illusionary space nor a space of illusion as in other performance events, but rather it is an active constituent of the event itself.

Within the event all of those involved—humans, horses, hounds, and foxes—have their participation and contribution variously and differently configured and judged in terms of how capably they perform by the people who participate. Such perspectives are internal to the event and come from those who are themselves participants. Foxhunting does not take place, nor is it enacted, for anyone other than those who are part of it. At the most general level I would like to suggest that there is no distanced, unconnected audience for foxhunting, there are no spectators who are outside of the event itself, and there are no mere observers of it.[11]

People go foxhunting for a wide variety of reasons, and they respond to it in different ways, but all of them are participants who feel themselves to be connected and engaged with it. No one going hunting attempts to find a position from which they have an overview of the event: each of them seeks to be part of it and in the thick of it. Foxhunting, in its totality, requires their presence for it to exist as an event.

Richard Schechner's notion of the "accidental audience" and the "integral audience" is one that can here usefully be extended from theater and ritual to the foxhunt.[12] The accidental audience of a theatrical event is comprised of those who have seen advertisements, or in other ways found out about the event, and chose to attend something that is open to all. They are like tourists watching a ritual ceremony. The integral audience is one that is comprised of people connected with the theatrical world, friends of the performers—an audience of people who know each other, who know what is going on. These differently comprised audiences are significant for performance in many different ways but what is particularly relevant here is, as Schechner points out, is that:

an accidental audience comes "to see the show" while the integral audience is "necessary to accomplish the work of the show." Or, to put it another way, the accidental audience attends voluntarily, the integral audience from ritual need. In fact the presence of an integral audience is the surest evidence that the performance is a ritual.[13]

Schechner's sense of the almost moral obligation felt by certain people to attend an event and the need for them to be there for an event to occur at all is particularly important for foxhunting. During my fieldwork I was struck by the commitment to hunting from those involved in it. There was a strong sense that, as members of a particular Hunt, they ought to be out with them on as many days as possible during the season. Certainly this was connected with the obvious point that they found immense pleasure in the event. Beyond this, however, there was a strong sense that as foxhunters it was proper to be out with the Hunt on a hunting day; that, although it was not as strong as a compulsion, there was a sense of obligation that it was necessary to make time for hunting. A huntsman out with his hounds on his own could certainly hunt foxes but this would be a much reduced and impoverished sense of foxhunting and much more akin to the solitary farmer with his gun. The integral audience is necessary for the totality of foxhunting as an event.

There is one point on a hunting day in which the Hunt is, as it were, on display and at which point there will possibly be an audience or spectators who view the Hunt as a spectacle. If the meet, described earlier, is held outside a pub, on a village green, or in any similar public space there will be people who arrive as spectators of the gathering: an accidental audience with no particular connection with the event. Even though they might live locally, such people are sightseers who attend to observe a moment of what is treated as a colorful tradition that stands out from everyday life.

To return to the sense of the obligation to hunt, having made this general claim, it is necessary to offer a more nuanced account of the gradations of participation. It might seem that an obvious distinction could be drawn between the horse-mounted participants in their formal equestrian dress and those who attend on foot, dressed in everyday country clothing. The former might seem more obviously connected with the main activities of foxhunting, and constitutive of those activities, whereas the latter might seem to form more of an audience whose participation is limited to watching. This distinction is, however, misleading and would only be made by an outsider, someone unconnected with the foxhunting world. All of the people who come together on a hunting day are part of that Hunt's local world and all of them would regard themselves as fully, although differently, participating in what constitutes a day's hunting.

It is only the huntsman and his hounds who are directly hunting the fox. No other participants are permitted to attempt to find, chase, or kill foxes in foxhunting. Both those on horseback and those on foot are following the central activity of huntsman, hounds, and fox and may not directly intervene in that activity that is the performative core of the event. The ebbs and flows of the relationships between the fox and the hounds dictates and governs the rhythms of the Hunt in its totality. The mounted riders have, perhaps, a more immediate relationship to this than those on foot or following in cars in that they hope to follow closely where the fox and hounds lead, although they must remain in a group under the guidance of the field master who will lead them across the countryside. While the huntsman is stationary and waiting for his hounds to explore a particular terrain; the riders will be at rest, hoping and waiting for the hounds to find a scent and begin a pursuit. If the huntsman is ambling along with the hounds as he follows them through a wood or along a hedgerow they will be allowed to follow at a suitable distance behind him, as they will if he trots or canters to a new location. For some riders, those who are aficionados of the practice of hunting itself, the fact that they are in sight of the huntsman working with his hounds is the central pleasure of the day. For the majority of riders however, this is hardly the excitement they hope for. Once the hounds have picked up a scent and begin to increase their pace in a very directed way then the potential exists for a much more challenging performance of equestrianism. To keep up with the hounds they must cross the countryside at speed and confront the obstacles that present themselves. Here riders judge their horses and those of others in terms of their performance—how they have jumped or faltered, who showed skill, style, and daring, who got in the way of other riders, who was competitive, who fell, and who was able to keep up with the action.

Those who follow on foot will also comment on the equestrian aspect of hunting, but this is not their passion. They are not there to see an equestrian show. The spectacular nature of the foxhunt is of no particular interest to them and is rarely commented on. Their passion consists of being in a position from which they can observe the hounds at work. This brings me back to the point suggested previously. Those who participate on foot do not do so in order to see the pageantry of the Hunt as it flows across the countryside but rather to enter the flows of hunting itself. Few foot followers actually walk across the countryside all day. The vast majority make use of motor vehicles of various kinds on the roads and lanes that crisscross the landscape to get them to a point where they will be able to walk to see the best of the action. Unlike the mounted followers who must follow the hounds, the foot followers will attempt to predict where a fox might be found and how it might run and attempt to get there as efficiently as possible. They too must know the countryside and how to get across it. They make judgments about the local conditions, about how the hounds might respond, and where a fox might lead them, and they then act on these judgments. Foot followers are enormously proud of their skill and ability to be in the right place at the right time, and many have a high reputation for this. Years of experience of hunting in the same country makes them extremely knowledgeable. To successfully predict how the Hunt will develop and to be present at its key moments is the aim of most foot followers and is, in itself, a perfect performance for them. One regularly hears foot followers proudly announcing, "I was the first to see the fox," "I was at the corner of the wood when the hunted fox came past me," or "I was there when the hounds were right with their fox."

This is not simply the skill of getting to the right places, it is also a narrative performance: they tell stories about what happened at a particular location in the past and they recount their previous experiences. Conversations consist of commentaries on what is going on, predictions about the chances of finding foxes, views on how the hounds are hunting, opinions on what might be expected given the conditions of that particular day, and judgments about where next to move in order to view the predicted developments. People will disagree with each other: some will stay where they are, convinced that the main activity will quickly swing back toward them, others will move off in different directions, each convinced that they have best understood the relationship between the fox, hounds, and terrain. This deep knowledge of hunting is not simply directed toward informing a critical, distanced judgment of the performance of others but it is rather an understanding directed toward an experience in and of the natural world for themselves. It allows them to be fully, immediately, and actively present.

In foxhunting what is sought is an engagement between a fox and hounds that has duration across time and space, an engagement that, in terms of the perceptions of the human participants, allows both sets of animals to reveal and display their particular qualities and to create a performance. The importance of the development of a relationship is highlighted by its opposite. It sometimes happens that hounds, entering a wood or undergrowth, will find and immediately kill a fox. This is referred to as "chopping" a fox. When I first witnessed such a killing I was surprised by the evident disappointment of the people present. I suggested to them that this was a good result: the hounds had quickly found a fox and killed it with no effort. The hounds had been both efficient and effective. Their response was that this was not what hunting was about; it was not hunting at all. It was not that the hounds had done anything wrong but it was, as it were, a waste. There had been no contest and challenge, and no interest and excitement. Although the people with whom I spoke about this did not express it in these terms, the expression "chopping" conveys a sense of sudden and immediate violence, perhaps even destruction. The fox offered potential but it was cut down before it could reveal it. It was killed as an unknown animal, one with which no relationship had been developed. (See Figure 2.1.)

The fox should have the time and space to present a series of challenges to the hounds as it attempts to avoid being found, pursued, and caught. The

FIGURE 2.1: Dead fox mauled by hounds. Tetcott Foxhounds, October 5, 1982. Mike Huskisson, Animal Cruelty Investigation Group.

fox is unwittingly and unwillingly drawn into the performance of the Hunt, and its behavior in this context is interpreted, commented on, and judged as a performance. A fox, when it is aware that it is exposed and the subject of the attention of the hounds, will take evasive action. It might run through difficult terrain or across spaces containing livestock whose scent might disguise its own; it might run straight and fast or in potentially confusing loops; it might attempt to conceal itself or seek refuge somewhere that hounds cannot enter. All of this behavior is of intense interest to the human participants who comment on it in terms of a set of opinions, views, and cultural beliefs about the nature and character of foxes. For them, foxes are regarded as clever animals, wily rogues, and tricksters, which are not easily caught, and hunting allows them to display their essential foxness. During a hunt they are admired for the skills of deception that they are judged to be employing to outwit the hounds, and for their bravery, strength, drive, and stamina when under pressure. In the commentaries on the behavior of a hunted fox there was a clear sense that what the fox was doing was something beyond responding to or relying on its natural instincts; it was no mere automaton driven by its biology but rather a thinking, aware, creature who was an active agent and who in some sense understood the processes of hunting and who created a performance out of the demands of the situation.

As a final point here it is also important to emphasize that the failure to catch and kill the hunted fox does not indicate a complete failure for the human participants. A fox that has created a series of interesting challenges for the hounds but who has finally outwitted or outrun them is admired by those who have been present. Such a fox has been a worthy opponent and a worthy victor of the contest, one that has outperformed the hounds that have pursued it.

Although the issue of animal performance for the foxhounds is more complex than that for the fox, there is a shared element in that the actions of the foxhounds are perceived to be governed by something other than a response to their biological nature. Foxhounds have a long history and pedigree through which they have been selectively bred and trained to fulfill one role only—that of hunting foxes. However these animals are not simply bred for their physical conformation and robust stamina but also in terms of aesthetic qualities such as the color of their coat and the melodious quality of their voice and for other qualities directly related to their role in foxhunting—their scenting ability and the more difficult to define quality of fox sense that refers to how humans think that foxhounds understand and respond to foxes.

There are two levels of performance associated with what is expected of a foxhound. At a minimal level a hound is expected to be effective in fulfilling its role as a hunting hound. It should be able to find the scent of a fox, be skilled and active in following it, and have the necessary stamina to pursue the fleeing fox. There is, however, a more complex notion of performance in terms of what the human participants expect of an individual hound and of the pack as a whole. There is a strong sense that these animals have an awareness of, and respond to, a sense of responsibility to the breed of which they are a member. Although hounds are referred to as working animals it is not expected that the work of hunting should be a chore for them. Hounds are spoken of as not only expressing a willingness when hunting but also a joy. A significant part of the aesthetics of foxhunting (an aesthetics constructed by the people who hunt) is carried by the hounds. Not only are they admired as pedigree animals and physical specimens, the embodiment of foxhoundness, but in terms of how their behavior can be interpreted as performance. Individual hounds will be singled out for attention and comment, but the performance of any individual is expected to contribute to the total performance of the pack. Many huntsmen commented to me that within their pack they had particularly good individual hounds—one might have an uncanny ability to sense where a fox might be found or where it might have gone; another that could find the slightest trace of a scent and hold that scent in the most difficult conditions; one would always persevere when the rest of the pack was becoming dispirited. Such individuals were valuable but, the huntsmen would add, these foxhounds should not become star performers or indulged prima donnas. The individuality of the pack should be expressed in the quality of the pack not in terms of the qualities of its individual members.

On the hunting field people comment on how hounds work at a scent, how they communicate finding the first traces of a scent to others in the pack, the quality of their voices (their baying, also known as the music of hounds), how they form into a close pack (often described as being so close that one could "throw a handkerchief over them") and flow rhythmically across the countryside. Although the hounds are expected to be effective hunters—they should regularly find and kill their prey—this is not expected to be a mechanical process and the hounds are not regarded as efficient killing machines. The pleasure for those who participate in order to watch hounds hunting is the style in which they do so. This is a performance of another order and more akin to interpreting and expressing a role.

The huntsman, who is the catalyst of the relationship between the central animal performers, must exercise control over his hounds despite having no physical contact with them. At all times he is expected to strike a fine balance between leaving them alone and helping them along. He should feel, sense, and understand the natural world around him and be responsive to everything that makes up that world. The nature of the landscape; the relationship between open fields, hedgerows, woods, and roads; the changes in local climate, the direction of the wind, and the rising or falling of temperature; and the condition of the very ground over which he is riding are all elements that have an influence on the progress of the Hunt.

Throughout the day people will comment on the huntsman's performance. There will be different views about whether he is leaving his hounds alone too much or whether he is interfering when they are best left alone; about whether he is using his voice and horn too much or not enough to encourage the hounds; about whether he has really understood and responded to the conditions properly. He might be criticized for being too out of touch with his hounds when they have found a scent and then not being able to keep up with them, or he might be admired for the way he brought the pack back to him when he was convinced they were not on the true line of the hunted fox. Different groups on the hunting field will also evaluate his performance differently. Those who participate in order to ride will be enormously pleased with a huntsman who moves along at a cracking pace, whether or not the hounds have convincingly settled onto the line of a fox, and creates plenty of opportunities for an exciting ride. Others, who often consider themselves purists in such matters, will be disappointed with a huntsman who is too hurried and does not allow the hounds to display their full hunting capacities.

One of the key images often used of the relationship between the huntsman and his hounds is that of the invisible thread that connects them. The huntsman and his hounds should form an ensemble linked by mutual purpose, understanding, and feeling. Although a pack of foxhounds is often spoken about as being a natural hunting unit they are not hunting for their own purposes; they are hunting with and for the huntsman. He should not continually impose his will on them, he must not continually command, but neither should he blindly follow where they lead. The thread by which they are connected is composed of the inflections of voices, both human and canine, commands and obedience, encouragement and reprimands, and understanding and mutual respect. It is a thread that sometimes has to be given out and sometimes drawn back in; sometimes it is taut, often it snaps.

This performance is at the heart of foxhunting. Human imagination and agency have created a domesticated animal to engage with a wild animal within the variously configured natural and cultural spaces of the countryside. The people who hunt come, in part, to witness this performance—not as distanced spectators who merely observe, criticize, or praise, but as participants who immerse themselves in the excitement, the disappointments, and sometimes the boredom it creates.

Finally, I want to consider the sensory and experiential aspects of hunting: the immersion of the hunter in the process of hunting. Here I will not be referring to any one specific form of hunting but perhaps we can imagine the case of a person going into the woods to hunt an animal such as a deer or out to the marshes to hunt duck and geese. Forms of hunting that can be classified as hunting by deceit require a movement of a different order toward the animal. Hunting events of this kind are characterized by the human attempting to remain unobtrusive and undetected in the landscape in order to find, follow, and approach the hunted animal. This is a close, direct, and personal engagement between the human and the animal; it is not, however, an open engagement. Although the hunter does not in any way cease to be human, he or she must adopt many of the ways of a wild animal—a process that Ortega y Gasset intriguingly refers to as "being open to the animal" and "a vacation from the human condition."[14] Although I do not, in any way, wish to suggest that hunting is in some way an inherent or a natural part of the human condition, many hunters do express the view that the practice and experience of hunting is a movement toward nature and would agree with the suggestion of Erich Fromm that "[i]n the act of hunting, a man [sic] becomes, however briefly, part of nature again."[15] Essential to that process of becoming part of nature is the creation of the hunter as a nonpresence to others while at the same time being keenly aware of their own presence. The hunter must sense in order not to be sensed.

I will later discuss how hunters express the nature and the pleasures of this total bodily sensing but here I need to consider how hunters act upon, change, and discipline their everyday bodies when in hunting mode. Each hunter is intensely aware of his or her body as an intruding body. The body must be disguised or camouflaged by means of clothes that allow him or her to blend into the environment, to become one with it, to be able to see without being seen. Unlike hunting by disturbance, which depends on creating movement, or flight, this form of hunting depends on stillness and gradual movement. Here movement has to be disguised; the hunter must learn to walk silently, with stealth, or to sit in wait without moving at all, perhaps in a so-called hide. Adrian Franklin, writing about the skills of angling, captures this perfectly with the simple, but elegant, phrase "mastering quietness."[16]

Human presence is also carried on the air and lingers on the track that the human intruder has taken. In some forms of hunting the hunter uses a scent that masks his or her own scent and in all forms of hunting the hunter must understand how the air is moving and how to remain downwind of the quarry. All of this understanding and skill based on sight, hearing, and smell is instinctual to the animal, part of its repertoire for survival, and the human must become adept in using and responding to such senses when hunting. The hunter must be fully alert to the animal in order not to alert the animal itself; to attempt to be absent, a nonpresence, to the eyes, ears, and noses of others in order to defeat the animal. This form of hunting depends essentially on deceit and an out-animaling of the animal. The hunter needs to close the gap as silently and secretly as possible—a characteristic of other predator–prey relationships. The moment of the lethal shot is entirely human—no animal can kill at such a distance—but that moment cannot arrive unless the hunter has been successful in becoming partly animal.

Hunters often speak of having to immerse themselves in, and be fully attuned to, the natural world and to become at one with it.

An evocative account of the senses of a hunter and how he places himself in the landscape is given in David Mamet's novel *The Village* (1994). Marty is a deer hunter. As he slowly settles himself into a position in the woods to wait for the deer that he is sure will pass during the day he reflects on what, and how, it is to be in the woods when hunting. To be silent is essential: "he was silent in the woods, as he always was, and never made an unnecessary sound, or spoke a word at all if he could help it,"[17] and he comments that sometimes, when out hunting with an "an unschooled companion" he would have to raise a finger to his lips if they spoke, to indicate that they should be quiet. Quietness is part of the woods and "you had to be like it if you wanted to be part of it."[18] Marty's inner commentary lasts from early morning to dusk.

> [H]e'd been out there, his back against the tree, since before dawn, and he was satisfied that he'd moved in nicely, and quiet, the wind in his face, his field of vision good, down the slope, to the bank of the stream, where he commanded a field of view some hundreds of yards to either side, down the stream, and, across the bank, back into the thick woods.[19]

He reflects on how he has been sitting, ever more stilled, with even his breathing slowed, "gradually becoming part of the forest."[20] For hours he sits intensely alert, observing but not reacting to whatever happens around him. He sits until the evening light fades to almost nothing,

> when the four deer came down the bank. He made out the buck's horns. "Well, all I have done is wait for you," he thought, "but I have waited for you." As the doe's hooves clattered a stone in the stream he raised his rifle, to see if the scope could catch enough of whatever light there might be, to allow a shot. He saw the buck through his scope, and picked his spot on the buck's shoulder.[21]

The narrative of this story ends at the point of sighting. What is unknown is whether this fictional hunter actually takes the shot or not. But whether he shoots or not, that part of the encounter between the hunter and the hunted is at an end. The human hunter has been successful in his mode of being, he has hunted successfully, he has achieved the closeness that he desired when he set out in the morning, and he has had the satisfaction of bodily experiencing hunting.

Concentration, alertness, and awareness are fundamental to the hunter's mode of being and in turn generate some of the key experiences, pleasures, and satisfactions of hunting. For example a hunter interviewed by Jan Dizard, a sociologist of hunting, commented:

> When I am on a walk, my mind wanders and inevitably drifts back to something that's been bugging me or something I ought to have done better. But when I am hunting, I am focused. All I care about is figuring out if that slight noise I just heard is a deer coming into my stand. I am totally absorbed, in a completely different world.[22]

All the hunters I have spoken with mentioned the pleasures of being in a state of heightened awareness of, and intensely attuned and responsive to, the places in which they hunt. This receptivity to the natural world is not a distanced aesthetic response, but rather it emerges out of a purposeful engagement with it and a participation in it. Although hunting cannot be understood as mere killing, the intention to kill, the anticipation of killing, and actual killing are clearly of immense importance for the experience of each hunter. There is an emotional intensity in hunting that comes from being prepared at any moment to kill an animal, and hunters speak about a special engagement with the natural world because theirs is a deadly pursuit. Hunters certainly look for animals and, if they find them, watch them attentively, but they are not spectators of nature. Two hunters in a recent anthropological study by Carmen McLeod of duck hunting in New Zealand convey the sense of intense involvement in the natural that often figures in hunters' accounts of their practices:

> People from the city seem to have the idea that nature is something that you go to look at but "don't touch." But a hunter like me wants to get involved with nature—we like to touch and to be part of natural processes—and killing is just one of those processes.[23]

> They are involved with more of a ... I can't even put it in words either, you know—they are in their waders, it is cold, it's frosty, they are in situations at times and places where the average person who uses the outdoors doesn't see or doesn't venture. Cold frosty mornings, windy cold horrible weather on a lake in a boat, there's mud, your dog smells ... and there is anoxic mud all over your dog and there is cold water running down your neck and hail hitting in your face and you are thinking: 'gee if we don't get across this lake soon the tide is going to be out and we are going to get stuck in the mud'. ... So ... you don't just go and see the Shoveller on Lake Waihola—you shoot one and you touch it and you can see its feathers so you have a much more intimate appreciation, "intimate appreciation" are the words I am looking for ... for the natural world.[24]

The engagement with the dead bird opens the way into a further realm of sensing body and its experiences in hunting. To balance my account of foxhunting I have here focused only on the act of hunting but, as with foxhunting, there are a range of complex practices both before and after hunting that need to be explored on another occasion in order to complete any analysis.

Prior to hunting the hunter must prepare his or her equipment and hunters report taking pleasure in this physical activity and the sense of anticipation it creates while doing so. For example, if they are used, guns must be cleaned and oiled, decoys prepared, and animal callers practiced with. Perhaps special foods and drinks are made to take with them. Certainly most hunters will re-clothe themselves in particular ways for hunting. Many will have to travel to the countryside from their everyday spaces and places of living as they begin the journey out to the animal. If the hunting trip is successful it will result in an animal traveling back to those spaces of the hunter.

At the moment of killing, the targeted animal is responded to and engaged with in new ways because it can no longer offer any resistance to the hunter. Often the dead animal is photographed with the hunter; an act of visually recording, marking, and celebrating the mastery of the hunter. What was once a free, wild animal now belongs to the hunter and enters a process of domestication. Usually the animal will be dismantled. It will be skinned or plucked, eviscerated, cleaned, and butchered, all activities that involve a complex amalgam of the senses of sight, touch, and smell as they encounter flesh, blood and guts. Through such processes the natural animal becomes a cultural product—meat—that will be prepared and consumed in the social and cultural practices of cooking and eating in which smell, taste, and texture feature strongly. The animal passes into and makes the human. But not all animals in hunting disappear without a trace. Some will be converted into taxidermized trophies. Here the disembodied animal is reassembled, although in a reduced form, and brought into a semblance of life, even though it is a life that is only skin deep. Like the trophy photograph of the dead animal, this approximation of the living animal is the celebration of the skill of the hunter, and both are evocative for the hunter. The animal that was once closely watched and observed is now looked at in another setting, and through this visual encounter memories and experiences are evoked. The hunter who was silent in the act of hunting is now able to indulge in the pleasures of speech, as she or he uses the animal to speak to others about how it was to have hunted.

It is clear that if I wanted to understand this sort of hunting as a cultural practice in all its complexity I must find a way to pay attention to these multi-sensual ways of experiencing the world. Hunting does not just mean something to hunters, it is something they do. My problem as an anthropologist is with what I can capture at the moment of its occurring and I can represent it, recreate, or evoke hunting for others who might be interested in understanding it without experiencing it directly. Hunting as it is spoken about before and after the event is perhaps less problematic to record and represent while, of course, being open and sensitive to the issues of writing cultures. Visual anthropology, ethnographic film, and ethnographic sound recording offer powerful and evocative domains of representation—but most of us probably work at the reduced level of words to represent the sights, sounds, touch, smell, and tastes of what we have experienced of the experience of those with whom we study. A restaurant critic's report of a memorable meal is a necessarily impoverished version of that meal but it can be evocative of that experience. Experience-rich anthropology is certainly something to be strived for but its realization seems extremely difficult—how do we capture and evoke scent, taste, and touch? In terms of my own research there is still a good deal of experiencing to be done and understanding to be developed in order to represent hunting in its full complexity. As an anthropologist I have certainly been closely engaged with foxhunting and foxhunters, but I need to expose myself to many other forms of hunting in order to get closer to those practices and experiences. This can be tricky. I have been with Spanish friends on wild boar hunts—I sit silently with them because that is how they are and because that is what they demand of me but I think I am doing something very different from them.[25]

CHAPTER THREE

The Present and Future of Animal Domestication

MARGO DEMELLO

Even though the majority of the animals used or kept by humans today were domesticated many thousands of years ago, the process of selectively breeding animals for human purposes continues up to the present. In fact, when we examine the scientific advances of the past twenty years (particularly in the field of agricultural sciences and most notably developments made in animal cloning), we might even say that the process of domestication has accelerated in recent years, changing the shape and very nature of today's domesticated animals and creating a radically new set of relationships between people and animals.

As has been long noted by archaeologists and historians, animal domestication—as opposed to simply taming animals[1]—first occurred between ten and fifteen thousand years ago, with the domestication of the dog (for hunting), followed by the goat, sheep, pig, and the cow (the first domesticated food animals). Horses (the first beast of burden), cats, chickens, llamas, alpacas, and camels were next, and were finally followed, less then two thousand years ago, by smaller animals such as rabbits and guinea pigs. As has been demonstrated by a number of scholars,[2] of the fourteen or so animals to have been truly domesticated, most (the cat is a notable exception) can be defined by a number of behavioral traits, including a tendency toward scavenging, a rapid maturity rate, reasonable size, a calm disposition, ability to be bred in captivity, a gregarious nature and willingness to live with others in close quarters, and a hierarchical social life. These traits make animals such as the dog or horse amenable to living with humans, in exchange for feeding and care. Of course the animals themselves must have had something to offer to humans as well, such as food, clothing, an ability to work as hunters or beasts of burden,[3] and later, the promise of companionship.

While the species that were ultimately domesticated fit the aforementioned criteria, making them natural choices for domestication, the process of domestication itself was a result of both natural and cultural evolution. First, specific behavioral and physical traits of individual animals who scavenged or hung around human encampments were favored by natural selection in the process of domestication. For example, those individuals who demonstrated less fear and more curiosity of humans, traits that tend to be found among the juveniles of the species,[4] would be among the first individuals to approach human societies; after reproducing, those traits would continue in their offspring. Second, humans most likely adapted their own behavior to that of the animals, incorporating them into human social and economic structures and later, manipulating the physiology and behavior of the animals themselves. As we will see, domestication in the twenty-first century has moved from natural selection to artificial and has been shaped almost entirely by human hands.

As we know, the domestication of animals, especially combined with the cultivation of plants, was a truly revolutionary stage in the development of modern civilizations. Domestication allowed for not only development of the early city-states with their complex division of labor and high degrees of inequality (thanks to the large numbers of people who could be fed with domesticated plants and animals), but eventually the political and economic dominance of a handful of European and Asian societies over much of the rest of the world (thanks to their unique geography and the animals and plants available to them, not to mention the epidemic diseases carried by domestic animals that helped to wipe out much of Native America).[5]

But the results of domestication for the human–animal relationship, and for the animals themselves, were no less revolutionary. As Tim Ingold points out,[6] the relationship between animals and humans among traditional hunter-gatherers was often one of mutual trust in which the environment and its resources are shared by both animals and people; animals that were hunted by humans were seen as equals. Domestication changed this relationship into one of dominance and control, as humans took on the role of master and animals that of property, becoming items to be owned and exchanged.

Domestication also had long-range consequences for the animals themselves, as the very nature of the animals changed throughout the process, typically not in the animals' favor. Through domestication, once-wild animals become increasingly more dependent on humans, both physically and emotionally. Because a handful of traits (like curiosity, lack of fear, willingness to try new things, food begging, submissiveness, etc.) found among the juveniles of species are selected for in domestication, the physical traits of the young (shorter faces, excess fat, smaller brains, smaller teeth, etc.) will also be selected for, leading to modern domesticates who are physically and behaviorally unable to live independently, and who are, in fact, perpetual juveniles—a condition known as neoteny. (See Figure 3.1.)[7] And of course once humans began selectively breeding their animal charges (and killing both those domesticates who do not fit the bill as well as wild competitors) in order to emphasize or discourage certain physical or behavioral traits (a process that intensified after the discovery of Mendelian genetics), the animals changed even further, resulting today in animals that are, for the most part, smaller and fleshier, more brightly colored, with shorter faces, rounder skulls, and more variations in fur and hair type as well as ear and tail appearance. And as Juliet Clutton-Brock points out, these changes also result in a permanent loss of genetic diversity within the species.[8]

According to both Frederick Zeuner and Stephen Budiansky, the process of domestication was one of mutual benefit in which both the early domesticates and our human ancestors had something to gain from joining forces.[9] The question we must ask ourselves now, ten thousand years later, is this: If nonhuman animals did in fact benefit from aligning themselves with human societies, gaining protection from predators, easy access to food, and shelter from the weather, do modern domesticated animals experience the same benefits?

FIGURE 3.1: Maya the pug illustrates some of the most extreme characteristics of neoteny. Photo courtesy of New Mexico Pug Rescue.

Indeed, a survey of the variety of venues in which domesticated animals are kept and used today reveals a startling dichotomy in terms of the way that we relate to domesticated animals. If we start with the most recent, and certainly most mutually beneficial, of the forms of domestication—companion animals—we see animals who are loved and treated as family members and lavished with gourmet food, glamorous clothing, an enormous variety of toys and entertainment, and even exotic travel opportunities. But we also see animals who spend their lives imprisoned in a fish bowl or cage or at the end of a rope or chain; animals who get little to no medical care, the most meagre of provisions, and no shelter, love, or nurturance at all. And while the most cherished of our companions live and die surrounded by love, millions of others are bred for profit, and die alone and unwanted. Animals used for food rarely receive even a fraction of the positive treatment lavished on some of our companions, and generally face a much shorter, harder life, and a much more brutal end.

The story of animal domestication did not end with the creation of today's major domesticated animals. As we shall see in the chapter that follows, domestication continues to this day, imposing new shapes and traits upon animals, finding new uses for these so-called improved creatures, and creating new benefits and profits for humans. As the Neolithic Revolution gave way to the Industrial Revolution, animals became industrial products: their reproduction, feeding, housing, and death managed according to the modern principals of the day. With industrialization came a separation of most Americans from farm life and a new relationship to animals in the form of prepackaged foods and puppy mill pets. And finally, the information revolution of the modern era brings with it an almost complete scientific and technological mastery over animal species through the development of biotechnology, food engineering, cloning, and the like. Yet at the same time, as mentioned earlier, even as some animals become products in entirely new ways, other animals become embraced as members of human families. Ultimately, as scientifically enhanced domestication continues through the twenty-first century, with its cloned cats and bioengineered cows, these contradictions will no doubt continue, and our relationship with animals, already full of contradictions, will continue to evolve as well.

THE MODERN ANIMAL AGRICULTURE INDUSTRY

We have come a long way from our Neolithic ancestors in Europe and Asia who first domesticated the earliest food animals and beasts of burden, the pigs, cattle, horses, goats, and sheep. Early farmers in ancient Egypt and Mesopotamia used domestic cattle primarily to pull carts and plows, as well as to provide milk and manure, only killing them when they become too old to work (and then using every part of their body for some purpose). Nomadic pastoralists of east and central Africa have for millennia lived closely with their cattle (whom they primarily use as beasts of burden and for blood, milk, and manure), naming them and integrating them into every aspect of their religious, social, and economic life. But modern cattle farmers and their cattle enact a very different relationship today. From the days of the big cattle barons of the nineteenth century to contemporary corporate meatpackers like Tyson or Cargill, cows have become meat-producing machines, manufactured and maintained for the highest profit. The story of this transformation is the story of industrialization and its impact on farming and the modern meat industry, as well as the relations between humans and animals farmed for meat.

FROM FAMILY FARM TO FACTORY FARM IN THE UNITED STATES

As many have lamented, the family farm is now effectively extinct in the United States and is rapidly becoming an endangered species in Europe and elsewhere in the world. The raising and slaughtering of animals for meat was, for thousands of years since domestication, a local and typically family endeavor (either in mixed-crop family farms or on larger cattle or sheep ranches). But since the end of the nineteenth century, and especially during the twentieth century, farming has increasingly become controlled by large national and international corporations, which are organized in order to maximize profit through technological advances and rational management techniques.

The first major innovation with respect to modernizing livestock production in the United States was the expansion of the railroad into the south and west, and the development of the refrigerated railroad car. (See Figure 3.2.) Prior to this time, in the nineteenth century, cattle, which were raised in western states like Texas and California, could not be easily converted to meat and brought to market in the northeast, where the large cities were. The expansion of the railroad into the south and west allowed cattle to be transported into Chicago, where large stockyards were constructed to house the animals before slaughter. After slaughtering, the refrigerated railcar allowed the fresh meat to be shipped east, increasing meat consumption among Americans,[10] and also, separating for many consumers the final meat product from its source, the animals—a change that would have long-standing consequences. (In fact, Adrian Franklin points out that this was also the time that saw the development of the automobile and with it the demise of the horse-drawn carriage, eliminating one of the last animals—the horse—to be in close contact with urbanized populations until the practice of keeping pets became widespread.[11]) The railroad and other forms of mechanized transport revolutionized farming in other areas as well, as it allowed for locally produced cheeses, eggs, and other agricultural products to be transported from agricultural communities to markets further away.

FIGURE 3.2: A Pullman Company livestock car from the late
1800s. Pullman Neg. 288. Photo courtesy of the Arthur D. Dubin
collection, Lake Forest College library Special Collection.

Besides the railroad, the single greatest development with respect to modern
animal-raising techniques in the early part of the twentieth century was the
introduction of methods drawn from a rapidly industrializing Western world.
Adrian Franklin[12] and Barbara Noske[13] both outline these revolutionary changes,
which can be summed up as large-scale, centralized production and intensive
animal rearing, which concentrated animals into small spaces and controlled
food, water, and temperatures, enabled easier health monitoring, and controlled
unnecessary and inefficient animal movements. In addition, automation and rational management over production and labor (which became highly special-
ized, tightly monitored, and racially stratified) turned both human workers
and animals into cogs on the production line. The animals are housed in large
facilities known as confined animal feeding operations in which all aspects
of the animals' lives are completely controlled and humanmade: no outside
air, no dirt, no sunlight, and no capacity for natural movement or activities
like grooming, play, exercise, unaided reproduction, or the like. This type of
confinement can be compared to the total institutions experienced by residents
of prisons or mental hospitals. Ironically, the same social behaviors that allowed these animals to be domesticated in the first place are eliminated since
the animals' social structure must be subverted in favor of total confinement,
either alone, or crowded together into nonkin groupings; thus the importance
of practices like tail docking and debeaking to keep down aggression.

Some animals experience the effects of these intensive practices more than
other animals. For instance, egg-laying chickens ("layers") experience the most

FIGURE 3.3: Chickens in battery cages. Photo courtesy of Compassion over Killing.

extreme example of not just intensive confinement but complete control over the animals' lives. (See Figure 3.3.) Over 90 percent of eggs worldwide are now produced in battery conditions, where tightly packed and stacked cages of birds are kept in a large facility with light, temperature, food, and water tightly controlled and a steady stream of antibiotics used to keep the birds healthy. This phenomenon developed in the 1920s but has accelerated in the last thirty years. This system is so efficient that one person can care for as many as thirty thousand birds.

"Broiler," or meat, chickens are kept in a similar environment, but because they are slaughtered much earlier than layers (at six to seven weeks of age as opposed to a year or two), the effects on the bodies of broiler chickens of this kind of confinement are lessened. Pigs, too, live a very different life today than they lived on small farms for the past ten thousand years. Traditional pasture systems have been replaced in the West by confinement in large warehouses, with sows experiencing the greatest degree of control, kept pregnant almost full time in gestation stalls that completely restrict movement, and with antibiotics again being an important part of the diet.

Cattle today experience a range of conditions in their lifetime, depending on whether they are being raised for meat or to produce milk. Veal calves (the offspring of dairy cows, from whom they are separated immediately after birth) undergo the greatest degree of confinement, kept in veal crates in which

FIGURE 3.4: Two or three times every day, dairy cows are hooked up to milk machines. Photo courtesy of Farm Sanctuary.

they cannot turn or walk and fed a milk substitute lacking iron in order to produce the anemic flesh so prized by gourmands. Beef and dairy cattle production has also been intensified in the past fifty years, with feedlots gradually replacing pasture, grains replacing grasses, artificial milking machines used to increase milk production, and weight maximization achieved through hormones and antibiotics. (See Figure 3.4.)

Compared to chickens, cows, and pigs, rabbits are relatively minor players when it comes to domesticated food animals, with only nine million rabbits raised for food each year in the United States (compared to nine billion broilers), and most "fryers" still raised in small scale or backyard operations. However, because rabbits are so small, they are easily adapted to the type of factorylike conditions that are now favored for poultry and pigs in this country. Ironically, it was Europe (which has typically been slower to embrace factory farming conditions than the United States) in the 1960s that led the way in intensive production systems for rabbits, with facilities that can house as many as ten thousand rabbits together, artificially inseminating them to obtain more pregnancies, and using other technologies to increase production.[14] Interestingly, only sheep and goats, two of the first food animals to be domesticated, have yet to experience intensive confinement or other modern farming techniques because they tend to not survive well under those conditions.

Finally, aquaculture, or commercial fish-raising, is increasing worldwide as wild fish populations decline and fish consumption goes up, thanks to the public's current interest in eating high-protein, low-fat foods. Like the other forms of modern farming we've seen, the farmed fish live in intensive confinement, requiring the same inputs of medication and chemicals, not to mention wild-caught fish (as food), to keep them healthy.

While the family farmer is replaced by the automatic feeder and milking machine, pasture is replaced by grains, milk, and parts of other animals,[15] the animals themselves change as well, as pigs cannot support the enormous weight of their bodies with their legs; veal calves find that their muscles have completely atrophied due to nonuse; broilers and layers can barely stand; and turkeys fall over from the weight of their breasts. All of these bodily changes are designed to produce the most meat in the shortest amount of time.

Clearly, relations between farmer and farmed animal have changed in the past century, as have understandings of consumer and product. As pigs, chickens, and cows, and the slaughtering, butchering, and meatpacking facilities that disassemble them, became separated from the cities where most people lived, and farming became an occupation practiced by fewer and fewer people, consumers became increasingly distanced from the products that they consumed, and meat itself became separated (metaphorically as well as physically) from the animals who produced it. This could be one factor in the increasing consumption of meat in the United States from the 1940s to the 1970s, but the bigger reason, most likely, is that, thanks to the new industrial techniques introduced during this period, the cost of meat dropped to such an extent that it could easily be consumed by the masses on a daily basis. Finally, to the farmers, some of whom began keeping tens of thousands of animals in a single facility, the animals lost the individual identities that small-scale farmers and pastoralists once recognized, becoming little more than fur or feather-bearing machines, "animate vegetables, all bred to look identical and reared in rows of cages to be harvested when required."[16]

Another modern development that has had a tremendous impact on animal agriculture has been the increasing consolidation among the largest corporations, with a handful of chicken, pork, and beef producers and processors dominating the U.S. market, edging out not just the small family farms but the medium-sized farms as well. Ten companies currently produce over 90 percent of this country's poultry, and only four produce over 80 percent of the nation's beef. Government subsidies, too, benefit large corporate farms rather than small or medium producers, to the tune of billions of dollars per year.[17] In addition, corporate giants like Cargill, Tyson, IBP, and ConAgra are now vertically integrated in that they own the facilities to not only produce the animals, but also the grain companies to feed them, the feedlots to fatten them, the chemical companies to provide the hormones and antibiotics, and the meatpacking facilities to slaughter them and package the meat as well. This type of integration allows companies like this to control every aspect of production, making it near impossible for smaller farms to compete.

The final area in which animal agriculture has been radically changed in the twentieth century is science. New developments in animal science are aimed at improving the productivity of food animals, and the field ranges from animal behavior to genetics, nutrition, and physiology to growth and metabolism. One new development is the use of antibiotics to prevent illness in otherwise healthy livestock. For the past forty years, penicillin, tetracycline, and other antibiotics have been routinely used to keep livestock healthy in unhealthy factory conditions. Additionally, the use of hormones such as testosterone and estrogen are commonly used in the United States (but are banned in Europe) to stimulate growth and meat production in livestock.[18] Even animal feed has been modified, as genetically engineered grains are now being fed to livestock (as well as to humans) thanks to the integration of livestock, grain, and chemical industries.

Since the early part of the twentieth century, farmers have been experimenting with creating new livestock breeds, via careful crossbreeding, in order to maximize size, productivity (for egg, milk, and meat production), pest resistance, or other favorable traits. This type of artificial selection, done prior to the discovery of DNA, resulted in new breeds of animals, able to survive in ever-harsher conditions with increasing levels of productivity. With the development of artificial insemination at the turn of the century, and the ability to freeze semen in the 1940s, cattle farmers were able to breed their prized bulls and cows more selectively, as well as to sell the semen from the most valued bulls to other farmers. Today, artificial insemination is routinely used for most large livestock, demonstrating the near-total control exerted by humans over animal reproduction.

Genetic engineering of livestock is a relatively recent (since the 1970s) development with long-range consequences, both to the animals themselves and to the human–animal relationship, as consumers become even further distanced from the animals that they eat. After all, modern pigs, beef cows, and chickens are now produced and even engineered for one purpose: to be consumed. Genetic engineering (changing the genetic makeup of an animal by manipulating and transferring selected genes from one animal to the next) represents an advance over the more simple artificial insemination, allowing scientists much greater control over traits such as tenderness of flesh, disease resistance, and level of fat; it is even being used to produce meatier salmon, yet it remains extremely controversial, both among some elements of the public as well as a number of scientists who are concerned about unintended consequences.[19]

Cloning breeder animals, and perhaps even animals to be consumed, is the wave of the future, since Dolly the sheep was successfully cloned in 1996. (See Figure 3.5.) Cloning offers scientists the greatest level of control over offspring, promising higher yields by copying only very productive or disease-resistant animals, although the health of the clones is currently in question, since Dolly

FIGURE 3.5: Dolly was the first mammal to be cloned from an adult cell. Photo courtesy of the Roslin Institute.

herself died at the relatively young age of six, and for every healthy clone produced, a majority of deformed clones are born or miscarried. So far, the focus has been to clone only prized breeder animals, but it is not yet legal to produce food animals themselves, although scientists involved in cloning have published studies maintaining that the cloned animals meet industry standards and compare to normal animals in most every respect.[20] Once the public feels that they are ready to eat cloned animals,[21] which can occur only after the Food and Drug Administration rules on the safety of cloned animals being used for human consumption, we may be able to journey to the grocery store to purchase meat from a cloned cow or pig (chickens have not yet been successfully cloned), moving us yet one more step away from the traditional human–animal relationship that has existed for the past ten thousand years.

CHANGES IN ANIMAL AGRICULTURE IN DEVELOPING COUNTRIES

According to *E Magazine*, worldwide meat consumption has quadrupled over the last five decades to reach an all-time high of 20 billion farmed mammals per year, an increase of 60 percent since 1961. Over the same period, the number of chickens, ducks, and turkeys raised for meat has nearly quadrupled from 4.2 billion to 15.7 billion.[22] In the next two decades, the World Bank predicts that "a significantly changed livestock sector is projected to produce about 30 percent of the value of global agricultural output and directly or indirectly use 80 percent of the world's agricultural land surface."[23] Most of this production will certainly be from further industrialized means of production and will most likely put strong pressure on global natural resources.

Part of the increase in global meat production can be traced to U.S. and U.N. campaigns (under the Food and Agriculture Organization) to convince developing countries experiencing famine that animal protein is necessary for human health, even when, by the 1960s, it was widely known that it was not a lack of animal protein that was causing hunger, but inefficient food production and distribution.[24] Even today, while over a billion people around the world are undernourished, thanks in part to a third of the world's grains being fed to livestock, intensive meat production continues to be promoted as the most rational way to combat hunger in developing countries.

Barbara Noske traces the move away by developing countries from sustainable agriculture and subsistence farming toward industrialized farming techniques to the green revolution of the 1960s.[25] This revolution brought mechanized farming, cash crops (raised from seeds introduced by Western companies), fertilizers, monocrops, and other hallmarks of modern farming to communities that until then primarily produced food, using local varieties of plant and animals, for themselves. And even though more than half of the world's people (and most of the world's poor) live and work closely with livestock (either as subsistence farmers or pastoralists),[26] changing to industrialized farming has not been either easy or beneficial for many populations. One drawback of modern techniques has been the loss of grasslands because overgrazing has turned these once fertile lands into desert, a problem that has been magnified by irrigation systems that drain the water tables. Even east African pastoralists, who have lived for thousands of years with cattle, are suffering as the governments of their countries, aided by international development organizations, encourage them to give up their nomadic ways and settle down to farm. Whereas moving small bands of cattle from place to place over the semiarid African land doesn't harm the land and provides a form of insurance for people in times of drought, converting to farming in this arid environment is known to cause damage to the land while forcing a dangerous dependence on rainfall or irrigation.

Local animal breeds that have adapted over thousands of years to diverse environments in Asia and Africa are also being lost, thanks to the introduction of a handful of Western, high-yield species.[27] Even cloning, as inefficient[28] and expensive as it currently is, is being promoted as the solution to the hunger woes of developing countries. In an article published by BBC News, Animal

Science Professor Jerry Yang of the University of Connecticut compared the extraordinary milk production levels among American dairy cows to Chinese and Indian cows, saying, "cloning could offer technology for duplicating superior farm animals."[29] Whether or not cloned animals make their way to India remains to be seen, but so far the replacement of local animals with highly bred and engineered Western livestock species, combined with the emphasis on industrialized, profit-oriented farming, represents not only a loss in genetic diversity for livestock as a whole, but a radical change in local cultures, for whom livestock (particularly cattle in Africa and India[30]) traditionally had multiple social, religious, and kin-related functions.

FROM FAT TO LEAN AND THE ORGANIC MEAT MOVEMENT

While meat consumption and a reliance on Western livestock and modern farming techniques rise in developing countries, many Westerners have been seeking exotic new animals for consumption, like ostriches, kangaroos, bison, and crocodiles. These animals aren't technically domesticated but are being raised commercially for food and profit. While part of the reason for the new taste in exotic animals is undoubtedly a quest for culinary adventure, the most common reason given by the marketers of exotic meats for eating buffalo, yak, or ostrich is health. According to Exoticmeats.com, for example, the meat of these animals is naturally high in protein but low in fat and cholesterol, making it highly attractive to weight- and health-conscious Americans. In fact, the interest in exotic or game animals can be seen as a cultural backlash against the modern agricultural industry's attempts over the past fifty years to breed bigger, fattier (and tastier) animals. Modern Americans' finickiness can also be seen in this country's growing organic food movement. Fueled by consumers who want to eat healthier, support environmentally sustainable farming, and relieve some of their guilt over eating animals, organic meat, free-range chicken, grass-fed beef, and free-range eggs are becoming increasingly common at grocery stores around the country.

Thanks to the impact of outreach efforts aimed primarily at teenagers and young adults, animal rights groups like People for the Ethical Treatment of Animals have succeeded in converting a large number of Americans to vegetarianism. But more Americans have given up red meat than have given up meat entirely; according to a Vegetarian Resource Group poll taken in 1997, 1 percent of all Americans self-define as vegetarian, but 5 percent abstain from red meat.[31] These dietary changes, fueled in part by morals but probably more by health concerns, have helped to restructure the American agricultural industry in favor of chicken and fish over beef and pork, and with a new emphasis on organic and lower-fat meats.

Since 2002, the United States Department of Agriculture has regulated animal products labeled organic. According to the department, organic products must "come from animals [who] are given no antibiotics or growth hormones,"[32] and farms must provide animals with access to the outdoors. However, the industry raises less than 1 percent of animals according to these standards,[33] and increasingly, factory farms use the organic label by exploiting loopholes in the regulations such as labeling milk as organic even when the cows have never had access to pasture (because they are in a "stage of production" such as lactating), or allowing an egg producer to use the organic label, despite the fact that the producer had only planned to construct two thirty-foot-square balconies to provide outdoor access to six thousand chickens.[34]

Other meat producers are responding to consumer demands for healthier meat by selectively breeding animals such as pigs to produce less fat and creating in the process boutique or specialty meats (which can be sold at a higher cost to high-end consumers).[35] The future, however, lies in technology, as genetically enhancing animals to produce the leanest, yet most tender, meat is the direction biotech firms have been following.[36] Gentech, for example, has discovered a gene marker that will allow scientists to breed pigs with leaner meat, while the Meat Animal Research Center has developed a way to test for genes for lean meat production ("double muscling") in cattle.[37] As American tastes change, we see that animal bodies themselves change as well in order to conform to dietary and culinary trends.

THE RISE OF PET KEEPING AND THE DEVELOPMENT OF THE MODERN PET INDUSTRY

For urbanized Westerners, the human–pet relationship is the only real relationship—other than through the consumption of meat—that most of us ever have with nonhuman animals. In the United States alone, more Americans (63%) now live with a companion animal than have children of their own. Americans spent $36 billion on pet food, toys, clothing, travel paraphernalia, and more in 2005, and even more on traveling with their pets (which now number almost 360 million in the United States alone), taking them to dog parks, special gyms, spas, and even luxury hotels.[38]

While pet keeping has been practiced in societies around the world for millennia, it has only been in the last hundred or so years that pet keeping in the West has exploded, creating multibillion dollar industries focused on producing, feeding, caring for, medically treating, and even disposing of millions of animals per year. How and why did this transformation take place?

James Serpell and other anthropologists have noted that people have long kept animals as companions, even hunter-gatherers with no domesticated animals (the animals kept by such groups were tamed wild animals such as dingoes or wild pigs),[39] and archaeologists have noted the presence of pets in ancient civilizations going back at least five thousand years. And for much of history, animals in small communities served multiple purposes throughout their lives, often serving as a source of eggs, milk, or fertilizer, or perhaps acting as a working animal, while also being a source of companionship, and often, ultimately being slaughtered for food. Indeed, animals were rarely absent from human lives in both hunter-gatherer and farming societies, whether in the form of wild animals or livestock. But for centuries, pet keeping was confined in the West largely to elites, and pets were viewed by many in Europe and America as irrational creatures placed here for the comfort of humanity, with the relationship developing between pets and people as disturbing at best.[40]

But with industrialism, and the changes in the agriculture industry outlined previously, animals largely disappeared from many people's lives, leaving a gap (compounded by the fact that middle-class families were having fewer children) to be filled by the development of the modern pet industry.[41] While urbanites can still travel to their city zoo, or even take a wildlife tour on vacation, in order to view animals, it is clear that a need to live close to and touch animals cannot be satisfied by a trip to the zoo or wildlife park.[42]

Widespread pet keeping as we understand it now (with domesticated animals that are purpose bred to be pets, who are then named and housed indoors or at least in close company with humans) began in the eighteenth century and was enabled in part by the rise of a middle class, with incomes to support what had been an elite, somewhat frivolous, hobby. It was also fueled by a desire on the part of Victorian families to use animals to teach children middle-class, bourgeois virtues, like kindness and self-control. According to historian Katherine Grier, parents and moralists saw having a relationship with a pet as a way to instill positive virtues in a child, which she calls the "domestic ethic of kindness," and which she saw as playing a role in reducing some of the casual violence toward animals prevalent at that time.[43] And finally, according to sociologist Adrian Franklin, pets became critical to modern Westerners as their ontological security (the knowledge that there was some stability and comfort in life that could be taken for granted, in the form of the traditional communities to which most people belonged) began to falter in the late twentieth century, with the increase of urban and financial stresses and the erosion of social policies and family and community networks to buffer them.[44]

Besides the billions spent per year on animal food and supplies, Americans spend another one to two billion dollars per year on purchasing animals from breeders and the various pet stores and dealers who sell, transport, or otherwise profit from them. No figures are available on the amount of money spent adopting animals from shelters and rescue groups, but Humane Society of the United States estimates show approximately three to five million animals adopted per year. Pet industry groups have a vested interest in ensuring that profits in the pet-producing business remain high, fighting any legislation that restricts the breeding, showing, or sale of purebred animals. Another way that the industry maintains profits in the face of a growing humane movement focused on reducing euthanasia and increasing animal adoptions from shelters is by creating new breeds of animals, which are more valuable than mixed-breed pets or more basic purebreds that have long been available. The practice of selectively breeding animals in order to emphasize desired traits is, of course, not unique to the agriculture industry and has been a part of the pet world for hundreds of years.

FANCY BREEDING AND BREED CLUBS

Domestic animals, including pets, are the product of controlled breeding for human purposes, a process that for many of our companion animals goes back many thousands of years, and has affected everything from the size, shape, and color of the animals who live with us to their temperaments, and even to their relationship with us.

Dogs and cats, the most common companion mammals,[45] have been selectively bred by humans since domestication. While there are currently 800 recognized dog breeds and approximately fifty breeds of cat, most of the dog breeds have been created in the past 400 years, and particularly in the past 200 years with the formation of the modern breed clubs and breed standards. The vast majority of the cat breeds originated only in the twentieth century. While the early breeds of dogs were focused on working traits (hunting, retrieving, herding, fighting, and sledding skills), recent breeds have been geared more toward aesthetics and temperament. Because of the lengthy history of dog breeding, and the utilitarian focus of so many of the breeds, dogs, more so than other domesticated animals, demonstrate an enormous range of size (from the teacup Chihuahua to the Great Dane), shape, color, and temperament. Since cats are not working animals (other than as mouse catchers), most cat breeds have been created for aesthetic purposes, with an eye toward color, size, fur type, tail, ear, and body type.

Rabbit breeds, too, exploded in the eighteenth through twentieth centuries, with dozens of rabbit breeds being created since then, differing greatly in size (from the three-pound dwarf to the fifteen-pound Flemish Giant), color, hair type, ear type, and shape. Since most pet breeds today were actually bred for meat, hair, or fur, the range of fur textures and colors could be traced to fashion trends in fur, and body types were primarily selected for meat breeds. But even as early as the eighteenth century, rabbits were being bred for traits like lopped ears that are more useful for pets or for show than for meat, demonstrating a movement at that early date toward seeing rabbits as pets.[46]

Organized dog, cat, and rabbit shows developed shortly after the introduction of specialty clubs like the Westminster Kennel Club, Cat Fancier's

Association, and American Rabbit Breeders' Association, giving fancy breeders an opportunity to show off their prized animals and sell their offspring to other enthusiasts. Prior to the massive commercialization of the pet industry, pet shows were the primary way for people to see and purchase purebred pets.

Today it remains hobby breeders and show breeders who create the new breeds and continue to breed and maintain the older breeds of dogs, cats, and rabbits. These are usually small breeders who breed and sell one (or a few) breeds of animals and consider themselves to be promoters of the breed, registering their animals with the major breed clubs and showing their prized specimens at the breed shows.

On the other hand, in the last fifty years, a new breeding model has developed to create greater numbers of puppies, kittens, bunnies, and birds[47] at low cost for the pet market. Popularly known as puppy mills (but more generally known as commercial or class A breeding operations), these facilities are large, often unlicensed, and usually dirty facilities, typically found in rural areas, in which puppies as well as other animals are bred in large numbers, usually to be sold to pet stores, via brokers. Dogs in these facilities spend their entire lives in wire cages and are bred over and over again, producing litter after litter, and the animals born in these conditions often develop ailments due to the lack of medical care and proper treatment, conditions that often don't develop until the animal is sold from a pet store. Unfortunately for many consumers, it's difficult for most people to know how many such facilities exist, and whether the puppies sold at their local pet store, for instance, come from a puppy mill.

But even animals carefully bred by responsible breeders can and do develop serious illnesses as a result of their breeding. In fact, over 350 inherited disorders are now known to be associated with various dog breeds and are an accepted side effect of the process of creating purebred dogs. Some of these are side effects of neoteny, or the retention of juvenile characteristics like short noses, smaller teeth, and excess fat into adulthood, through domestication and selective breeding. Dogs, especially, are at risk for problems associated with the odd proportions in body, legs, and head that are bred into many of the modern breeds. Even without specific genetic defects associated with dog or cat breeds, many modern breeds of dog or cat are unable to survive without close human attention. While dependency has been bred into domestic animals since the earliest days of domestication, it has accelerated in recent years with the production of animals such as Chihuahuas, who are physically and temperamentally unsuited to survival outside of the most sheltered environments. (See Figure 3.6.)

The breeding of purebred pets today is, not surprisingly, governed by a number of the same scientific and rational techniques associated with modern livestock husbandry, including intensive confinement (for puppy mill pets), but especially in the areas of reproduction, in which all aspects of a dog or cat's reproduction are tightly controlled via methods such as artificial

FIGURE 3.6: Milo is a four-pound Chihuahua who cannot survive without human care. Photo courtesy of A Leg Up Rescue.

insemination, culling of offspring with unwanted traits,[48] genetic engineering, and even cloning.

Even the language used to describe breeding pets (stock, earning units, bitches, queens, studs, cocks, bucks, etc.) sounds suspiciously like the language used to describe livestock breeding, with its emphasis on product. Breeders choose studs or bucks based on the physical characteristics of the animal, with an eye toward complementing the attributes, and correcting the faults, of the bitch, doe, or queen. In some breeding operations, the breeder may own both the males and the females, while in others, the breeder will have to pay another breeder a stud fee to access a male's sperm; stud fees can range for a dog from $500 to $2,000 and for a cat from $100 to $1,000, or the cost of a puppy or kitten from the litter.

The increasing reliance on cosmetic surgery for dogs is one result of the focus on breed perfection. Certain breeds of dogs require, in order to conform to standards, docked tails (Australian shepherd, rottweiler, fox terrier, corgi, poodle, and sckipperke), cropped ears (Great Dane and American pit bull terrier), or both (boxer, Doberman pinscher, miniature pinscher, and schnauzer). According to the American Kennel Club, these standards are "are acceptable practices integral to defining and preserving breed character and/or enhancing good health."[49] For years, pain medication was not given by the veterinarians who performed these procedures, and while medication is becoming more common, some veterinarians still do not medicate the animals for pain. Some dog behaviorists worry that because dogs use their tails to communicate with other dogs, tail docking puts them at a disadvantage when socializing and may impair physical functions such as stability as well.[50] Because of these concerns, a number of countries have now banned or restricted the procedures, and California is considering a bill to ban ear cropping.

Even after many years of education on the part of international humane organizations, and the movement of many people to adopt rather than purchase animals, the drive to improve current dog and cat breeds and to create new ones continues to this day. While mixed-breed dogs are not considered by breeders to be economically valuable, there are a number of new dog breeds created by the purposeful interbreeding of two distinct breeds, such as the labradoodle (Labrador–poodle cross) and the maltipoo (Maltese–poodle), both of which are gaining popularity. Some of the newer breeds of cat, on the other hand, were not created through crossbreeding but by selecting often harmful genetic mutation, and breeding for them. Japanese bobtails (bobbed-tail) and Scottish folds (folded down ears) were early examples of this trend, both created in the 1960s and 1970s. Hairless cats have appeared and been bred throughout the twentieth century, and American curls (with curly ears) were created in 1981. More disturbing are cats that go by the name of twisty-cats, squittens, or kangaroo cats, all of which have a form of radial hypoplasia that results in drastically shortened forelegs or sometimes a flipperlike paw rather than a normal front leg (because they cannot walk, they must hop somewhat like a kangaroo), and that are being selectively bred by a handful of breeders. Other new cat breeds have been created by crossbreeding domestic cats to wild cats, such as the Bengal, created by crossing a domestic shorthair with an Asian leopard cat.

A NEW FRONTIER OF PET CREATION

While the science of artificial pet breeding is not yet as advanced as it is in the world of animal agriculture, partly due to the higher profits to be garnered from the sale of prized cattle or pigs (the cost of a cloned calf today is estimated at $19,000, but one clone recently sold at auction for $170,000),[51] and partly due to the outcry from animal rights advocates, the pet industry is quietly catching up with the new technologies.

Because dog breeding has been around for such a long time, breeders have long exercised careful skill when selecting individual dogs to mate and documenting the results of their couplings, in order to improve on individual traits. But new methods of both selecting and modifying animal traits are now becoming available, as well as ways to more carefully control the breeding process, eliminating any possibility of error due to the inefficiencies of sexual reproduction among animals. For example, artificial insemination, offered by veterinarians, is becoming more popular today, especially for dogs.

Genetic engineering, too, is starting to take off in the pet-breeding world. Glofish—zebra fish modified with sea anemone genes to make them glow—were introduced in the United States as a novelty pet in 2004, unleashing a string of controversy and legal actions. But the primary focus in genetic engineering for the past few years has been to produce, via genetic modification, an allergen-free cat. While Transgenic Pets, the first company to undertake this project, went out of business due to a lack of funds, a biotech firm called Allerca expects to offer the first genetically modified cat, or lifestyle pet, for sale for approximately $3,500 in 2007. But the final frontier for breeding pets is now cloning.

Genetic Savings & Clone (GSC), the only U.S. firm working on pet cloning, started in 1997 with the Missyplicity Project, a project undertaken with Texas A&M University to clone a mixed-breed dog named Missy (the project was funded by her wealthy owner before her death). Missy has not yet been cloned, although her DNA is kept in a PetBank run by GSC, for future use, but the company did succeed in creating CopyCat, or CC, in 2001, the world's first cloned cat (who ironically does not look like her donor, Rainbow). (See Figure 3.7.) In 2004, GSC sold the first cloned cat, Little Nicky, to a Texas woman who was mourning the loss of the first Nicky. Little Nicky's cost was $50,000 but the cost of current cats is now a bargain $32,000.

Even though the Missyplicity Project began with the intent to clone Missy, GSC has not yet succeeded in cloning the more reproductively complicated dog. In 2005, a scientist from Seoul National Unversity, Hwang Woo-suk, announced that he had cloned the world's first dog, an Afghan puppy named Snuppy, by taking genetic material from the ear of an adult male Afghan and inserting it into an empty egg cell, which was inserted into the womb of the surrogate mother, a Labrador. Since the announcement, however, it has been revealed that Dr. Hwang fabricated the results of some of his other (human) cloning work, casting doubt on the story of Snuppy's origin. Genetic Savings & Clone, however, continues its work on dog cloning (a potentially much more lucrative venture than cat cloning) and hopes to have the first cloned dog within the next year.

As Susan McHugh points out, the pet cloning projects currently undertaken by GSC are very different in intent from those carried out by universities and biotech firms that clone livestock.[52] While the intent of agricultural cloning

FIGURE 3.7: CC, shown here at seven weeks old, was the first cloned cat. Photo courtesy of College of Veterinary Medicine, Texas A&M University.

is profit on the part of the cloning companies and increased productivity for livestock (and thus increased profit) via the cloning of highly valuable animal specimens, GSC's aim is to reproduce economically worthless animals such as the mixed breed Missy, or the tabby cat Nicky. Certainly GSC aims to make a handsome profit from their efforts, but cloning a mixed breed dog or cat for the private pleasure of a person is a very different enterprise from cloning a prized Brahmin bull. And while animal protection advocates decry the practice of pet cloning (given the millions of dogs and cats euthanized at animal shelters every year, the $50,000 spent to purchase one cloned cat seems distasteful at best), the existence of GSC and the devotion of their clients to their pets, most of whom appear to be mixed breed, testifies to an overwhelming love of companion animals among at least a portion of the population, a love that seems to override rational and commercial concerns.

THE ROLE OF COMPANION ANIMALS TODAY

Companion animals occupy an ambiguous position in contemporary society. There is no doubt that the companion-animal relationship can be one of the richest, most fulfilling ways that humans and animals can interact, bringing happiness to both person and animal. Yet the production of those animals in a world already filled to capacity with domestic animals who either have no home or are living lives of abuse or neglect is driven primarily by profit, rather than a concern for animal welfare, and necessitates the wholesale destruction of millions of no-longer-wanted animals per year. To put it another way, while humans derive huge benefits from living with companion animals—studies show that pets provide us with a variety of physical and emotional benefits, from decreasing blood pressure and cholesterol levels to preventing heart disease to increasing opportunities for exercise and socialization to decreasing loneliness[53]—how much do we as a society do to ensure that the benefits go both ways? Clearly, companion animals have moved into our families and hearts in ways rarely seen before in history, and many would argue that they have certainly benefited from this increased level of intimacy.

Animals serve for many of us as surrogate family and friends, which according to some scholars, is an understandable but lamentable side effect of modern, alienating, industrialized life.[54] But I would argue that most people who live with companion animals don't see the role of pets in their lives as filling a gap better filled by human companionship, and most of us are not lonely old women living with fifty cats among piles of feces and old newspapers. As sociologist Leslie Irvine points out, humans who do choose to live with animals don't demonstrate any psychological weaknesses that would keep them from creating lasting human relationships.[55] Additionally, some preliminary recent studies may show a link between positive attitudes toward animals and a more compassionate attitude toward people.[56] Today, many scholars think that living with animals does in fact teach empathy and compassion[57] although at least one recent study challenges this notion, finding that living with pets is *not* correlated with empathy, but that living with cats is in fact *negatively* correlated![58]

Companion animals today are more ingrained in our lives than ever, and that fact alone is shaping our culture in ever more interesting ways. For some, particularly the rich and powerful, expensive purebred pets have always been a status symbol. While the current trend in Hollywood is for young celebrities to tote around small dogs (often Chihuahuas), others demonstrate their status through the purchase of exotic animals,[59] a trend made famous by Michael Jackson and his chimpanzee, Bubbles, and seen in Paris Hilton's most recent acquisition, a kinkajou. But while keeping companion animals was, for most of history, a sign of affluence (and was seen as wasteful by many commentators, an attitude that continues to appear after every well-publicized case of a suffering animal draws the empathy and financial contributions of large numbers of people), and those with money can still afford the best food, medical care, and luxury items for their pets, there is no indication that most pet owners today are either wealthy or use their animals to demonstrate status.

Besides the direct financial impact of living with so many pets, we can also see the ways that other businesses, at least in the United States, have changed as a result of the explosion of pets in this country. Hotels now routinely accept animals as guests, well-known companies known for creating products for humans now market products directly aimed at pets, pet foods are becoming more gourmet and diet conscious, dogs can now attend day care and pets can go to their own spas, and small dogs in carriers have become ubiquitous at celebrity and elite venues like fancy restaurants and department stores. In addition, an explosion of films and television shows that focus on both wild and domesticated animals has led to an entire television network, *Animal Planet,* demonstrating our need to see animals even when we cannot touch them.

On a different note, we can point to the tremendous growth of animal protection organizations over the past century, with millions of members and over $200 million in charitable contributions per year, as a possible extension of the way that we care for our companion animals. At least one recent study points to a correlation between positive attitudes toward pets and a more humane attitude toward other animals, indicating that pet keeping could lead to ethical food avoidances and membership in animal protection organizations.[60] Not only are Americans donating more money than ever to such organizations (and to animal-specific rescue efforts such as those organized after Hurricane Katrina), many ensure that their own animals will be cared for after they're gone by leaving them money in their wills or writing trusts to provide for them after their own deaths. And many thousands more volunteer their time by founding their own rescue, education, or advocacy organizations, or by helping with established groups and shelters. In fact, this is probably the best example of humans giving back to animals (companion and otherwise), for their service to us.

After dogs and cats, other animals have crossed that often fuzzy line separating food, laboratory, or working animals from pets. Rabbits, for example, classified as a multipurpose animal by the United States Department of Agriculture, have historically been bred and used primarily for food, fur, and medical purposes. Until the 1980s, even as pets, they usually lived in backyard hutches with little to no medical care or human attention, seen as cheap children's pets or starter pets. However, with the publication of the groundbreaking *House Rabbit Handbook*[61] and the founding of House Rabbit Society, the world's foremost rabbit advocacy organization, the status of rabbits began to change. Today, there are tens of thousands of people living with rabbits as indoor house pets around the world. These rabbits, like cats and dogs before them, are neutered and spayed, and provided with medical care, high-quality food, fancy toys, and much more. And while rabbits are perhaps the most extreme example of an animal that has so successfully moved from product to pet (although rabbits continue to be bred and slaughtered for food, fur, and scientific uses in the millions per year), other animals like rats and horses have made the jump as well. (See Figure 3.8.)

Finally, by looking at the recent attention paid by law enforcement agencies, animal advocates, scholars, and the media to the problems of animal abuse, we not only can see new and disturbing trends related to pet keeping but also a growing awareness of and empathy toward issues of animal suffering. High-profile cases of cats, dogs, and rabbits being set on fire, thrown out of cars, drowned, stabbed, and suffering other horrors have sensitized millions

FIGURE 3.8: Casper is a New Zealand rabbit, one of the most commonly bred rabbits for both the meat and vivisection industries. Photo courtesy of the author.

to the abuse many companion animals suffer. And while there's no way to tell whether companion animal abuse has increased in recent years, or has simply been more widely publicized, we do know that legislators have responded by increasing penalties for animal abuse. As of this writing, forty-one states and the District of Columbia have laws making certain types of animal cruelty felony offenses, thirty-six states provide for prohibiting the ownership of an animal for some point after sentencing, and twenty-seven states require psychological counseling for certain cruelty offenses.

Dangerous dog attacks have also either risen in the past few years or have been reported much more frequently. These often-fatal attacks have resulted in a spate of legislation banning dog breeds like pit bulls from various communities. Chained dogs, who are often the source of such attacks, and dogs who are kept for protection and fighting, are not surprisingly often found in inner cities that are plagued by violence, unemployment, poverty, pollution, and drugs, conditions that create a high level of misery for all occupants—human and animal alike. Because these problems won't be solved by the banning of a particular breed of dog, some communities have banned the chaining of dogs, a small step in the right direction.

Other forms of animal abuse also began to garner more attention in the last decades of the twentieth century, as sociologists and psychologists demonstrate the link between violence toward animals and violence toward people,[62] and law enforcement agencies respond with programs aimed at rehabilitating young abusers before their violence escalates from animals to people.

Another well-documented connection is the link between violence toward animals and domestic violence. Recent studies have found that anywhere from 71 percent to 85 percent of women who escaped their homes due to domestic violence reported that their partner had abused the family pets as well.[63] Feminist Carol Adams[64] also points out that many batterers force their partners to have sex with the family pet, which exploits both woman and animal. Other forms of sexual exploitation aimed at both women and pets are crush videos, which are videos in which women in stiletto heels crush small animals to death for men's sexual gratification, a phenomenon that came to light, and was criminalized, in the 1990s, and bestiality, practiced most likely since the beginnings of animal domestication but increasingly linked today with domestic violence and animal cruelty.[65]

Whether or not the increasing numbers of media reports on animal abuse represents an increase in incidences of abuse, at the very least we can say that it points to a rising awareness of the issue in modern society, an awareness—coupled with the growing interest in supporting animal welfare organizations—that will most likely continue to have positive repercussions for companion animals living among us.

DOMINANCE OR MUTUAL DEPENDENCE?

The earth trembled and a great rift appeared, separating the first man and woman from the rest of the animal kingdom. As the chasm grew deeper and wider, all other creatures, afraid for their lives, returned to the forest—except for the dog, who after much consideration, leapt the perilous rift to stay with the humans on the other side. His love for humanity was greater than his bond for other creatures, he explained, and he willingly forfeited his place in paradise to prove it.

—Native American folktale[66]

This folktale is one of many similar tales from around the world that purport to explain how the dog became domesticated. In all such stories that I've found, whether the dog was coerced or manipulated into joining the land of humans as is common, or whether he voluntarily joined human society, the end result is the same: he chooses to remain with humans, giving up his freedom, his wildness (and, according to the above tale, his place in paradise) for the privilege. I haven't found a single folktale that has a similar message regarding other domesticated animals, although I did find an African tale explaining how the goat became domesticated, but the story concludes with the goat ending up with humans only because she was chased there by a leopard.[67]

Certainly the lack of folktales demonstrating the voluntary nature of animal servitude cannot be taken as proof that domesticated animals do not benefit from their positions in human society. However, I do think that this lack could demonstrate that the people who domesticated the horse, cow, sheep, goat, and pig in places as diverse as Africa, Asia, the Middle East, and India don't necessarily view those animals as benefiting from their relationship with them. While the mutual dependence–mutual benefit theory of domestication suggests that animals chose to be domesticated because they recognized that life is better with humans,[68] I don't think, especially given the modern evolution of the agricultural animal, that this implies that their current lives must be better than what they would be if they still lived in the wild. According to ecologist Paul Shepard, "the benefit to animals of being domestic is fictitious, for they are slaves, however coddled, becoming more demented and attenuated as the years pass."[69] In any case, the point is moot because with the possible exception of the mixed breed cat, today's domesticated animals are so highly bred and engineered for human benefit that they could never again survive on their own. In short, we care for them because they could not live without our care, and they live with and obey us because they no longer have a choice in the matter.

But we also care for domestic animals because we have grown dependent on them. While this is perhaps more the case in preindustrial societies where animals' labor is and was a critical part of the economy, it continues to be the case today in modern society's dependence upon meat and other products taken from the bodies of animals, as well as in our dependence on pets for companionship, love, and affection.[70] But whereas the dependency of most domestic animals on humans is irreversible—even animal rights advocates do not foresee a day when domesticated chickens, pigs, and cows, much less Chihuahuas and Persian cats, can be wild again—that is not necessarily the case for human dependency on animals.

But while we no longer need meat, fur, or leather to survive, as the lives of millions of vegetarians demonstrate, most people seem unwilling or unable to shed our dependence on the products of animal agriculture. Even more intractable may be our connection to our companion animals. According to a 2002 American Animal Hospital Association pet owners' survey, 73 percent of Americans have signed a greeting card from their dog, 86 percent include pets in holiday celebrations, 46 percent plan all or most of their free time around their animals, 58 percent include pets in family portraits, and almost half have more photos of their pets than their partners.[71] Given this level of commitment, it is difficult to imagine most pet lovers being willing to live without animals.

Does this unwillingness to release ourselves from our dependency on domestic animals stem from love, greed, selfishness, or a desire to dominate others? Just as we have bred dependency into the domestic animal–human relationship, we have also bred its corollary, dominance, into that same relationship. Not only do we dominate farm animals, through every level of control exercised over their minds and bodies, but we dominate, albeit with affection, our pets as well,[72] from whom we demand unconditional love and absolute obedience.

Or does our dependence stem from a human need to stay connected to animals and to the wild from which they came, and by extension, to our own roots? Since the disappearance from human society of wild animals and even the farm animals on whom we still depend, Paul Shepard sees the presence and importance of pets as a testimony to an enduring and necessary link between human and nature, providing, albeit incompletely, "a glimmer of that animal ambience, sacredness, otherness."[73]

Today, the relationship between human and domestic animals continues to evolve. Companion animals are becoming ever more drawn into human lives, providing love and companionship but also, perhaps, filling a more complicated need for humans to connect with other species. Agricultural animals, on the other hand, are becoming increasingly distanced from us, shut away in factory farms and slaughtered in secret. But both farmed animal and pet are moving physically further away from us as well, as they are genetically engineered and even cloned to ever more exacting human specifications, losing much of their animalness in the process. And finally, we react to the pain and suffering that domestic animals endure—the suffering of livestock, while intentionally mystified by the agricultural industry, is well known to anyone who thinks about the food that they eat, and the deep suffering of pets is obvious in the millions who die at shelters every year because they were no longer wanted— by passing legislation and demanding more oversight, but never, never losing our dependence on those animals, and that suffering. While humans would suffer without animals, animals suffer, much more, in order to serve us.

CHAPTER FOUR

Zoo Animals as Entertainment Exhibitions

DAVID HANCOCKS

No era stands on its own. What happens today has origins in yesterday. Civilization exists because there was a global climate change at the end of the last great glacial advance, about twelve thousand years ago, which led to the spread of grasslands. Hunter-gatherers in the grassy habitats of what is now southeastern Turkey and western Iran came to realize that collecting and planting grass seeds guaranteed a new crop each year: thus the simple genesis of agriculture. It was the beginning of a move from a lifestyle that had persisted for over one hundred thousand years.[1] In less than a few centuries people in the region were living in settled communities.

Life in permanent abodes is characterized by ownership of nonessential goods—a luxury unavailable to nomads—and the imperatives of social status demand an excess of such objects, preferably rare and exotic. Ownership of wild animals, as opposed to mere utilitarian beasts, was a very powerful and primal symbol of status and a bold way to demonstrate importance. A peasant was fortunate to hold a few chickens, but princes might own lions. Zoos have therefore always been obvious examples of social rank, and they emerged at an astonishingly early stage of civilization, the first appearing 4,300 years ago in Ur, in what is now southern Iraq, only one thousand years after the first farming villages had emerged, in Mesopotamia.[2]

By the twentieth century, modern zoos in the Western world regarded themselves as repositories of knowledge for the public good, like botanical gardens and libraries. They also claimed to be science-based educational institutions, and in the closing decades of the modern era began to position themselves as latter day Arks, saving endangered wildlife from extinction. A closer examination, however, reveals the paucity of these claims.

EARLY ZOO DEVELOPMENT OF THE MODERN ERA

The modern zoo first blossomed in England, when the Zoological Society of London opened its new zoological gardens in The Regent's Park, in 1828. During its first century it pioneered many traditions, from taxonomic planning to architectural finery, and even first use of the word *zoo*. It became the archetypal zoological park, setting the style for a massive global program of zoo development throughout the nineteenth century, initially in the port cities of Britain, across Europe, and on to North America and major cities around the world in the European colonies as other communities sought to ride the abundance of popularity that had flowed into Regent's Park.

The London Zoo probably received more media publicity throughout the era of Victorian Britain than any other public institution apart from the British royal family, and throughout the nineteenth century almost all the new zoos enjoyed enormous public success as a constant stream of new animals, exotic creatures rarely or never seen before, fed one public mania after another. Vast amounts of money were expended in building new zoos, yet there was very little fundamental change in zoo standards or styles during an extended period of almost frantic zoo development.

Many of the new zoos, though initially based upon the exhibition philosophies and designs of the London Zoo, overtook their Regent's Park progenitor in size and in sumptuousness. Dutch zoos built stronger and broader scientific platforms. German zoos in particular invested much greater sums of money than any of the British institutions. Architects Ende and Böckmann produced extraordinary buildings of a scale and grandeur for the Berlin Zoo that has never been surpassed and that spoke power and authority with immense confidence.[3] American zoos in the first years of the twentieth century, notably in New York and in Washington, DC, began to proceed with a scale of development far in excess of anything imagined in Britain.

The huge expansion of zoos in the latter half of the nineteenth and early years of the twentieth century had produced fantastical exhibits that replicated castles, cottages, Greco-Roman and Far Eastern temples, alpine chalets, renaissance pavilions, whimsical ruins, and other follies. But virtually nothing was known about the natural life history of wild animals, and thus their most basic requirements typically went unmet by designers and by zoo managers.

Most zoos devoted their energy to acquiring new animals, in huge numbers, to fill the constant vacancies from rapid death of many animals that entered zoos. With no direct knowledge of the wild, and no apparent interest in learning of that, zoos in blind ignorance copied each other, focusing only upon trying to look grander and more opulent than their rivals.

In the first decade of the twentieth century, however, animal dealer and trainer Carl Hagenbeck, after experimenting for many years with novel exhibition techniques, introduced into his new Tiergarten in Hamburg the most spectacular exhibits in zoo history. In company with Swiss sculptor Urs Eggenschyler, who made three-dimensional models for the new zoo based upon rock formations and gorges sketched from real life, he developed exhibits that were unique in many ways: the first to combine naturalistic landscapes, barless enclosures, and regional groups of mixed species.[4] Comprised of an African and Arctic panorama, they were of a scale and grandeur never before seen or attempted.

The clue to the success of these grand panoramas of large open enclosures, other than their impressively bold size, was the successful adaptation and expansion of a device from eighteenth-century English landscape gardening: a ditch with one vertical side faced with brick or stone and one sloping face covered with grass created a concealed boundary to a garden area, keeping animals out of the cultivated landscape but allowing uninterrupted views out to the countryside.[5] Originally a French military invention called an ah-ah, the English reinterpreted it and called it a ha-ha: a more playful use and a clearly onomatopoeic expression. (Fantasy and humor writer Terry Pratchett created a character "Bloody Simple" Johnson who invented things of mangled size, such as a triumphal arch that fitted into a matchbox, a gazing pool one-inch wide and 50 yards long, and a ho-ho. This variation on the ha-has was 20 feet deep; its name derived from the sound the property owner made when someone fell in it.[6])

The ha-ha was employed at the Hamburg Tierpark in its traditional role, keeping people and animals separated without visible fences. Even more cleverly, however, and of special significance in the history of zoo exhibit design, these ha-has also kept different types of animals separated from each other (notably predators and their prey) and thus allowed enclosures to be used as if they were a series of theatrical stages, each one at the back of and slightly higher than the other, thereby creating a totality of scenic landscape. These very large and integrated exhibits, with a great diversity of animals from one type of habitat all apparently living together in replicas of surprisingly realistic geological formations, were immensely popular with the public.

In his biography Hagenbeck said, "I desired, above all things, to give the animals the maximum of liberty. I wished to exhibit them not as captives, confined within narrow spaces, and looked at between iron bars, but as free to wander from place to place within as large a limit as possible, and with no bars to obstruct the view and serve as a reminder of captivity."[7] He aimed to demonstrate to the zoo scientists and managers as well as to the general public that tropical animals could acclimate to live outdoors in temperate climates. At a time when allowing tropical animals to have access to outside cages was considered dangerous for their health, he promoted the revolutionary notion that they would thrive in the fresh air. He also wished to demonstrate the benefits of giving zoo animals larger spaces and of displaying them in environments that looked natural. Many zoo professionals, however, ridiculed these ideas, especially the senior members of the more highly prestigious and supposedly scientific institutions of the time. (See Figure 4.1.)

Ludwig Heck, director of the Berlin Zoo, abhorred the new approach, with its focus upon naturalism and visual drama, believing it would threaten the taxonomic zoo layout that had been introduced at the London Zoo in 1828.[8] This concept, in which visitors were intended to gain better understanding of the natural world by viewing taxa in orderly groupings and by then comparing differences between species, as if they were objects in a museum like so many pots or eggs or suits of armor, was considered central to the scientific basis for zoo planning. It is, surprisingly, still favored by a few zoo managers and educators.

FIGURE 4.1: Media campaigns against the enclosing of wild animals behind bars began to emerge in the late 1960s. Bars reminded people too uncomfortably of prisons. Ironically, however, the iron bars were often the only components in the naked cages that animals could interact with and climb upon. Visitors were much more accepting of moated enclosures: though equally as barren as typical zoo cages, the islands did not have intrusive metal bars to mar the view. Photo by David Hancocks.

William Hornaday, director of the New York Zoological Society, harboring a hatred for Germans following World War I, dismissed Hagenbeck's approach as a "fad" and was assisted by Emerson Brown, director of the Philadelphia Zoo, in persuading America's zoos to boycott it.[9] Other zoos, however, were more open minded or at least made special note of the Hamburg Tierpark's strong public appeal.

Denver Zoo's mountain habitat exhibit, built in 1918, was the first example of this new style in America. It even set new standards in detail and accuracy by using plaster models of rock formations from the Hogback Range west of Denver. The St. Louis Zoo, in 1921, built large grottos for displaying bears that also took levels of authenticity to a higher level, making direct copies from natural limestone bluffs, and giving special attention not just to the rock detail but also to the natural stratification of the geological formations. The Houston Zoo similarly produced a good early example of the style with its sea lion pool, and the San Antonio Zoo created exceptionally naturalistic examples with its bear and monkey exhibits in the 1920s. The Detroit Zoo employed members of the Hagenbeck family to design many of their animal exhibits built between 1928 and 1938. The Vincennes Zoo in Paris, opened in 1931, also modeled itself on the Hamburg Tierpark, as did the zoos in Cologne and Antwerp.

Unfortunately, as more and more zoos began to copy this style, they increasingly neglected the principles and philosophies of the original. Increasingly, they were mimicking one another, as zoos still so persistently do, rather than looking at nature and analyzing wild habitats directly. They also too often failed to approach the problem of building for animals with the same sort of conviction and avidity for dramatic and naturalistic scale as Hagenbeck. When the London Zoo built its Mappin Terraces in 1914 they produced something merely lumpish and drab. (See Figure 4.2.) It was admittedly a vast improvement on the cramped cages that they superseded, and the setting for bears, wild goats, and deer was generally well regarded at the time of opening, but the Mappin Terraces were eventually seen to represent "some of the worst aspects of enclosing animals for public display."[10] An audience more conversant with televised images of bear habitats came to recognize the relentlessly barren enclosures of depressingly gray concrete as little more than elevated versions of the old menagerie bear pits. (Figure 4.3.)

Before Hagenbeck, zoo designers never looked to nature as a source of inspiration but instead relied upon architectural copybooks and cultural or mythological stimulus for their designs. Zoo architects and managers would have considered it ridiculous if not unsavory to examine wild places or to consider the wild habits of the animals they were designing for. Constructing ornate, impressive, and exotically flavored zoo buildings, conversely, guaranteed praise and awards from the socially elite.

FIGURE 4.2: In 1913, the London Zoo built the Mappin Terrace exhibit. It was not based on any natural geological feature but was instead a poor copy of a naturalistic style developed at Hamburg Zoo. The result was visually and experientially mind-numbing and unremittingly gloomy, for both animals and visitors. It was, however, one of the London Zoo's major attractions for most of the twentieth century. Photo courtesy of Carl Hagenbeck's Tierpark, Hamburg. Photo by David Hancook.

AWAY WITH THE OLD

The naturalistic approach pioneered in Hamburg coincided with a shift in design philosophy in the modern Western world. After the excessive decoration that adorned so much nineteenth-century design, and in concert with other social and political revolutions ablaze early in the twentieth century, modern architecture set about creating a brave new world. It consciously rejected history as a source of inspiration, and sought boldness, simplicity, and what it considered to be unadorned honesty. In 1908 Adolf Loos, one of its great theoreticians, thundered, "Ornament is a crime!"[11]

In the heady atmosphere of the early 1920s, the London Zoo, confident in its position as the foremost general public attraction in the British Empire's premier metropolis, began a series of new developments aimed at making itself appear modern and up-to-date. It introduced several novelties and experimented with new technologies. Special consideration was given to lighting (appropriately, for gloomy London) partly for theatrical effect, as with the introduction of skylights above the animals in the exhibition houses for insects,

FIGURE 4.3: Bear pits were a very common feature of nineteenth-century zoos and symbolized all that was wrong with those inadequate institutions. Most zoo visitors today would not tolerate such conditions. When a bear pit is disguised by well-made artificial rock walls, however, it seems to be perfectly acceptable, even if it is in many ways more inadequate than any menagerie's. This example, constructed at the Baltimore Zoo in the 1970s, did not even provide the traditional pole for the bear to climb up high. She was thus unable to ever see anything beyond the rim of the mockingly naturalistic walls that enclosed her. Photo by David Hancocks.

reptiles, and small mammals, but also for animal health. It was an era when sunshine and fresh air was rather suddenly recognized as vital. Artificial sunlight via quartz incandescent lamps was provided for primates, and ultraviolet light for reptiles. Hygiene was considered to be paramount in this new regime. Concrete was the preferred material for floors, and walls were built of glazed bricks or tiles so they resembled bathrooms. It was a trend that persisted in zoos worldwide for many decades.

There should have been significant changes in zoo exhibit design in the 1960s, following the publication of two important books by Swiss zoo director Heini Hediger. He wrote of the need to consider the psychology and behavior of zoo animals,[12] arguing for a biological approach to zoo design. He explained the concepts of territory and of flight distance and examined the importance of play for captive animals and of preventing stereotypic behaviors by creating opportunities for active interaction with a richer environment than the typical sterile enclosures. He made it clear that designers and managers must concentrate on the content and the quality of the spaces.

Hediger's words were, however, largely ignored. Zoo enclosures were typically designed for sluicing by keepers rather than to meet the behavioral needs of living wild animals who had evolved to interact with complex and living natural environments. As a recently graduated architect employed in the architect's department at the London Zoo in the late 1960s I was advised to provide specially reinforced concrete for animals that liked to dig.

The most numerous as well as the most historically significant examples of zoo modernism are the works of Berthold Lubetkin, founding partner of the Tecton Group in London, who designed many projects for zoos in Dudley, Whipsnade, and London in the 1930s. His design for the gorilla house at Regent's Park in 1933 was the firm's first contract, followed by the penguin pool of 1934 (copied from a 1928 set design by Russian constructivist El Lissitzky for Moscow's Meyerhold Theatre, and one of the most famous zoo structures ever built) and various works at the Whipsnade Zoo including the elephant house in 1935. (See Figure 4.4.)[13]

Tecton's zoo design work was simple and elegant in form and featured swirling concrete planes in clever articulations. It was an early and influential example of international modernism in Great Britain—the Dudley Zoo designs were the first example of modern architecture in the English midlands—but none of these zoo designs were progressive in terms of functional needs for the animal clients. The precisely detailed structures were radical only in form and structure. Lubetkin's daughter, Louise Kehoe, when interviewed for a London newspaper, likened the controlling world of the penguin pool to the way he treated his own children: "That's the way he saw nature. He liked the contrast between the perfect man-made symmetry … and the wobbling idiocy of the animals. The penguins are just instruments to display man's ability to control nature."[14] Her analysis throws light on an aspect of zoo exhibit design that is unfortunately commonplace. Lubetkin's much admired zoo exhibit buildings have always been inadequate for their principal purpose, and are all today abandoned, much to the chagrin of many architects who adore their forms and plead for their renovation.[15] One can only hope, however, that wild animals never again have to eke out their existence in any of them. The sterile plainness of the buildings so loved by those architects who paid only lip service to the notion that form follows function were never suitable for living wild beings.

Most zoos, however, characteristically stayed away from anything radical or even vaguely intellectual. Indeed, at the same time that the London Zoo was experimenting with radical architecture and new technologies, it was also introducing another type of new exhibit, the chimpanzees' tea party: a classic example of the dichotomous attitudes so prevalent in the history of zoos—part science but equally also part show business.

FIGURE 4.4: When modern architects began designing zoo exhibits, they, like their predecessors, ignored the needs of the animals and concentrated almost entirely on form and style. Architect Berthold Lubetkin created several modernistic exhibits for British zoos in the 1930s. His smoothly sweeping concrete planes were perceived as radical and attracted abundant praise from the design professions. His elephant house at the Whipsnade Zoo was only a more elegant version of what had gone before, written in even more stark language. The animals, to Lubetkin, were strange and decorative pieces amid the pristine forms of his structures. All his designs are now defunct but with heritage listings applied to protect them from demolition. Some architects plead to have them restored to use. Photo courtesy of Architectural Review.

Chimpanzee tea parties rapidly became an essential part of the fun of going to the zoo, especially in Europe and in zoos of the British Empire. (See Figure 4.5.) Being able to laugh at animals that were so disturbingly similar to humans would have been a welcome source of relief for many visitors, especially in an era that exhorted racial differences and in societies that believed Whites were superior to people with darker skins. But these chimpanzee fiascos persisted for a surprisingly long period, and in the 1950s even expanded into a very lucrative arena for the Twycross Zoo, in the English midlands, which for forty-five years rented out chimpanzees to promote the country's most popular brand of cheap tea in Britain's longest-running television advertising campaign.[16]

The chimpanzees appeared dressed in such guises as Tour de France cyclists, as movers trying to get a piano down stairs, as James Bond characters, and especially as ordinary folk in a suburban home, in curlers and cardigans, with a pipe, a newspaper and, always, a cup of tea. Both the Twycross Zoo and the tea company resisted many years of complaints from those who saw the advertisements as demeaning the chimpanzees. Like all modern zoos, Twycross has always claimed that it played an important role in creating a public that supported wildlife conservation. But its rigid adherence to supplying chimpanzees for public humiliation was probably more for commercial gain than for promoting a sense of compassion and support for chimpanzee conservation.

Unfortunately, primates, and especially chimpanzees, have long been used for money making tricks such as posing for photographs with tourists—the animals typically abused, often drugged, and invariably presented in ridiculous clothing, sometimes almost as badly dressed as the tourists—and especially in the sort of vacation spots favored by the market segment of tea drinkers who would prefer Britain's leading brand of tea. The fact that one of Europe's major zoos was so intimately involved for more than four decades in activities that mocked chimpanzees hampered the attempts of animal welfare campaigners who worked so hard to outlaw the use of chimpanzees and other wild animals in the tourist hotspots of Europe and Asia.

While Britain's Twycross Zoo was renting out its chimpanzees to be dressed up for television advertisements, America's St. Louis Zoo was drawing huge crowds with shows featuring trained lions, tigers, and especially chimpanzees dressed as baseball players or anything else the trainer thought might bring a laugh. These shows were the mainstay of the zoo until the 1970s. The trained chimps were then sold: once stars of the show, some went to other zoos, some to private owners, and some ended up in medical research laboratories. The story of a female chimpanzee, Edyth, born at the St. Louis Zoo in 1964, characterizes the type of misery that many zoo animals endured across the twentieth century. Edyth was sold in 1968, and at the time of writing is in her fifth place of residence, a Texas roadside zoo called, to its shame, a Wildlife Refuge. This sort of activity would not happen in St. Louis today: the zoo now operates with

FIGURE 4.5: Because chimpanzees are so like humans they have often been displayed as comic characters: incomplete or deformed versions of our own kind. Derision can separate them from what is, to some people, an uncomfortable closeness. It is an attitude that makes Jane Goodall's decision to study them seriously in the wild all the more remarkable. She grew up in a culture and an era in which chimpanzee tea parties were standard fare in British zoos. In 1925 the St. Louis Zoo began specializing in animal shows and continued the tradition for more than fifty years. This scene from their 1961 "Barnyard Jamboree" is a typical example. When the shows finally stopped many of the chimpanzees were sold. Some ended up in road-side zoos and medical research laboratories. Photo collection of David Hancocks.

very different standards, but a frank exposure of past sins and a willingness to engage in open and honest public debate on future directions is essential before the world's major zoos can honorably progress toward their fuller potential and pursue the more enlightened goals that are so urgently needed.

MONKEYS AND MADNESS

The conflicts inherent in zoos were sadly and clearly evident in new developments at the London Zoo in the 1920s and 1930s. At the beginning of the modern age, the Zoological Society of London was eager to retake its position as leader in the zoo world. It set about doing this through the application of modern architecture.

Sir Peter Chalmers Mitchell was Secretary of the Society when the London Zoo approached its centenary in 1928. He had high ideals, encouraged innovation, employed innovative architects of high caliber, and promoted the latest design philosophies and technologies. He wanted not only to ensure greater public success, but also to demonstrate excellence in exhibit design, to obtain maximum open air for the animals, and to create better facilities and circulation for visitors.[17]

A proposed new exhibit, Monkey Hill, must have seemed to represent everything that London Zoo wanted to become. It offered healthy sunshine in a spacious enclosure under the open sky, with heated quarters beneath large formations of artificial rockwork quite skillfully representing the animal's natural rocky habitat. Rather than just a solitary animal or only a pair on display, it would house a *hundred* baboons, guaranteeing constant activity and a great public attraction. It was, however, an immediate disaster, and continued to be so for many disquieting years.

The exhibit was the brainchild of the recently graduated and ambitious primatologist, Solly Zuckerman, who had been hired as the Zoo Society's first research anatomist. Later he would become president of the Zoological Society. (After several decades assiduously courting the socially influential and the royal glitterati he would also receive a knighthood and later be elevated to the Upper House of the British Parliament and become Lord Zuckerman.)

Modeled on Hagenbeck's idea of separating people and animals by ha-has, the new Monkey Hill was an island configuration measuring 100 feet by 60 feet (30 meters by 18 meters) surrounded by a concreted dry moat. It featured two large piles of rocks, beneath which were heated rooms as a retreat for the animals. It was grand by zoo standards, but it proved to be an astonishingly cruel experiment.

The species selected for display on Monkey Hill was the Hamadryas baboon. These baboons live in the arid northeast regions of Somalia, Ethiopia, and Sudan in groups comprised of a dominant male and his harem of up to six females, and occasionally in groups of bachelor males. The association between a male and his harem lasts for life: he is constantly devoted to keeping the females cowed and close to him, threatening and biting them if they stray, and fending off other males. It is a tough existence of endless aggression in a harsh environment. Even so, the baboons were unprepared for coping with the disaster that was Monkey Hill.

In the spring of 1925 about one hundred Hamadryas baboons were released on to the island. Only six of them were female. War immediately broke out with prolonged fights to the death. Within two years the population had been halved. Many visitors must have been horrified, but it was a major draw for others: one observer noted that fights attracted "crowded houses from nine in the morning until sunset."[18] Male baboons killed in the fights were repetitiously replaced, and more than thirty female baboons were also added. Over time, eighty male and all the female Hamadryas were killed, in fights that sometimes lasted for several days. Even after a female had died from her injuries, demented males bit at her body and pulled at her corpse in attempts to steal her body. Zuckerman records the last fight, in which four female baboons were killed, as being so protracted and so repellant ("from an anthropocentric point of view") that it was decided to remove the remaining five females and to keep only males in the exhibit.[19] But it was not until ten years later, in 1940, that the sordid sorry experiment was finally abandoned. Apparently the interior cages during all those years had never been entered for cleaning: "in the dismal clean up ... the cages were found to contain several long defunct (mummified) baboons."[20]

The sad history of Monkey Hill reveals some equally sad truths about the inadequacies of its designer, and of zoological parks themselves. It also illuminates much about the strange and paradoxical phenomena that zoos represent, exposing the perpetual dichotomy that besets our ambivalent relationship with other animals. Zoos urgently appeal for visitors to indulge in the human pleasure of being close to wild animals yet too often fail to provide for the animals' basic behavioral, social, and psychological requirements, and they display wild creatures as objects of fascination while simultaneously crushing their very wildness.

Zuckerman's intent, always and foremost, was to make the London Zoo a scientific research institution. His own research concentrated on the role of sex hormones and the mechanisms that controlled them, and he would not have regarded the baboon escapades at Monkey Hill as a tragedy so much as a rich source of information. He based his most famous studies on the doomed inhabitants of this exhibit, regarding the situation as a suitably scientific basis for the study of animal behavior. He noted that the restricted space of the exhibit and the inability to escape from aggressors resulted in fights being carried much farther than they would in the wild. "This, however, adds to their interest."[21] It is not difficult to imagine a certain glee in what he observed there. It would have been unique, dramatic, and his alone to dissect.

There is no doubt that in the 1920s and 1930s very limited information would have been available about the natural life history of Hamadryas baboons. But even if more had been known, there is no evidence to suggest that the same awful situation would not have been created. The animals' natural history and their psychological, social, and behavioral needs have typically not figured in the calculations when designing spaces for zoo exhibits.

As recently as the mid-1990s, for example, zoo curators John Seidensticker and James Doherty, of the National Zoo and the Bronx Zoo, respectively, documented an experience where they had been employed to advise what they discreetly described as a well-known zoological park in the design of a new exhibit for jaguars. Both Seidensticker and Doherty have a strong record of concern for animal welfare and are advocates for developing zoo exhibits that "help visitors gain perspective on the world and their place in it." Their consternation must have been fraught when faced with the situation they described:

> The designers were working to obtain for the visitor a visual image of a jaguar lying on a log in the sun at the edge of a tropical river backwater. The space allotted to this was less than 300 square feet (28 square meters) and the designers were insistent that this was adequate; the design ... had also proceeded too far to allocate more space.[22]

INHERENT PROBLEMS IN ZOO DESIGN

For almost the entire modern era of the twentieth century, zoos persisted in employing architects to design their exhibits unless they decided to produce their own monstrosities without professional assistance. Unfortunately, architects tend not to be the best profession to design facilities for animals in zoos. Their principal focus, as with the buildings they produce for humans, is characteristically upon appearance and aesthetics and is thus often superficial.

University of Chicago ecologist Alfred Emerson cleverly described the intricate nest structures built by termites as "frozen behavior."[23] The structures created by human architects, however, are more concerned with style and fashion, and only rarely take account of the behavioral or psychological needs of the inhabitants. This has especially unfortunate consequences for animals that have to live in the confines of zoo exhibit spaces.

Architectural critic and professor of urbanism at the University of Pennsylvania Witold Rybczynski points out that architects vehemently deny that they design according to any stylistic mode, but the evidence is plain to see.[24] Fashion is central to all commercial design, and while it is lauded and expected in areas such as graphic design, automotive design, and especially clothing, fashion as a central component of architecture is rigorously denied by the profession.

Be that as it may, architects usually bring the wrong set of skills to zoo design. Trained to think in terms of structures and in the assembling of manufactured materials, architects pay excessive attention to form and very little to function. Thus, when the principal purposes are (or should be) to satisfy the physiological, behavioral, psychological, and social needs of wild animals, together with the need to design exhibit spaces that connect people emotionally and intellectually with those animals and their habitats, it is clear that architects are ill equipped for the task.

Landscape architects, conversely, and especially those trained in North America and in Australia where university courses in landscape architecture place more emphasis on ecology than just on garden design, work much more with landforms, natural systems, climate, and microhabitats, as well as with plants. It is odd, then, that landscape architects were ignored for zoo exhibit design work until the mid-1970s: a time increasingly perceived by some commentators as marking the premature end of the end of the twentieth century and the close of the modern era.[25]

Throughout the years, zoos had complained about architects and what they perceived as their proclivity to design monuments. Peter Crowcroft, director of the Brookfield Zoo and previously of Sydney's Taronga Zoo, included in the index of his book *The Zoo*, "architects, snide comments about."[26] Zoo directors as eminent as Bill Conway of the New York Zoological Society, and Heini Hediger, director of first the Basel Zoo and then the Zurich Zoo, Switzerland, and the profession's principle advocate of designing for the behavioral and psychological needs of wild animals, each reputedly described architects as "the most dangerous animal in the zoo."[27] More eloquently, Conway explained that zoo animals "respond poorly to the usual conventions of human architecture. Zoo architects usually respond no less poorly to the needs of animals."[28] Yet, puzzlingly, zoo mangers persisted in turning to the architecture profession for designers of their zoo exhibits.

In 1976, however, a recently formed company of Seattle landscape architects, Jones & Jones, produced a master plan for the Woodland Park Zoo that, as University of Washington professor of landscape architecture David Streatfield has written, "transformed the design of zoos, and considerable enriched their interpretive function."[29] Anne Elizabeth Powell, then editor in chief for *Landscape Architecture* magazine, remarked that it was "an astonishing departure from conventional zoo design because it reflected a pronounced shift in philosophy."[30]

Instead of taking a zoo tour to see what other zoos had built, and rather than focusing on the superficialities of style and form, the landscape architects set about measuring and analyzing virtually every aspect of the existing zoo site. They diagrammed its shade and sun patterns, slopes, natural drainage, soil types, vegetation cover, and notable trees and overlaid this data as the basis for preparing a plan that thus responded to the natural environment.[31] The plan established the most appropriate locations for establishing ten different bioclimatic zones. Within this layout the design team then prepared a set of exhibit scenarios based upon a concept that Grant Jones began referring to as "landscape immersion." The term has since become ubiquitous in zoo design, but its principles have faded away and are rarely now employed. (See Figure 4.6.)

FIGURE 4.6: The landscape immersion concept for zoo exhibits was introduced at the Woodland Park Zoo, Seattle. It was intended to bring benefits to both zoo animals and zoo visitors. The first of its type was opened in 1978, for gorillas. The concept was not greeted enthusiastically by other zoos, who saw it as wasteful of space, paying too much attention to plants, making animals difficult to see, placing too much distance between visitors and animals, and generally disruptive to the business of displaying animals. The concept spread slowly from Seattle, first to the neighboring city of Tacoma: shown here is the polar bear exhibit at Point Defiance Zoo in the 1980s. Australia's Melbourne Zoo in 1990 was the first outside Seattle to adopt it for gorillas. The Dallas Zoo, San Diego Zoo, and then others across North America followed suit. The concept has rarely been adopted in Europe (although Switzerland's Zurich Zoo has developed some of the world's finest examples) and never in England. The principal objective of landscape immersion was that all the senses of both people and animals would be absorbed within a replica of the animals' natural habitat. Today the concept has been reduced in many zoos to only a superficial view. At the same time both visitor and animal spaces are again becoming littered with artificial paraphernalia. Zoos have nevertheless become increasingly attached to the notion of calling their exhibits habitats, no matter how much the spaces may be composed only of concrete and other nonnatural materials, shaped and crafted merely to look natural. Photo by David Hancocks.

Jones & Jones had been asked to test the feasibility of reorganizing the zoo on the basis of bioclimatic zones. The logic behind this request was that the vegetation patterns induced by climate determined the distribution of wild animals, and that this, rather than any artificial factor, should determine the placement and relationships of exhibits. Zoo visitors would therefore be able to see that specific habitats and specific animals were connected and interdependent.[32] As an extension of that logic it was important not only that the individual exhibits be habitat based, but also that visitors should experience those habitats with all of their senses, to make the identification of that interconnection between animal and habitat especially memorable. This would underscore the zoo's educational message that loss of certain habitat types meant loss of specific animals.

The landscape architects responded positively to the challenge of creating a more perfect illusion of nature than had been achieved before in zoos and especially to eliminating any sense of separation between animals and people. Their new landscapes, with exquisite attention to landscape detail, saturated all of one's senses and were dramatically powerful, intended to appeal as much to the eye as to the mind, to the emotions as much as to the intellect.

The Arizona–Sonora Desert Museum, opened in 1952 on the dusty outskirts of Tucson, naturally immersed its visitors within the desert habitat and saguaro forest of its site. As they toured the museum grounds, people enjoyed exhibits about water (or the lack of it) and cactuses, geological formations, botanical transects, and wild animals (the latter unfortunately in quite nonnaturalistic enclosures), and were at the same time engaging with the landscape that these exhibits related to and came from. The Desert Museum demonstrated how appealing and how powerful that educational and landscape approach could be. The vision was not, however, picked up by zoos until landscape immersion was introduced at the Woodland Park Zoo.

The notion of taking great care to represent habitats as realistically as possible was based upon the notion that a wild animal seen in any environment other than the habitat in which it had evolved could not be fully comprehended. Outside of its natural habitat it must inevitably be seen as incomplete, even distorted, or a freak of some kind. Fifty years earlier naturalist Carl Akeley had pursued the same belief when pursuing realism in his stunning dioramas for Chicago's Field Museum and the New York's American Museum of Natural History.[33]

Landscape immersion was intended to create scenarios in which both zoo visitors and zoo animals would literally be immersed in the same type of habitat. Unfortunately, the difficulties in maintaining vegetation and animals together have not been recognized by zoos as a problem sufficiently worthy of their attention. Although protection of some plants is usually inevitable, today almost all the vegetation in so-called landscape immersion exhibits is placed out of bounds by some means, usually by electrified or hot wires. Thus, while the animals may appear to visitors to be in lushly planted spaces they are in fact typically confined to corridors of flattened grass and well-worn dirt.

The opportunity to give zoo animals an interaction with live plants, if it is employed at all, is now most usually restricted to the temporary provision of cut branches. The joys of climbing and dismembering live trees, of lounging amid shrubs, and of playing among tall grasses have been deliberately removed. These types of interaction, however, were an essential and fundamental component of the basic intentions for landscape immersion. Replacement costs for mature trees and other living plants is small in relation to the very large benefits it brings, principally to the animals but also for the enjoyment of visitors. When the gorillas at Zoo Atlanta in the late 1980s began destroying the vegetation in their new exhibit area, the designers and horticulturists implored director Terry Maple to install protective electric wires. He responded, rightly, with the advice that they instead plant cheaper trees: an extraordinary attitude among zoo directors. He is, in many ways, an unusual zoo director. A scientist and former president of the American Zoo and Aquarium Association (AZA), Maple argues that although AZA members voted in 1980 to establish conservation as the association's first priority, he would prefer animal welfare to be at the top of the priorities.[34]

In the early 1920s the distinguished Bronx Zoo director William Hornaday, after some thirty years of contemplating, learning about, and managing zoological parks, prepared a list of rights for zoo animals. Close to the top was this one: "An animal in captivity has a right to do all the damage to its surroundings that it can do."[35] If all zoo directors since then had observed this dictum we would find zoos to be not only much better and more useful places, but also that the quality of life for zoo animals would be greatly enhanced. Zoo animals do have this right, and zoo visitors have the right to see and learn about wild animals in replications of wild landscapes. These rights, when combined, impose upon zoo managers a responsibility that is admittedly taxing but that, inexcusably, has been almost universally disregarded.

Zoos, and especially zookeepers, have instead and much more enthusiastically embraced the concept of what is termed *enrichment*. Rather than providing the sort of behavioral enrichment opportunities that wild habitats provide naturally, zoos prefer to turn to technology: they create artificial diversions. Increasingly, therefore, zoo exhibits resemble trash heaps, with multicolored objects, plastic toys, and many other synthetic alternatives littering the enclosures. These may create diversions for the animals, but they destroy the very basic purpose of inviting people to see the animals in a zoo in the first place, which should be to reveal the connections and interdependencies between animals and natural habitat. A wild animal seen outside its natural habitat is seen out of context and cannot be fully appreciated or understood.

PACKAGING AS A SUBSTITUTE FOR GOOD DESIGN

The language of humbug and hokum, so loved by marketing and advertising agents, has long been a staple of show business. Aggressive promotion and media hype can not only be an effective substitute for a poor show, but it is also an indispensable part of creating the deceptions that characterize public entertainment and that sometimes appear as magic and sometimes as fakery. It is often manifested in discomfiting ways in the zoo industry. Zoos commonly refer to the animals in their collections as ambassadors for their wild cousins, but the treatment zoo animals typically receive does not reflect the deference accorded to officials of such high diplomatic ranking. Zoos also routinely describe the most barren exhibit space, even those made entirely of concrete and steel, as a habitat. A recent article on exhibit design in the AZA's newsletter advises, "murals can be used to transform the most ordinary space into an exotic habitat."[36] As if paint on a wall could make any useful contribution either to a wild habitat or to an animal's behavioral needs. Why the term *immersion* is still so persistently employed and is now almost regarded as the norm for zoo exhibit design is rather puzzling, for it has moved far away from its original intentions.

There was much public criticism of the old zoo and menagerie cages that were so barren and sterile and induced such severe boredom for the animals. Today, the exhibits often *look* green, but they typically contain cleverly camouflaged devices designed to shock animals or in some way keep them away from any live vegetation. The paying public is unaware of the unfortunate similarities in practical ways between so many new zoo spaces and those of the old menageries.

The appearance is as much an illusion as anything intended by the landscape immersion concept in which hidden barriers were intended to deceive visitors into thinking they were in the same space as the animals, but now the deception has a negative not a positive reason. Clever barriers no longer separate animals from people or animals from animals, but instead animals from vegetation. If visitors could see exactly how much of an area of so many new zoo exhibit spaces was out of bounds to the animals, they would see the similarity between the paucity and the scarcity of space that is so often provided today and the more obvious and recognizably inadequate spaces of the old zoo cages. If the animals are admittedly less bored due to the diversity of artificial toys with which they are provided, the question of the purpose for their being confined in the first place is left begging for an answer.

DISTORTED VISIONS

It may seem unfair to concentrate on the shortcomings of conditions for zoo animals when the situation for circus animals is so much more seriously deficient.

Circus animals are not only restricted to much smaller and more inadequate quarters but also are on the move for months at a time, swaying in the dark carriages of trains or trucks in extremes of heat and cold, publicly presented as oddities and freaks, trained in harsh ways to carry out completely unnatural behaviors.

It is however a mark of shame against the zoo profession that they have not collectively spoken out against the standards and activities perpetuated in circuses. Zoos and circuses have traditionally maintained much the same general collections of species: lions, tigers, bears, elephants, camels, hippopotamuses, and so on. Zoos should be well able to speak authoritatively on behalf of these animals and to call attention to their needs. Is the silence from zoos about circus conditions due to uneasiness about casting stones from within glass houses? Is it a fear of attracting attention to shortcomings in zoo conditions? Is it mere professional courtesy? Or is it a mark of acceptance by zoos of the standards of care in circuses? All these possible translations are left hanging. It would therefore be a signal of both courage and encouragement if zoos would take a stand on this issue. In the absence of this, the inevitable public perception of some sort of mutually supportive partnership between zoos and circuses must continue to linger.

Zoos of past days perpetuated false images of animals as bad as any circus show, with bears in dank pits, lions in cramped cages, and monkeys in jailhouses. Zoos today may concentrate more on learning, and especially on having fun, but their methods of presentation can still be depressing. Their continuing focus on displaying just a narrow band of wild animal species conveys completely wrong perspectives to their visitors. Botanic Gardens tumble just as easily into the same trap and similarly focus on unusual and gigantic forms, presenting these as separated pieces rather than attempting to present and interpret interconnected holistic habitat displays.[37]

Typical zoo collections restrict themselves almost entirely to diurnal, colorful (and mainly African) large animals. Compare, for example, the diversity of animal species on the planet with the composition of zoo collections. Of the probably thirty million species of animals on earth, about 1,640 are mammals. The average collection of an AZA-accredited zoo in the late 1990s contained fifty-three mammalian species; a ratio of 1:31, or one type of mammal in the zoo for every thirty-one species of mammals in the wild. For birds, the ratio is less than one third that figure, 1:98. It reduces even further for reptiles, with a ratio of 1:104. When we move to the realm of small creatures the deficiency is even more alarming. Amphibians are represented in the average AZA zoo at a ratio of only 1:2,000. For invertebrates it drops to just one in several millions.

Shortly before Ted McToldridge retired as director of the Santa Barbara Zoo in the late 1990s, and after creating one of the most appealing and well-designed small zoos in America, he came to see that zoos needed to make radical changes in regard to their collection philosophies: "We have to stop exhibiting lions and elephants and start exhibiting spiders."[38] I have occasionally found similar views among other leading zoo directors, especially in recent years. McToldridge's energetic enthusiasm for presenting more holistic and realistic views of nature was, however, deflated by his recognition that a zoo director's desire to change things is so often thwarted by zoo board members who, though they generally have no knowledge, and have no oversight, are given exaggerated authority.

The rash of conversion that spread across zoos in North America in the latter decades of the twentieth century, whereby local authorities handed over operational authority of their zoos to a Zoo Society, probably insures that such ideological changes are doomed. The new masters will want measurable outcomes rather than pursuing qualitative agendas. They will have little interest in serving the public good. Changing public perceptions about nature will not attract their interest as intently as their focus upon birthday party rentals and concerts and the financial bottom line. This shift, a by-product of the narrow-minded economic rationalism of the 1980s, may yet prove to be one of the most unfortunate and far-reaching changes in twentieth-century zoo history as more and more technocrats are given authority and as the postmodern confusion of management with leadership grows deeper roots.

The large percentage of members from the corporate world who comprise the typical zoo society board, and the technocrats they are increasingly employing as CEOs, will almost certainly have no interest in the fact that their zoo collections reflect an upside-down view of the natural world. At the end of the twentieth century there was more social status in having an elephant in one's zoo than in any attempt to illustrate nature's diversity. More than 95 percent of all animals are small enough to fit in the cup of your hands and are completely unknown and unexplained in zoos. This is a critical deficiency because it is often the very small animals that illustrate the most interesting behaviors and that best illuminate the intricacies of ecosystems. Invertebrates especially usually have more biomass and thus greater influence and more vital and direct links to ecological functions.

Despite the fragmented view presented by their collections, zoos make extravagant claims about the impact of their exhibits on zoo visitors. They repeatedly use phrases such as "forging strong connections between people and wildlife" or "bringing people into contact with nature." There is not a shred of evidence that this actually happens. Even by the start of the twenty-first century, the AZA had still not instituted any formal means of gathering data to support the perpetual and ubiquitous claims by zoos and aquariums that they "inspire people to make a difference."[39]

Nevertheless, in defense of what it perceived as attacks from what it called the "hype" of "animal rights extremists," on the standards of care for zoo elephants, a 2006 AZA news release claimed that, "the public knows that elephants in zoos provide a crucial link to the conservation of the species in the wild."[40] At almost the same time, however, an AZA-funded review by the Annapolis-based nonprofit Institute for Learning Innovation (ILI) of the literature on studies of what visitors learn in zoos revealed that "little or no systematic research has been conducted on the impact of visits to zoos and aquariums on visitor conservation knowledge, awareness, affect, or behavior."[41]

That same study by ILI noted that the primary and most intense long-term impact emanating from all the energy and the millions of dollars that AZA zoos collectively invest in education programs is "heightened awareness of zoos and aquariums as conservation organizations." In other words, self-promotion. Unfortunately, zoos show very little and only belated commitment to environmental conservation. They enthusiastically promote themselves as agents of conservational change but are extremely careful to avoid making their visitors feel uncomfortable about the negative impacts that their personal actions have upon the environment, such as, say, excessive consumption of fossil fuels. Zoos may have genuine concerns about loss of wildlife habitat, but this will not prevent them from welcoming visitors who drive up in SUVs. One can sympathize: zoos are in business for customers. But when the AZA promotes zoos as leading conservation organizations they must realize that important responsibilities come with such an assertion.

Zoo staff members typically have strong concerns for conservation of specific animal species with which they work, and this may be why zoos tend to equate conservation with breeding. But zoos do not demonstrate many of the values that would be inherent in an institution strongly committed to capital-c Conservation. They have not been vigorous leaders in adopting green design principles for their building projects. They make no comment on unsustainable or unhealthy (or cruel) animal farming practices. They invariably have no official purchasing policies to consider the conservation impact of all their purchases, from paints and panel vans to carpets and computers. They do not promote public transport to bring families to the zoo. They very rarely offer organically grown food products in their cafés and restaurants.

The eagerness with which AZA promotes the image of zoos as conservation organizations may even serve as a disservice to conservation. Most people are not directly involved in conservation activities and know little about the real facts, but harbor a general uneasiness about loss of wildlife. It must be a great sense of relief if they think their local zoo is solving these problems. They can stop worrying and not have to bother making uncomfortable changes to their lifestyle. One can imagine some enterprising zoo introducing conservation confessional boxes. Visitors could confess their environmental sins, be told to walk once around the zoo, deposit $100 in the zoo's conservation fund, and go back to happily sinning all week.

The AZA likes to boast that attendance at their member zoos exceeds all American professional sporting events combined. Clearly, if these millions of zoo visitors were in fact gaining new understandings, new insights, and new enthusiasms for the protection and care of wildlife, we would not be facing the extreme situations that are decimating wild animals and their habitats all over the globe. Despite almost two hundred years of professionally operated public zoos in the West we have a citizenry that is alarmingly ignorant about wild habitat desecration, apparently uncaring about environmental degradation, and is biologically and ecologically illiterate to a disturbing degree.

If as much energy and dedication were applied to these problems as to trying to ensure visitors have an easy trouble-free day with lots of fun for the family, we would surely see a more energized and compassionate citizenry emerging from the zoo exit turnstiles. For all the feel-good aspects of a visit to a modern zoo, they remain institutions that reflect a darker set of realities.

SATISFYING THE NEED

In his foreword to Lyn Margulis's and Dorion Sagan's wonderful and astonishing *Microcosmos* (1991), Lewis Thomas explains that the book is about "the inextricable connectedness of all creatures on the planet, the beings now alive and the numberless ones that went before." He draws the distinction between this viewpoint and a series of university seminars he attended many years ago, on "Man's Place in Nature." Mostly, Thomas says, the seminars looked at human control, exploitation, and management of the natural world. "The general sense was that Nature is a piece of property, an inheritance, owned and operated by mankind, a sort of combination park, zoo and kitchen garden."[42]

That is the view often promoted by zoos, and even then only by the more progressive. It is a simple concept to grasp, suggests that everything is fixable, and fits comfortably with our inherited mindset that the whole place is ours for us to look after and to do with it what we want (see, for example, the Bible's Genesis 1:26).

Many millions of people have visited zoos around the world over the past century, passing by labels that every zoo educator knows they never read, gazing upon animals in spaces invariably too small and inadequate, learning nothing essentially useful about wildlife conservation, and gaining no intelligent insights about wild places.

If most zoos had set out to do more than simply put wild animals on display, like mere curiosities, and had not restricted themselves even further by focusing almost entirely upon the charismatic, the cute, and mainly just mammals and birds, their continuing existence would rest upon a more justifiable foundation.

And if some part of all the money and human effort invested in zoos had been directed toward encouraging visitors to recognize that humans are an integral part of nature, each of us biologically connected to every other living thing, then perhaps some proportion of these many millions of visitors might over time have developed a very useful and very different perspective.

A zoo that aimed to reveal the complexities and interdependencies of life forms, that exhibited ideas and not just objects, that presented an ecological appreciation, that appealed equally to the intellect and the aesthetic, that treated the animals in its care with the respect that is warranted for ambassadors, giving them the sort of conditions they would request if they could but speak, and that held some higher ideals than just increased attendance every year, would be a zoo that had little connection with the vast part of zoo history. They would be the sort of zoos that had the potential to be truly valuable institutions to help guide a citizenry increasingly separated from contact with nature and increasingly devoid of understanding how terrible that is.

CHAPTER FIVE

Scientific Animals

*Reflections on the Laboratory and Its
Human–Animal Relations, from* Dba *to Dolly
and Beyond*

KAREN A. RADER

No animal is more iconic of science than the laboratory mouse, and the ambivalence of its contemporary meanings finds many expressions in American popular culture. One of the most brilliantly satirical of these is an animated television program called *Pinky and the Brain*. Produced by Warner Brothers (1995–1998), the series' two lead characters—both talking lab mice—were imagined as the consequence of a genetic engineering experiment gone awry. Instead of taking part in the original (unspecified) Acme Laboratories' protocol for which they were intended, their genes were accidentally spliced, using the company's commercially successful Combination Bagel Warmer and Gene Splicer. The result: one superintelligent mouse (the Brain) and one loveably insane sidekick mouse (Pinky), whose collective goal each episode was to escape their laboratory cages and conquer the world. Such immodest aims, the theme song reminds viewers, stemmed from truly humble ambitions: "To prove their mousey worth/They'll overthrow the Earth."[1]

But in each encounter with the world Pinky and the Brain demonstrated they knew human technoscientific culture very well and even occasionally embraced becoming a part of it. Sometimes their knowledge was revealed through sarcastic commentary on sci-fi entertainment, as when Brain writes (during each show's opening sequence) a complex but ambiguous formula on the blackboard entitled "The Universe Explained," with the resulting answer being THX 1138—the title of the first film ever made by *Star Wars* creator George Lucas. But other plots more profoundly explored the agency and domination of animals in laboratory culture, as in the episode where the mice become proud parents to Romy, created from the accidental merging of their DNA by Brain while he was trying to create a mouse "master race." "With these multiphasic transrepliclonator pods," Brain exclaimed, "I shall create a single clone in my own image. After a modicum of study, I will take a new sample from the prototype and make two more clones, then they'll make two clones, and they'll make two clones, and so on, and so on. Thousands of me, all working toward the same goal—taking over the world!"[2]

The numbers of animals used in laboratories today is actually orders of magnitude greater that Brain's vision: a 2004 U.S. Department of Agriculture report estimated 1.1 million warm-blooded animals were used in U.S. research (government and industry sponsored), but this number excluded the tens of millions of mice, rats, and birds that are still (as of this writing) not regulated by the Animal Welfare Act.[3] Still, as difficult as it is to determine their exact numbers,[4] it is also nearly impossible to imagine a time in history before their presence was anything but an inevitable part of scientific culture. Part of what makes the premise of *Pinky and the Brain* work so well is precisely that the "mousey worth" of its characters has been almost completely circumscribed by science; laboratory mice have, in some sense, already taken over the world by virtue of the widespread application of biomedical knowledge obtained from them. Still, as late as 1953, mouse geneticist Clarence Cook Little worried about how to give the laboratory mouse a better public image, and he concocted a plan to arouse Walt Disney's interest in doing "a factual, or partially factual film, to tell the story of the mouse in science, which might easily be a brother or sister ... of Mickey [Mouse]." At the same time, geneticists themselves were engaged in important methodological debates about the use of animals in research: should so-called model organisms be simplified models of real life, as bacterial geneticists often argued, or bits of real, complex life on which biologists can experiment, as mouse workers claimed?[5]

Thus the use of particular animals in twentieth-century scientific laboratories was not inevitable, and the history of these developments raises important issues about interdependent relationships between humans and animals[6] in both science and society. Decisions about what animals became recurring fixtures in various routine scientific and experimental practices were the product of a delicate and ongoing negotiation of two key tensions: the relationship between natural and technological systems in the realm of biological experiment, and the relationship between humans and various animal species in Western culture. In this chapter I explore three case studies to illustrate this point: early and contemporary use of the inbred mouse for genetic research; competing constructions of dogs used in biomedical research; and public and scientific reactions to various contemporary forms of animal cloning—including Dolly, the first human-engineered cloned sheep.

THE MOUSE: HUMANS AND ANIMALS IN THE DOMESTICATION OF GENETIC SCIENCE

Early geneticists recognized that specific variants of highly inbred animal populations—in scientific parlance, mutants—could be used effectively as tools to sort the many heritable features of organisms into biologically identifiable processes. Initially such efforts were frequently taken on by so-called amateurs: for example, German high school teacher Hans Duncker combined his rudimentary knowledge of genetic science with the bird breeding expertise (ability to select for color and song) of fancier and shopkeeper Karl Reich in a quest to create what biologist Tim Birkhead claims was the first genetically engineered animal: a red canary.[7]

The mutants used most productively in early academic genetic research did not come initially from highly prized cultivars, but from animals culturally classified as pests—such as the fruit fly, drosophila. As historian Robert Kohler has shown, Columbia University zoologist T. H. Morgan and his then-graduate-students Calvin Bridges and Arthur Sturtevant exploited this organism's proximity to humans and its biological capacity as a "breeder reactor"; drosophila bred fast and generated copious mutants, which enabled Morgan's team to construct the first animal genetic map of its four salivary chromosomes in 1921.[8] For Kohler, such laboratory domestication of the fly was continuous with its biological evolution and domestication more broadly and it created the kind of mutual dependency between the human and animal actors that Stephen Budiansky argues is the hallmark of domestication itself.[9] As Kohler writes, "when fruit flies crossed the threshold of the experimental laboratory, they crossed from one ecosystem to another quite different ones, with different rules of selection and survival. ... Once in the lab, drosophila ... revealed an unexpected and very remarkable capacity for experimental heredity and genetics which soon made it and its human symbionts famous."[10] Soon after, more technological processes—such as the X-ray and chemical mutagenesis—were developed that allowed scientists to create (rather than merely find) even more fly mutants, which sealed drosophila's fate in the development of classical genetics, and thereafter, in biological teaching laboratories.[11]

Like drosophila, mice have also been hangers-on to human culture for thousands of years, so their identity—cultural, as well as biological—derived first and foremost from that relation. Taxonomically, mice are the smallest members of the order *Rodentia,* or "gnawers," and their evolutionary appearance dates to the Eocene epoch, fifty-four million years ago. *Mus musculus* proper "shared

with the European his recent conquest of the globe" as ocean-vessel stowaways
to all habited regions of the Asiatic seacoast and to the Americas.[12] While
the internationalization of the house mouse is a relatively recent phenomenon
as measured by evolutionary time, ancient cultural traditions expressed many
mouse mythologies and narratives. Some such legends were pejorative: for example, Aelieanus (ca. 100 CE) of lower Egypt speculated disgustedly that mice
developed from raindrops because they were so plentiful in that area. More
recently, anthropologists have suggested that the Egyptians' hatred of mice accounts in large part for their well-known deification of the cat. Yet other stories
and cultural images cast the mouse in a positive light. More than a thousand
years before Christ, Homeric legend reported a cult of the mouse god Apollo
Smintheus, whose popularity reached its height around the time of Alexander
the Great. White mice, because of their relative rarity and their associations
with purity, were thought to forecast prosperity. (See Figure 5.1.)[13]

The multivalent aspects of this ancient cultural legacy persisted in the West
through the early decades of the twentieth century. Modern heirs to the an-
cients' negative portrayals of mice included various accounts—both scientific
and folkloric—of mice as harbingers of disease and "spookers" of women. Yet
by the 1930s, these representations existed simultaneously with positive cultural
depictions.[14] Perhaps the most famous of these was Walt Disney's personified

FIGURE 5.1: White mice are used in research at the Children's Hospital Los Angeles
Research Institute, Los Angeles, California. Credit: Aaron Logan.

Mickey Mouse, who made his public debut in 1928 and proved phenomenally popular.[15] But in 1929, the popular magazine *Nature* also ran an article called "White Mice," which described the daily activities of the author's real pet mice. The author gave a particularly pointed and modern spin to Egyptian pure white mouse myth: "If cleanliness is next to godliness, as the soap advertisements say, then Plato was wrong and our animals do have souls."[16]

For genetics, however, the most significant early twentieth century human activity centered around mice was a hobby called mouse fancying. The exact origins of mouse fancying are obscure, though textual sources (believed to be early breeding manuals) indicate that the collecting and developing unique strains of mice in captivity dates as far back as seventeenth-century Japan. But the formation of many local and national mouse fancier organizations in the early 1920s indicates that mouse fancying clearly enjoyed increased popularity in America and Britain beginning in the early twentieth century. Fanciers who belonged to the American Mouse Fanciers club, and its many British counterparts, selected for certain standard physical features and preserved the specimens that exhibited them.[17] As described by a 1930s popular magazine article, fanciers thought "the perfect mouse should be seven to eight inches long from nose-tip to tail-tip, the tail being about the same length as the body and tapering to an end like a whiplash."[18] Fanciers most often kept these mice as pets and would travel with them to local or national mouse shows, which awarded small cash awards to the owners of visually unusual and interesting specimens. Other mouse breeding enterprises had more lucrative commercial interests in mind. In 1930s England, for example, mouse breeders could cash in on the demand for full-length women's coats made of mouse skins, which took 400 skins and sold for $350 retail.[19]

One fancier, in particular, was of significance for the development of laboratory mice: Abbie Lathrop, who ran the Granby Mouse Farm in Granby, Massachusetts. Lathrop founded this institution around 1903 as an alternative to her failing poultry business. Mice and rats, for sale as pets, provided an inherently quicker turnover, and Lathrop probably believed the growing community of fanciers in the New England area would be her main market. But instead of receiving requests for a few mice of exotic coat color from mouse fanciers, she soon began to get large orders for mice from scientific research institutions and medical schools, many of whom were using mice to do drug testing and cancer research. Lathrop's farm quickly became the East's largest supplier of mice for research in the first two decades of the twentieth century. She took orders from laboratories all along the East Coast and from as far west as St. Louis.[20]

By 1913, the Granby Mouse Farm had become such a local curiosity that a Massachusetts newspaper (the *Springfield Sunday Republican*, October 5, p. 12) devoted a feature article to it. The details of caretaking provided in the reporter's account reveal clearly that Lathrop's mouse breeding for research was a large and resource-intensive undertaking, requiring extensive practical knowledge of proper mouse husbandry. Her stocks had gradually increased to 10,000 since her humble beginnings with "a single pair of waltzing mice which she got from this city." Lathrop housed her mice in wooden boxes, with straw as a bedding material, and since cleaning the cages had become too much work for her alone, she periodically hired town children at seven cents an hour for this purpose. The mice were fed a diet of crackers and oats, and Lathrop reported going through twelve-and-a-half barrels of crackers and a ton-and-a-half of oats each month. Furthermore, the cages were given fresh water daily "in little jars which are first boiled as protection against disease germs." Lathrop even appears to have experimented with a primitive water bottle device, from which "a thirsty mouse has only to stand on his hind legs to quaff a cooling drink."

But although Lathrop's fancy mice can rightly be called the raw materials for the creation of laboratory mice, the boundaries between the field and amateur knowledge-making of fanciers, and the laboratory professional science of genetics remained porous for several decades. Fanciers learned from and exploited their relationship with scientists, and vice versa. For example, Harvard zoology professor W. E. Castle attended mouse fancy shows and encouraged his students to do the same—some even acted as judges. Also, Lathrop herself was interested in science and worked with University of Pennsylvania pathology professor Leo Loeb to breed and analyze patterns of tumor inheritance in several strains (most importantly, one that fanciers had named silver fawn for its coat color, but geneticists renamed *dba* as an abbreviation for its coat color genes: dilute, brown, and nonagouti).[21] One Castle student in particular—C. C. Little—sought out Lathrop's particular variants and the use of these materials shaped his own genetic research, which aimed to make Mendelian sense of mouse coat and eye color inheritance, as well as mammalian cancers. Little ultimately translated his vision for the role of inbred animals in research into the Jackson Laboratory, a Bar Harbor, Maine, research institute and mouse supplier he founded in 1929 and that is still going—stronger than ever—today. Another of Castle's students, Freddy Carnochan, cofounded a commercial animal breeding farm called Carworth Farms and continued to work closely with card-carrying mouse geneticists—especially, L. C. Dunn of Columbia—to identify and develop new mutant stocks.[22]

Some early mouse geneticists self-consciously used the metaphor of domestication to argue that there was no important boundary between past and present practices. Particularly powerful in this regard was the idea that laboratory domestication represented a process continuous with *Mus musculus*'s evolution as a human symbiont—a biological term meaning a participant in a close, prolonged, often mutually beneficial association between different organisms of different species. For a scientific audience, Castle's student Clyde Keeler wrote *The Laboratory Mouse: Origin, Heredity, and Culture* (1931), a handbook-*cum*-homage to his favored laboratory creature. It aimed (as Keeler noted in the introduction) to collect comprehensively "literature upon the house mouse, its origins, history, distribution, development, the nature of its variations, the hereditary transmission of its varietal characters, as well as methods of rearing it suitable for the needs of laboratories" in order to "present it in a useable form." But what counted as useable form amounted to a kind of claiming of past domestication efforts in the name of genetics. The book, for example, provides a list of the most important Mendelian unit characters in mice—the first being dominant spotting in 1100 BC and the last being George Snell's dwarf mutant in 1929—in order to show that out of eighteen then extant, eight have been recorded since 1900. Likewise, in another article for the popular *Scientific Monthly,* Keeler led his readers on a journey "In Quest of Apollo's Sacred White Mice," only to conclude that while much of the mouse's ancient history lies buried "in the religious auguries of Babylon and Troy ... we may say definitively that Apollo's mice were albinos of the species *mus musculus* and that our laboratory mice are probably descended from the temples of Apollo. [This is] the longest heredity of a simple variation of which we have a written record."[23]

At the same time, other genetic scientists mobilized existing cultural boundaries between nature and culture to help advance their own domestication work in the laboratory. In 1935, for example, Little penned a *Scientific American* article he called "A New Deal for Mice." First, he juxtaposed gains the mouse had made in science during the last decade (in cancer and other medical research) with the animal's prevailing cultural stigma; Little described this stigma as follows: "Do you like mice? Of course you don't. 'Useless vermin,' 'disgusting little beasts,' or something worse is what you are likely to think as you physically or mentally climb a chair." Then against this background, Little cast himself as "attorney for the defense" and argued that through their involvement with science, mice had been positively transformed. Inbred laboratory mice—as opposed to their "not very convenient" wild mice relatives—"provided a particular service" to both science and to humanity. Little invited his lay readers to visit the domus through which this became possible: the Jackson Laboratory's mouse house or, in another more Progressive-era description, one of the "mouse laboratory 'cities' with its cleanliness, orderly arrangement, and activity." Such arrangements testified that thoroughbred mice (a concept Little acknowledged some people would find "amusing") had become "an integral part of man's helpers." "Under these circumstances," Little concluded, "perhaps mankind will accept and develop his relationships with mice in a different light."[24]

In all these cases—some rhetorically self-conscious, and others practically strategic—domestication functioned as an active, relational, if sometimes contradictory, meaning-making metaphor that united and ultimately naturalized the coexistence of diverse domains of science and culture in mouse–human relations. Mouse fanciers routinized the activity of mouse breeding in captivity before scientists became interested in this animal—and in so doing, established traditional husbandry assumptions while lowering the practical thresholds to mouse use in the laboratory. Fanciers provided genetic scientists with both a unique mammalian material resource and a broader practical context in which the controlled breeding of these animals for human ends was an accepted cultural activity.

But scientists' active collaboration with this group of animal producers and pet owners also highlights the kind of ambiguous and fluid boundaries that separated domestic fancy animals (even nonagricultural ones) from humans. While the cultural turn to mice as pets that the mouse fancy represents could potentially have resulted in increased emotional attachment to the species[25]— and the refusal to use them in laboratories—in practice, the reverse happened: fanciers sought to use the new science of genetics to understand their own breeding process and get a leg up on the competition (other commercial breeders and competitors at mouse fancy shows). Thanks to the existence of fancy mice, mice did not need to be trapped messily from one's home or field to be obtained for research. Instead, mice could be ordered from a scientifically minded breeder, making contact with them in their natural state unnecessary. The metaphor of domestication was one about whose relevance early mammalian geneticists and fanciers agreed on and, in turn, this metaphor was itself a potent resource through which mice crossed the threshold from field to laboratory.

Nearly a century later, contemporary scientific work on so-called designer mutant mice has employed new tropes of domestication, influenced in large part by subsequent genetic research. In mass media representations from the 1990s onward these creatures have appeared as generic aggregate types—genes for X mice, where for X, one can substitute medical conditions as diverse as Alzheimer's disease, male-pattern baldness, obesity, and aggression (to name only a few).[26] But occasionally such mice have also emerged as individual fait accompli, with unique names and commercial applications attached to their identities. One of the most widely reported animals of the latter genre was called Doogie, the Smart Mouse. In mid-September 1999, Princeton University neurobiologist Joe Tsien created this animal and named him after the TV child prodigy Doogie Houser, MD. Doogie was a so-called smart mouse: his memory has been enhanced through genetic manipulation of NR2B, a gene whose product pairs with another gene's product, NR1, to open what biologists believe to be the physical mechanism of memory in the brain. Doogie's forebrain produced some extra NR2B product, so his memory mechanism stayed open an extra 150 thousandths of a second. This was enough time, Tsien and his colleagues say, for the creature to outperform other normal mice its age on standard tests of rodent intelligence. *Time* magazine proclaimed that

Tsien's work "sheds lights on how memory works and raises questions about whether we should use genetics to make people brainier." Meanwhile, Princeton filed for a use patent on the NR2B gene, which would give the institution the right to develop drugs to enhance NR2B production in humans.[27] As a material incarnation of the practical and ideological values of genetic-based experimental biomedicine, then, designer mutants like Doogie have been presented by scientists and the media as true domesticates as well as true cyborgs. Doogie is part nonhuman animal, in so far as scientists have altered his genes and experimented on his body in ways ethically unthinkable for members of our own species, but Doogie also bears a human name and performs functions significant only within human culture.[28]

Critics of genetic engineering sought to mobilize these contradictory representations to challenge to biomedical research values and assumptions. The environmental advocacy organization Turning Point Project, for example, ran an advertisement in the front page section of the *New York Times* in October 1999 featuring a photo of "the mouse with a human ear on its back." This creature was produced in 1995 in the lab of Charles Vacanti. Vacanti collaborated with a chemical engineer to create an earlike scaffolding made of biodegradable polyester fabric to distribute human cartilage cells onto the form and to implant it onto the back of a hairless (or nude) mouse that lacks the immune system to reject human tissue.[29] The resulting ear-shaped human cartilage was then removed—and the mouse lived. At the time of Vacanti's initial publication, *AP Newpapers* reported: "Someday, ears and noses for cosmetic surgery will be grown in a test tube using the patient's own cells and custom-designed scaffolding." But the Turning Point Project asked readers to reject this formulation: "Whether you give credit to God or to Nature ... there is a *boundary between life forms* [emphasis in original] that gives each its integrity and identity ... Biotech companies are blithely removing components of human beings (and other creatures) and treating us all like auto parts at a swap meet. ... Some of these experiments may save lives, but so far, there are few successes and an equal or greater chance for terribly negative consequences." In this formulation, then, cultural dissonance sprang from biomedicine's misguided intrusion on what might be called natural mousehood; no knowledge obtained from these mice could be natural and the creatures themselves were artifacts of a dangerous arrangement between science and society.

Likewise, persistent biotechnology critic Jeremy Rifkin collaborated with developmental biologist Stuart Newman to create a series of laboratory protocols for making a human–mouse chimera they call Humouse™. One method, for example, merges an eight-cell human blastula (the structure resulting from a fertilized egg) with a mouse embryo at the same stage of development. Another introduces human embryonic stem cells into early stage mouse development, then implants the resulting embryo into the uterus of a mouse to gestate. Newman argues that such procedures would "take only a day of laboratory work" to complete successfully, but neither method has been tried. Instead, Rifkin and Newman submitted the protocols to the U.S. Patent Office in 1997 in an attempt to force the legislative hand of the federal government on the question of patenting of human life. In April 1998, the Patent Commissioner broke a long-term policy of not commenting on pending application to tell reporters: "There will be no patents on monsters, at least not while I'm commissioner."[30]

Throughout the twentieth century the lay public has for the most part tolerated the tensions of scientific mouse and scientific human coexistence. A recent (1999) National Science Foundation Science Indicators Survey noted that public approval of the use of mice in research was approximately 66 percent—significantly higher than the use of animal models generally. At the same time that the Minnesota-based Alternatives Research and Development Foundation took on the biomedical research industry by mounting a challenge to the Animal Welfare Act, forcing the U.S. Department of Agriculture (its administering institution) to include previously excluded mice, rats, and birds under its more stringent laboratory care provisions, the Web-based magazine *Fast Company* conducted a survey indicating that its readers rated the development of the laboratory mouse as the best of the best innovations in technology during the twentieth century.[31]

Incongruous images and beliefs about the standardized lab mouse, then, remain powerful resources for both scientists and their critics. Remarking on the genetic similarities between mice and humans, yeast geneticist Ira Herkowitz said in 2003: "I don't consider the [laboratory] mouse a model organism. The mouse is just a cuter version of a human, a pocket-sized human." But such translations of the domestication metaphor can go both ways; if (as Jean Baudrillard infamously declared) "Disneyland exists to conceal the fact that America is Disneyland" then (as Marc Holthof has argued) the laboratory mouse exists to conceal the fact that humans are also mice.[32]

RESEARCH DOGS: CULTURE AND THE CONSTRUCTION OF SCIENTIFIC SUBJECTIVITY

Beginning in the scientific revolution, dogs featured prominently in medical and anatomical research—and this work bequeathed important cultural and material legacies to twentieth century biomedicine. Robert Hooke performed an open thorax experiment on a dog for a public audience at the Royal Society and reportedly was so distressed by the experience that he never experimented on these animals again.[33] But physiological research, begun in seventeenth-century England by William Harvey and performed in earnest throughout the nineteenth century by Francois Magendie and Claude Bernard in France, made extensive use of vivisection and dissection of dogs to study respiration and anatomy. In 1928—the tercentenary of Harvey's publication of *On the Motions of the Heart*—the importance of this laboratory method was commemorated by the Royal College of Physicians and Surgeons through a film reenactment of Harvey's experiments, showing the hearts of live fish, frogs, and dogs in the hands of unidentified modern scientist demonstrators.[34] Likewise, Louis Pasteur's laboratory work, in which he injected the rabies virus into the brains of anesthetized dogs, was celebrated by the mainstream French and American media as a medical breakthrough: "the experiments, cruel as they may appear at first sight," wrote one reporter, "are made in the interest of humanity, and M. Pasteur is careful not to inflict needless suffering on the dumb creatures that he subjects to the operation."[35]

By the 1920s, however, antivivisection advocacy had coalesced in America and Britain, and laboratory dogs were a particular focus of efforts to represent scientific work as a threat to accepted human–canine relations. The proliferation of special breeds of dogs as domestic companion animals (or pets) distinguished them in middle-class urban areas from working or agricultural animals—as well as from the feared mutts that roamed the city streets. In 1876 Parliament passed the first federal legislation that attempted to regulate animal experimentation: the Cruelty to Animals Act, which required all medical researchers who used vivisection to register and become licensed to perform the procedure by the state. Antivivisectionist such as Frances Power Cobbe featured sketches of dogs undergoing physiology experiments in her pamphlet *Light in Dark Places,* and dogs like the one begging a scientist for mercy in Charles John Tompkins's infamous 1875 painting *Vivisection* became central to an ongoing antivivisection campaign.[36] Twenty years later, leading American physicians mounted a successful effort to block similar legislation in Washington, D.C., but the U.S. antivivisectionists exerted continued pressure on the research medical community throughout the 1930s, with a special focus on abolishing experimentation with dogs. By the 1930s an estimated eight million Americans owned dogs, and between 1929 and 1933 seven state legislatures had pending bills against using dogs in laboratories. At the federal level this same legislation was introduced repeatedly over the next several decades: in 1919, 1926, 1930, 1938, 1943, and 1946.[37] As medical school Dean George Hoyt Whipple told a congressman in 1930: "The people who are proposing this bill first proposed an all-inclusive bill which prohibits all experiments on animals. Failing to get this bill through, they fell back on the dog as an entering wedge, knowing that there is more sentimental affection for this animal than any other."[38]

Some antivivisection concerns grew out of problems with laboratory animal supply. With the rise of experimental biology and medicine in the early twentieth century, larger numbers of animals were required by laboratories, which gave rise to new mechanisms for obtaining and managing what scientists represented as their necessary research materials.[39] Many American universities and hospitals initially relied on animal dealers, who purchased dogs with unknown histories at auctions; dealers themselves often obtained dogs and cats from individuals who raised animals or collected strays. To prevent the use of stolen or lost animals in laboratories, in 1909 the American Medical Association promoted a voluntary code that a research facility hold an animal for one to two days before starting experiments. But reports of stolen pets discovered in medical school kennels, as well as widely reported cases of pet-napping by dealers, drew public attention to the ambiguous distinction in this system between valued family companions and abandoned street animals. By the 1920s researchers turned increasingly to city shelters for animals and experienced less public resistance: American medical researchers successfully blocked many attempts through the 1930s to obstruct the use of pound dogs in laboratories. Still, this practice remained a source of tension with animal advocates because shelters were often run by the local Humane Society.[40]

Medical researchers made careful efforts to represent their dog subjects in ways that either meshed with mainstream cultural understandings of their use or obscured the aspects of laboratory work that might be displeasing to animal advocates. As historian Susan Lederer has shown, Rockefeller Institute for Medical Research Director Francis Peyton Rous developed guidelines for manuscripts submitted to the *Journal for Experimental Medicine* that included mandatory and detailed discussion of any anesthesia used; the substitution in discussion of procedure of "impersonal medical terms" such as hemorrhaging for bleeding; and the restriction of photographs to only the specific part of the animal body involved (e.g., the limb or lesion) rather than the whole animal. "The invisibility of the 'naturalistic' animal was enhanced," Lederer argues, by the elimination of references to dogs whenever possible, substituting the word *animal* or each subject's experimental number (altered in ways so as not to reveal the total numbers of animals used in an experiment—e.g., dog no. 897 would be called subject 8–97). At the same time, strategies for counteracting the negative media images of dog experimentation reintroduced aspects of pet keeping to the laboratory. For example, in the 1930s and 1940s, the New York Academy of Medicine and the National Society for Medical Research both gave out research dog hero awards—on behalf (in the case of the NYAM prize) "of their ancestors who had contributed to fundamental research." These awards, which the media deemed "the canine equivalent of the Nobel Prize," were given to dogs with names—Duke, Bozo, and Flossie, to name a few—but nevertheless underscored the persuasive argument (especially after Frederick Banting's 1922 discovery of insulin working with diabetic dogs) that some animal sacrifice was necessary for scientific medicine to be able to treat successfully human disease.[41] Walter B. Cannon argued as early as 1909, in well-received popular essays, that dog use was at the center of American advances in both medical science and clinical practice.[42]

Decisions about how to represent experimental practices with dogs also affected knowledge claims scientists could make with their research. For example, in the first decade of the twentieth century Russian scientist Ivan Pavlov conducted extensive Nobel Prize–winning experimental work on the physiology of conditional reflexes in dogs. (See Figure 5.2.) Historian Daniel Todes argues that Pavlov's dogs were literally technologies, "particular kinds of 'machines' designed and produced in the laboratory to generate particular kinds of facts."[43] Surgically creating dogs with intestinal and gastric fistulas, and especially those with isolated stomachs that enabled Pavlov to collect gastric juice and analyze the effects of what he called "sham feeding" (the food never reached the dog's stomach), was difficult and complex; researchers seeking to replicate Pavlov's results were reliant on him for animal subjects. But (as Todes notes) the "tension between dog-as-technology and dog-as-organism was rooted both in the laboratory dog's 'lifestyle' and in the confrontation between its biological complexity and Pavlov's scientific vision."[44] As a biologist, Pavlov was committed to investigating the normal functioning of organs through physiological surgery and was in opposition to acute experiments (his term for vivisection) that he believed created undue stress in animals that

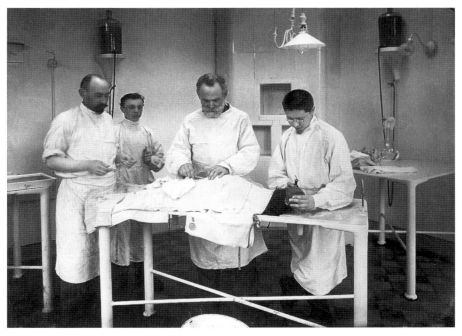

FIGURE 5.2: Dogs from Pavlov's laboratory undergoing experiments on gastric secretion, 1904. Wellcome Library, London.

interfered with regular physiological process to distort experimental results. (Many laboratory animal care workers make this same argument today, and an industry has arisen to mediate the effects of stress on experimental animals so that they will generate more accurate knowledge.[45]) Consequently, the normalcy of Pavlov's dog subjects was central to the legitimacy of his scientific arguments, and it was achieved in several ways. First, by facilitating traditional pet–master relationships between experimenters and animals (each dog surviving the surgery received a name, a personality description, and a daily walk by on the Imperial Institute of Medicine grounds), but also through a series of laboratory "interpretive moments"; when two identically treated dogs yielded widely divergent results, these "numberless factors" were invoked by Pavlov and his assistants to explain the discrepancies.[46]

Likewise, cultural assumptions shaped initial scientific understandings of behavioral genetics, which led researchers to use dogs as this field's preferred experimental subject. Historian Diane Paul details how C. C. Little (a former Boston Dog Show judge) wrote to Alan Gregg of the Rockfeller Foundation in 1941 to advocate for breeding a uniform strain of dog for cancer research at the Jackson Lab. Recognizing the resource-intensive nature of such an enterprise, Gregg suggested that Little apply the methods used by psychologists in breeding rats to breed for intelligence in these same dogs. In Gregg's view, most people would never be impressed with the demonstration that there are more and less intelligent rats. They would simply "dispense with that phenomenon in much the same way as we do with trained fleas." Psychologist Robert Yerkes supported the proposal, noting that dogs were the perfect subjects because they had strong emotional appeal for humans. Gregg even suggested that these laboratory dogs could be sold as pets, and that the owners of such "friendly and bright dogs" would be more inclined to thank experimental biology for producing their beloved pet rather than to be critical of animal experimentation. For the next fifteen years, scientists John Paul Scott and John Fuller produced and collected data on five breeds of dogs: African basenjis, beagles, American cocker spaniels, Shetland sheep dogs, and white-haired fox terriers.[47] The results were inconclusive, but Scott and Fuller blamed the experimental animals rather than their formulation of the scientific problem: "Nothing like the general-intelligence factor sometimes postulated for humans" existed for dogs, they argued in 1965. In turn, researchers sought out other genetic uses for these animals, with one grants officer even going so far as to suggest that Scott should attempt to produce "a strain of obviously schizophrenic dogs" in order to provide a living argument "for the hereditary arrangement of the human disease."[48]

Five decades later, dog genetics remain (in the scientific estimation of biologist Jasper Rine) "the hope of discovering the genetic basis of both mammalian development and behavior."[49] The so-called dog genome project launched in 1990 as a collaborative study involving scientists at the University of California, the University of Oregon, and the Fred Hutchinson Cancer Research Center, but it, too, involves breeders and fanciers: dogs are an especially useful species for genetic study because the American Kennel Club has tracked 150 dog breeds in its 120-year history. DogMap (according to media reports) aims "to do for dog DNA what the human genome project did for human DNA":[50] to produce a map of all of the chromosomes in dogs, which will then be used to map the genes causing disease and those genes controlling morphology (animal form) and behavior. Donna Haraway recently noted that part of what is at stake in these and other canine projects is ownership: for example, what commercial activity will surround the discovery of markers for dog diseases? But she also argues that the dog genome project allows for, even encourages, a necessary interrogation of the cultural category of companion species: these animals, she suggests, are our "partners in mutual constitution" and as such are understandable only in our "relentlessly historical" relations with one another.[51]

CLONED ANIMALS: ENGINEERING ANIMALS, FROM THE FARM TO THE LIVING ROOM

As we begin the twenty-first century, the vast enterprise of scientific breeding of animals for research in the laboratories now exists alongside an even vaster enterprise of scientifically breeding animals for other purposes—farming and companionship being chief among them. On the contemporary cultural landscape, the boundary between human and animal domestication and breeding—once firmly reconstituted, when the Western world acknowledged the horrors of Nazi-era eugenic practices in the 1940s—now seems more blurry, both practically and ideologically. Twentieth-century genetic technologies designed to further human ends—especially with regard to reproduction—have borrowed freely from knowledge obtained through the controlled breeding of domesticated animals and vice versa.[52] Furthermore, even when human reproduction was not an aim of a particular research program involving a genetically engineered animal, it has been frequently invoked—by scientists and pundits alike—in conversations about the application of results.

These trends are most evident in the recent history of animal cloning. For example, Ian Wilmut, the scientist and creator of Dolly, the first cloned mammal, has noted that the main objective of the controlled breeding program resulting in her birth was not achieving reproductive cloning (that is, the ability to create genetically identical animals through adult cellular nuclear replacement), but rather devising a strategy for genetic manipulation of farm animals. Dolly originated in a project to create a sheep (Tracy) that would exert in her milk large quantities of alpha-1-antitrypsin (AAT), an enzyme used to treat human blood clotting and lung disorders and formerly only available through its extraction from human blood plasma.[53] But interestingly, this animal "pharming"—and its implications for reframing political and social relationships between humans and animals, as well as for the health care economy—was not what captured the American cultural and scientific imagination in 1997; rather, it was the possibility that cloning technology itself could be applied to human reproduction.[54] Dolly died in February 2003 (ironically, of a lung infection and advanced arthritis), almost two years to the day after the decoding of the Human Genome Project was announced. The moral of Dolly, Princeton biologist Lee Silver argued, was that human reproductive cloning through nuclear transfer between two human cells was "a story that will come true. To believe otherwise is to misunderstand the power of the marketplace, and the power of individual desires to reach very specific individual reproductive goals."[55]

Dolly's appearance, then, challenged the relationship between natural and technological systems in science and society, as well as the relations between humans and animals in Western industrialized cultures. Subsequent critics of human reproductive cloning (many scientists among them) pointed to the ethical issues raised by both the low efficiency of the animal cloning procedure (from 244 mammary nuclei transferred, only nineteen healthy embryos could be implanted in surrogate lamb mothers—and of those, only one survived until birth), as well as emerging evidence of abnormal gene activity during clones' development (causing such things as skeletal and respiratory abnormalities) and in later life, premature aging.[56] But Dolly's birth also marked a significant step in the process that Sarah Franklin has called "the defamiliarization of what it means to do biology or be biological."[57] Silver, and other advocates of newer forms of genetic engineering and cloning, actively sought to blur the boundaries between humans and animals, at the same time that they renaturalized domestication itself. Now the success or failure of this natural domestication is framed as dependent not on biological or evolutionary forces but on the invisible hand of the marketplace and the inductive emergence of community values from individual reproductive and animal cloning decisions. Like all arguments about science policy, this move was not made in a vacuum: global biotechnological markets have themselves already reshaped critical relationships between humans and animals and between the public and private spheres. As Franklin has observed: "We are currently witnessing the emergence of a new genomic governmentality. ... This is necessitated by the removal of genomes of plants, animals, and humans from the template of natural history that once secured their borders, and their reanimation as forms corporate capital."[58]

Efforts to clone pet animals have reflected this same market-based logic. In February 2002, Mark Westhusin's laboratory announced that it had cloned a domestic cat, a tabby called CC (Copy Cat). This achievement began as the Missyplicity Project, a $3.7 million partnership between Texas A&M University's College of Veterinary Medicine and University of Phoenix founder John

Sperling, aimed at cloning Sperling's beloved Siberian husky mutt, Missy. But it ended, in 2002, when Sperling dissolved this arrangement with the university, and reinvested in a private California-based company called Genetic Savings & Clone (or GSC). Westhusin suggests that medical benefits for humans might come from continued research on animal clones: "Cats have feline AIDS and that's a good model for studying human AIDS." Sperling, in turn, wants to put the ability to replace lost pets within the reach of all consumers. For an initial fee of about $1,000, plus a $100 annual maintenance fee, GSC customers can now have their cat's or dog's DNA stored in the company's gene bank in anticipation of the day they can bring home a pet clone (target price tag: $20,000).[59] Either project, it seems, presumes a "maximal utility" relationship between humans and animals, where (even though the initial motive may be to confirm a caring ethos between human and animal companions) human money has all the power in shaping outcomes.[60]

Since Dolly, American and British media coverage of cloned animals has been more modest, sounding celebratory but also cautious notes. Nearly every first clone of a species has been assigned an individual name, ranging from the clever to the mundane. These include: ANDi, a rhesus monkey (January 2001), whose name is a scientific abbreviation for "inserted DNA" spelled backward);[61] Full Flush, a cattle bull (2001), named for a winning poker hand;[62] Ralph, a rat (September 2003);[63] Idaho Gem, a mule (May 2003);[64] and most recently, Snuppy, an Afghan hound puppy (August 2005) produced by the South Korean lab that fabricated its human cloning research.[65] In cases where a name has not been assigned, researchers and reporters alike stress the biological and medical benefits of cloning entire classes of animals, such as endangered animals or organ transplant animals.[66] Regardless of the type of clone—from farm animals to pets—scientists and policy makers continue to stress the technical difficulties associated with the laboratory procedures to create these organisms, noting the similarities with human-assisted reproductive technologies.[67]

But to the extent that animal cloning[68] has caused widespread ethical and biological concerns, boundaries between animals and plants seem as significant as those between humans and animals for shaping public discussion. As Carol Tucker Foreman, Director of the Food Policy Institute, noted at a 2002 Food and Drug Administration Workshop, mainstream opinion polls showed opposition to animal cloning has been significantly greater than opposition to genetically modified plants. Foreman suggested this was because human attachments to animals were more sentimental: "no one pulled up a stalk of corn and named it Bt Betty."[69] Research in science communication confirms this view: M. C. Nisbet and Bruce Lewenstein surveyed media articles in the period from 1970 through 1999 and noted that Dolly's appearance reframed popular discourse about biotechnology by shifting the emphasis from issues of economic progress and risk management to issues of ethics and morality.[70] Likewise, while economic interest in human–animal organ xenotransplants remains high, policy deliberations have focused more on the medical and environmental risks (such as animal diseases crossing the species barrier) than on the ethical issues surrounding animal-body manipulation and harvesting.[71]

CONCLUSION

In 1994 sociologist Arnold Arluke argued that images of animals in laboratory animal advertisements (a long-standing feature of scientific journals) allowed these creatures to be "seen and treated simultaneously as more object-like and more human-like than they actually are." Portrayed alternately as (in Arluke's classification system) "classy chemicals, consumer goods, or team players," lab animals were simultaneously impersonal objects (data), sacrificial symbols (scientific knowledge), and anthropomorphized sentient beings (laboratory pets). "Images of lab animals in advertisements may allow readers to both distance and identify with them," Arluke wrote, and it is this paradox that embodies the contemporary ideology of Western science: experimental knowledge is made by humans and yet is represented as impersonal and objective.[72] But just as the twentieth century was a period during which animals became an inescapable features of modern biological and medical laboratories, it was also a period in which scientific animals transformed human cultural relationships and meanings. As Donna Haraway wryly observed, these creatures are at once "powerful technologies and potent jokes: we inhabit their world and they inhabit us."[73]

Cultural understandings of laboratory animals thus remain significant as much for their ability to bring us together under the umbrella of common humanity these creatures serve as for their ability to tear us apart, in periodic waves of social and ethical conflict over the larger meaning of their use. For earlier generations this tension was captured literarily in Aldous Huxley's fictional *Brave New World*, a human genetic dystopia founded on eugenic methods formerly believed appropriate only for domesticated farm animals as well as (in America) the reality of Model Sterilization Laws enacted in 1914.[74] Likewise, for our own era, ambivalence about the converging roles of humans and nonanimals in the historical process of laboratory domestication is both fact and fiction: it is the finished code of the human or mouse or dog genome project but also the technoscientific urban imaginary of Zadie Smith's novel *White Teeth*,[75] the climactic scene of which features the public launch of celebrated (fictional) scientist Marcus Chalfen's FutureMouse©.

Smith's FutureMouse© is a transgenic animal in which fatal genes have been engineered to be turned on and expressed along a predictable timetable. This animal, Dr. Chalfen claims, is the "site for an experiment" into the aging of cells, the ultimate embodiment of human agency in the process of scientific development: "FutureMouse©, he tells the crowd, holds out the tantalizing promise of a new phase in human history where we are not the victims of the random but instead directors and arbitrators of our own fate." For Chalfen's middle- and working-class teenage children and their friends, however, Future-Mouse© is a metaphor for the degree to which their father's personal affections for them (and by extension, his concern for the problems affecting contemporary Western, especially British, society) have been distracted by science, technology, and other bourgeois values. Still, when asked by a group of animal activists (F.A.T.E.: for Fighting Animal Torture and Exploitation) to liberate the animal, Chalfen's oldest son Josh (mothered by his horticulturalist wife Joyce and with whom Marcus has an especially tense relationship) surprises everyone by resisting his friends and expressing what he holds to be a certain fatalism about this mouse's development: "this isn't like the other animals you bust out. It won't make any difference. The damage is done."[76]

FutureMouse© does eventually escape, and the creature gladly seizes its elusive and short-lived freedom and (literally) runs with it. Still, in this one act of resistance, son Josh redeems his personal relationship with his father and seals the fate of FutureMouse© in the world—and in so doing, his character encourages us to redirect our focus to what is interesting and important about scientific animals. Just as in *White Teeth*, Smith is not as interested in the issue of race per se as she is the juxtaposition and interaction of urban people from different ethnic groups living their daily lives, Josh is not as interested in the genetically engineered animal per se as much as the juxtaposition and interaction of animals and people domesticated by science as a cultural metaphor for life as it is, rather than life as we wish it to be.

CHAPTER SIX

Animal Philosophy

Bioethics and Zoontology

RALPH R. ACAMPORA

MORALITY

Animal philosophy of the past eighty-five years, at least in the traditions of western Europe and North America, has been dominated by ethical reflections and advocacy. These moral meditations and exhortations have evolved along a spiral trajectory—from an early emphasis on anti-cruelty kindness, through a later insistence on rights or liberation, to a most recent resurgence of interest in caring sympathy (similar but not exactly identical to the earlier welfarist concerns).

Emblematic of the first stage is Albert Schweitzer's ethic of reverence for life. Schweitzer represents something of the grand old man or godfather of late-modern animal ethics. (See Figure 6.1.)[1] An accomplished polymath in theology, music, and medicine, he came to be regarded as a genius of Renaissance proportions and earned international renown for his humanitarian enterprises in Africa. His period of greatest activity spanned the entire first half of the twentieth century, culminating in the award of the Nobel Peace Prize in 1952. Schweitzer's central doctrine was a vaguely biocentric compassion for all (at least animate) creatures. Though its core was decidedly humanitarian, Schweitzer was explicit and strong in articulating the inclusion of other animals under the doctrine: "To the universal ethics of reverence for life, pity for animals, so often smilingly dismissed as sentimentality, becomes a mandate no thinking person can escape."[2] Or again: "Every man and woman who thinks

FIGURE 6.1: Albert Schweitzer was a pioneer of animal ethics. Credit: Library of Congress.

simply and naturally cannot do otherwise than express love in action, not only on behalf of human beings, but also on behalf of all living things."[3]

As an ethos reverence for life imposes, or rather mediates, obligations of a positive or active as well as negative or passive sort: "Ethics consist in my experiencing the compulsion to show to all will-to-live the same reverence as I do my own. A [hu]man is truly ethical only when he obeys the compulsion to help all life which he is able to assist, and shrinks from injuring anything that lives."[4] There is in this position a metaphysical murmur of Schopenhauer's voluntaristic morality of sympathy. As Schweitzer puts it, "I am life which wills to live, in the midst of life which wills to live. ... Whenever my life devotes itself in any way to life, my finite will-to-live experiences union with the infinite will in which all life is one."[5] Also like Schopenhauer, he finds Western philosophy lacking in this area and takes inspiration for a compassionate outlook from Eastern traditions:

"In Chinese and Indian thought the responsibility of man to the animal creation plays a much greater part than in European thought."[6]

Yet Schweitzer goes beyond what he takes from the East, "for it is not as if Chinese and Indian ethics really solve the problem of the relationship of man to animals. What they have to offer in this regard is fragmentary and cannot satisfy us."[7] In transcending the Jain doctrine of nonviolence, or *ahimsa*, for instance, he is at pains to explain that we have not merely to refrain from harm but should also affirmatively intervene for the protection or betterment of animate beings.[8] Indeed, the burden of our obligations in this respect is compounded by the guilt incurred through participation in natural and cultural orders that ineluctably place us at odds with other forms of life:

> An ethic that tries to teach us reverence and love for all life must at the same time open our eyes in pitiless fashion to the fact that in manifold ways we find ourselves under the necessity of destroying and harming life, and that we are constantly engaged in grievous conflicts, if we have the courage not to let ourselves be stupefied by want of thought.[9]

Of course, Schweitzer was not alone in having this insight. Other animal welfarists, prior and subsequent to him, shared a similar sense of burdensome responsibility—but then they go on to discharge it by offering various exceptions or excuses. What makes Schweitzer distinctive in this regard is that he refuses such a maneuver altogether, eschewing entirely apologetic appeals to natural necessity or conventional contingency: "The ethic of reverence for life recognizes no relative ethic. It considers good only the maintenance and furtherance of life. It brands as evil all that destroys and hurts life, *no matter what the circumstances may be.*"[10] Ostensibly this claim is part of what dictates a proactive stance of animal assistance (compensation or restitution, as it were, for the huge debt always piling up), but we may be forgiven for noting also how nicely it sets up the need for human redemption through divine salvation latent in Schweitzer's not-so-crypto Christianity (he was, after all, a minister). Whatever the ultimate motivation(s) for his reverential vitalism, Schweitzer was clear that the exact nature and extent of its implications for ethical practice are matters to be worked out by individual conscience (everyone is culpable for inevitable compromises, in other words, but no one should judge anyone other than himself). And this is what exposed Schweitzer to critique from more trenchantly transformative or outright abolitionist animal ethicists later in the century, for apparently his own conscience was willing to countenance humane forms of vivisection, carnivory, and other modes of animal usage (e.g., hunting and husbandry).

In fact, as the 1960s ran into the 1970s, humane welfarism in general was challenged by the emergence of hard-hitting moral philosophies of liberation and animal rights.[11] The germ of this development was the publication in 1971 of *Animals, Men and Morals,* a collection of essays whose influence grew as it was covered by Peter Singer for the *New York Review of Books* (1973). Singer's review stirred up much interest, and he followed through with a book of his own—*Animal Liberation* was published in 1975, and it became something of a biblical ur-text for a new wave of uncompromising animal advocacy consolidating in the late 1970s. During that same decade protectionist off-shoots of the environmental movement (influenced by Aldo Leopold, Rachel Carson, and others) were successful in defending the interests of wildlife, to the point of securing passage of landmark legislation (e.g., the United States' Endangered Species Act).[12] In 1983 the foundational tome of animal rights theory, Tom Regan's *The Case for Animal Rights,* was published—and it was discussed with fervor by animal ethicists for the rest of the decade.

What was it about the late-century zeitgeist that made this powerful intensity of interest possible if not necessary? Bids at explanation vary. Sociologist Adrian Franklin views the phenomenon as a reaction to the misanthropy and psycho-ontological insecurity of post-Fordist society (turning to other animals for righteous relations makes up for humans' feelings of self-loss and species loathing).[13] Historian Richard Bulliet sees instead the ideological manifestation of a post-domestic episteme, whereby "those who become guilt-ridden about the productive beasts we cannot humanize feel a corresponding yearning to reconnect with the wild animals that our human ways are rapidly driving to extinction" and to liberate or grant rights to the domestic animals we drive through a machine of exploitation.[14] Some of the leading animal advocates themselves look at the development through Enlightenment lenses and perceive an orderly progression of liberal sensibility that expands enfranchisement across boundaries of class, race, sex, and eventually (ultimately?) species.

However their origins may be explained, it is important to understand the different content of the major first-generation theories of animal ethics. To begin with, the position of animal liberation staked out by Singer is *not*— despite a common misperception (abetted at times by loose rhetoric on Singer's part)—a rights theory. Actually, it is a thoroughly utilitarian account that self-consciously traces its historical roots back to Jeremy Bentham's principle of "the greatest good for the greatest number" of sentient beings, nonhuman as well as human. Unlike Bentham, however, Singer does not define *good* hedonically (i.e., in terms simply of pleasure over pain)—rather, his brand of utilitarianism is concerned with maximizing interests in more complex terms of preference satisfaction. Within this framework, the argument for animal liberation proceeds fairly straightforwardly: we know, on behavioral and neurological analogy with our own experience and anatomy or physiology, that most vertebrates (at least) are sentient interest-bearers with preferences that can be satisfied or frustrated; like interests must be considered equally (as a basic condition of impartiality or fairness, which does not always entail the same ultimate treatment); therefore, many nonhuman animals' interests—though they are often discounted by an-thropocentric custom—should be considered in any relevant utilitarian calculus of ethical action or policy.[15]

Using a term coined by psychologist Richard Ryder a few years earlier, Singer characterizes the failure to accept this argument's conclusion as "speciesism"—and claims it is no less arbitrary or morally repugnant than prejudices such as racism or sexism.[16] In this way he makes an explicit analogy between the cause of animal liberation and movements on behalf of feminism or Black Power, at-tempting to recruit supporters of the latter to adopt the former. What are the implications of adoption? For Singer, they are fairly thoroughgoing if not revo-lutionary: change of diet from omnivory to vegetarianism, dramatic curtailment of animal experimentation, phasing out of animal-abusive entertainments (rodeo, circus, etc.), and the like.[17] Still, consistent with the utilitarian frame-work, animal liberation stops short of calling for complete eradication of all animal usage. Depending on the empirical details of any given case, there may well be times when overriding amounts of preference satisfaction are probable enough to justify this or that utilization of nonhuman animals. For examples, some organic and family farms could be deemed sufficiently humane (relative to, say, intensive animal agribusiness operations), or there might be medical protocols that sacrifice so comparatively little to directly bring about so much benefit for so many that Singer would be committed to approve or endorse them. The test for such allowances would always be to ask ourselves if it would make any difference to us were the contemplated harm to be done upon humans—which is just a reminder that truly species-blind neutrality demands that like interests be considered equivalently (as per the original argument). As it turns out, in actual practice, situations that meet the net-benefit threshold on application of species-impartial utilitarian criteria are fairly rare.[18]

Nonetheless, it has struck many that any moral system capable of sanction-ing exploitive practices (however humane or infrequent) is inadequate as an animal ethic. The intuition on this view is that the central injustice of animal exploitation is the very usage of an organism—as if it were a thing the ma-nipulation or consumption of which was a matter of indifference to or for it. From this perspective a robust animal ethic must recognize and appreciate that (many nonhuman) organisms are the locus of vital interests that matter both objectively and subjectively to or for them. Clearly, such an outlook harbors an abolitionist tendency that will not sit well with utilitarianism of whatever stripe. Instead, it is more congenially defended from a deontological approach based on principles of duty and correlative rights. The preeminent champion of this rights view has been Tom Regan, to whose theory we now turn.

Regan's arguments for animal rights have two forms, a pure one from scratch, so to speak, and a rhetorical shortcut version. The latter starts out by taking human rights for granted; it then notes that there is no nonarbitrary way to delimit basic rights only to human beings; hence, at least some nonhumans have at least some basic rights. Regan tends to use this version when addressing audiences outside of academic philosophy to whom an assumption of human rights can safely be attributed in advance.[19] The second premise requires much elaboration for its support, which means a rehearsal of the best attempts to establish human moral uniqueness and a corresponding refutation of each and every one. Often such refutations instantiate a crucial subargument from so-called marginal cases: for examples, if someone holds that humans are morally special because they alone can speak or reason, it can be pointed out that we don't (and shouldn't) withhold moral standing from linguistically impaired or mentally deficient humans—and so neither language nor rationality is morally relevant. Thus, by dismissing various candidate capacities as essentially speciesist, it can be shown at least that the boundary of ethical considerability extends somewhere beyond the frontier of humanity as usually conceived.

Furthermore, according to Regan, the case for animal rights is not logically dependent on the assumption of human rights. He frames a foundational argument for the proposition that many nonhuman animals have rights on the basis of the following premises.[20] (1) All inherently valuable beings bear rights (by definition it seems). (2) All "subjects-of-a-life" have inherent value (apparently self-evident). (3) Adult mammals (at least) are subjects-of-a-life. Regarding the second premise, Regan argues that vital subjectivity is a sufficient condition for inherent value though he admits it might not be a necessary one. What is a *subject-of-a-life?* This pivotal concept is characterized as follows:

> individuals are subjects-of-a-life if they have beliefs and desires; perception, memory, and a sense of the future, including their own future; an emotional life together with feelings of pleasure and pain; preference- and welfare-interests; the ability to initiate action in pursuit of their desires and goals; a psychophysical identity over time; and an individual welfare in the sense that their experiential life fares well or ill for them[.][21]

In other words, sometimes used by Regan himself, subjects-of-a-life are those biological beings *who* are also biographical entities (in the sense that a coherent story can be told about the status and trajectory of their life *from their perspective*).[22] The scope of this term, as per the third premise, is alleged to be (at least) all adult mammals (those above one year of age). In support thereof Regan argues that a belief–desire account of mammalian activity is superior to a stimulus-response model (inasmuch as the science of cognitive ethology has superseded old-school behaviorist psychology).[23]

What, then, are the practical consequences of this theory? Regan has it that if we endorse animal rights of the sort he has argued for, then we should abandon vivisection altogether (indeed all scientific uses of animals), eliminate the meat industry (dairy as well as leather), and abolish sport, trophy, and commercial hunting.[24] "*Empty* cages, not bigger ones!" is the battle cry of the animal rights movement that takes inspiration from Regan's point of view—to which might be added, "*vegan,* not just vegetarian" and "*give* up, not clean up, hunting." Thus this deontologically grounded position is more stringent even than Singer's utilitarian call for animal liberation: the theory is totally uncompromising and the associated practices are truly radical in that they would require a revolution in the economies and cultures of modern civilization (beyond, that is, merely marginal or even intermediate-scale reforms).

Whether the rights view must condemn the kind of subsistence hunting traditionally practiced by premodern peoples (and their descendants, contemporary indigenes) is an interesting point of controversy that merits some notice in the present context. Certainly, for Regan, those who can nourish themselves otherwise should do so. What about those in cultures or climates that dictate venatic pursuits as a nutritional or spiritual necessity? The hardcore animal rightist will say that such peoples ought to change their lifeways and dwelling places. Yet this stance attracts the charge of ethnocentric universalism from indigenous foragers (especially those in Arctic regions), who will point out that they have rich heritages of land stewardship, species conservation, and respect for individual animals (the latter of which often requires rituals of permission or atonement for any killing). The Reganite animal advocate is generally unimpressed by such apologetics and retorts that it matters not to the hunted animal whether we say a prayer to or for its spirit before, during, or after inflicting death.

Here is not the place to (even try to) settle this score, but I shall offer a couple remarks before continuing our discussion. On the one hand, the animal rightists might usefully be reminded of the deontological tradition from which their ethic springs. Of particular import is the Kantian maxim (indeed one of the original formulations of the categorical imperative itself) that we ought not treat ends-in-themselves *merely* as means. The qualifier *merely* is all too frequently forgotten or ignored, as if we had always only a stark choice between respecting dignity and using resources. There is, however, at least the theoretical possibility of a hybrid attitude that could be called respectful usage.[25] I take it this is what a certain sort of subsistence hunter is implicitly invoking when he simultaneously claims to recognize the subjectivity of animals and kills them for food. On the other hand, indigenous (and likeminded) hunters need perhaps to acknowledge that the cultural, religious, or ritual status of a practice does not in and of itself make the practice immune from ethical criticism—even if holders of the tradition in question have been subjected to a history of colonial maltreatment. Indeed, the principle at stake—that culture can be submitted legitimately to critique (not necessarily from above, but from aside as it were)—constitutes the very fulcrum for condemnation of turpitude such as slavery and genocide (to which, of course,

indigenes themselves have been no strangers). And so maybe, then, peoples
with a tradition of subsistence hunting should ethically reconsider the nature
and perpetuation of that custom—at least, I want to say, it is not automati-
cally disrespectful to invite or encourage such reconsideration.[26]

At this juncture, having surveyed the dominant theories of late-twentieth-
century animal ethics, it will be well to address some challenging rivals that
have arisen since the 1990s.[27] To understand the place of these latter perspectives, certain aspects of their context must be brought into view. There has
been a fairly pervasive emphasis on reason that runs through much of the
mainstream analytic treatment of the subject at hand, not cognitively (say in
contrast to empirical theory of knowledge) but rather in the sense of intellec-
tualizing morality. First- and second-generation thinkers in the area usually
took or adopted this stance on ethical or more broadly philosophic principle,
but behind their foreground theorizing there was a sociohistorical setting
that placed structural demands of a rhetorical nature on their discourse. Before animal ethics became (in the 1970s and 1980s) a subspecialty within the
academic discipline of philosophy, there was an already venerable tradition
of animal advocacy and activism (in many countries, including the United States
and the United Kingdom). A number of ideological platforms and strategies of
action coexisted under various banners, most especially those of *welfare* and
humane. The principal message that broke through into popular consciousness, from the nineteenth up until (at least) the mid-twentieth century, can be
characterized justly as a be-kind-to-animals sentiment (à la Schweitzer). To the
chagrin of its self-consciously serious proponents, this essentially anti-cruelty
movement became branded by dominant humanist culture (especially estab-
lishment media) as sentimental in the derogatory sense—with the stereotyped
advocate portrayed as an overly romantic, bleeding-heart (pejoratively effemi-
nate) animal lover. Against this backdrop it is understandable, if not entirely
excusable, that early on (mostly male) animal ethicists as well as their immediate interlocutors and commentators would disown embodied emotion
and promote a purely rational basis for animal liberation or rights.[28] Such
a strategy, which was likely only half-conscious in motivations and implications, effectively served as a rhetorical bid for renewed stature in, and so
greater influence with, the educated public.

Yet over the past couple decades both the philosophical community and
that of animal advocacy have learned a good deal, theoretically as well as
practically, from the late-twentieth-century rehabilitation of embodied existence and emotional life conducted by feminist thinkers and activists as well as
other ethicists. "In particular," one may notice, "feminist approaches, ecofeminist analyses, and more holistic approaches that include broad environmental
concerns have made their way into the philosophical conversation regarding
animals."[29] Thus there are those who would correct for the fact that affective

and somatic aspects of the moral life were underplayed in some earlier animal ethics. Arne Vetlesen, for instance, points out that

> the act of [ethical] judgment we exercise presupposes and rests on an act of [moral] perception that logically precedes it ... feelings are required in the sense that there can be no successful act of moral perception, or [*a fortiori*] of moral judgment, without the participation of the faculty of empathy and hence of our emotional capacity, our elementary ability to feel.[30]

And as Josephine Donovan observes, "It is a particular qualitative experience that is missing in contemporary rationalist theory, the emotional sympathetic understanding of another creature."[31] I would add that this experience is originally mediated by physical sensibility.

Given these developments, therefore, it would be appropriate for us to examine now some of the newer accounts of animal ethics—in particular, feminist and European treatments. Taking the former first, we should note that recent feminist theorists have differed in the degree and variety of their criticism and constructive work in this area. Drawing inspiration from literary and legal theory, from ecocriticism and environmental philosophy, feminist thinkers have taken Singer and Regan to task on a number of fronts. The main charges include that the utilitarian and deontological approaches are too detached and calculating, are enthralled to a one-sided justice model of ethics, and remain cryptohumanist (i.e., are unsuccessful in subverting anthropocentrism). Those who make these allegations have called for, and some have themselves developed, alternative vocabularies for thinking through the multifaceted issues of animal ethics.

One of the first, as well as most vocal and prolific, feminist critics in this arena has been Carol Adams. The crux of her critique, however, will be treated below in a somewhat different context. Here I shall begin with the contribution of Adams' collaborator Josephine Donovan, a substantial critical and constructive force in her own right, and the allied commentary of Deborah Slicer as well. Chief among the criticisms lodged by these feminists against the animal ethics that extend utilitarianism or deontology to cover nonhumans is that they are beholden to a masculinist model of morality. This model finds its historical exemplars in such figures such as Kant and Bentham and was formulated as a developmental theory in the twentieth century by psychologist Lawrence Kohlberg. It stresses adherence to rational principles as the epitome of ethical thinking and presupposes that moral agents are in fact (or should be ideally) autonomous individuals. The business of morality on this model is to recognize or intuit fundamental axioms of ethics, deduce universally normative standards therefrom, and then apply such to specific cases of concern—with all of this activity being conducted impartially by level-headed reasoners. Over the last generation or so this standpoint has received substantial challenge, which was pioneered by Carol Gilligan and Nel Noddings in the early 1980s. Gilligan's research found that while many males do adhere to the model of abstract justice just described, girls and women tend to develop along a different trajectory of ethical growth, one that stresses instead nurturance of relationships in contexts of rich affect.[32] Noddings's theory used these results as a basis for articulating an "ethic of care" to rival or complement the established justice tradition of ethics.[33]

Donovan and Slicer mobilize such feminist critique against the received doctrines of animal liberation and rights. According to Donovan, the utilitarian approach is beholden to a calculative bias characteristic of androcentric scientism: "it requires a quantification of suffering, a 'mathematization' of moral beings, that falls back into the scientific modality that legitimates animal sacrifice" (as in, e.g., vivisectory research).[34] For Slicer, the deontological approach is overly formalistic (a typical shortcoming, allegedly, of masculinist models)—"general principles are too legalistic and abstract to be helpful in resolving unique, highly context-laden, nongeneralizable situations," she avers, adding that "a 'principled morality' leaves no room for virtue or affection."[35] Along a similar line of reflection, Donovan notices that "women animal [advocacy] theorists seem, indeed, to have developed more of a sense of emotional bonding with animals as the basis of their theory than is evident in the male literature" exemplified by Singer and Regan.

Another related charge brought by feminist theory is that of cryptohumanism: it is alleged that the discourse of animal liberation and animal rights masks a residue of anthropocentrism in that its candidate criteria for moral standing (sentience and subjectivity) tacitly rely on paradigms from our own species. "In effect," Slicer argues, "animals are represented as beings with the kind of capacity that human beings most fully possess and deem valuable for living a full *human* life."[36] Ecofeminist Val Plumwood labels this extensionist maneuver "minimalism" because it opens the sphere of moral considerability just enough to admit only the most humanoid entities; in other words, "this ethical stance minimally challenges or [rather] reinforces anthropocentric ranking regimes that base the worth of a being on their degree of conformity to human norms or resemblance to an idealized 'rational' or 'conscious' subject."[37] According to the feminist train of thinking under discussion, we need to root out residual speciesism in order to develop a truly progressive animal ethic. After all, Slicer continues, "There is no reason why animals' differences, independence, and indifference cannot be grounds for caring, for relationships characterized by such ethically significant attitudes as respect, gratitude, compassion, fellow or sisterly feeling, and wonder."[38] To undermine the nexus of anthropocentric and androcentric domination, then, "it is also possible—indeed necessary—to ground [animal] ethics in an emotional and spiritual conversation with nonhuman life-forms," Donovan concludes. "Out of a women's relational culture of caring and attentive love, therefore, emerges the basis for a feminist ethic for the treatment of animals."[39]

Those inclined toward an ethos of care or compassion, rather than rational justice or hedonic calculus, were never limited to feminism for inspiration, and by the 1990s they also turned to (or emerged from) continental European traditions of philosophy, including phenomenology, existentialism, and hermeneutics. I contributed to this development by taking up the posthumanist project of reappreciating bodily animacy as such in order to expand the range of caring regard in recognizing our status as animate zoomorphs.[40] I undertook that task by engaging a bioexistential hermeneutic of body in view of Edith Wyschogrod's observation that "classical phenomenology's account of the body subject [can be] recontextualized so as to highlight the body's receptive capacities, its vulnerabilities, its patience; it is thus replete with ethical significations."[41] Interpreting embodiment phenomenologically along these lines, I claimed that we could enter a mode of philosophizing fruitful for interspecies ethics—because the live body of experience is the primary locus of existential commonality between human animals and other organisms, and the appreciation of commonality undergirding differentiation enables the growth of moral relationships. I suggested that we might ground moral compassion for other animals in the sensation of sharing carnal vulnerability (rather than, say, various mental abilities).

This overview could stand some elaboration. On a somatic level, then, it seems to me that we are aware of our own physical vulnerability—susceptibility to injury, illness, and infirmity—just in virtue of being entities aware of their animate flesh. We might share this sort of somatic sensitivity with another (kind of) organism in the minimal sense of becoming conscious that our susceptibility to suffer harm is like that of the other organism. My claim on this construal is that such minimal mutuality of common carnal nature suffices phenomenologically to establish compassionate concern for the other—in the mode of his being the proper object or patient of ethical consideration. In another, stronger sense of sharing, the second party might also become aware of our vulnerability being similar to her own; this richer form of reciprocity is requisite, it appears to me, for interspecific compassion to take on the facet of respect—whereby both parties appropriately regard each other as moral subjects, agents, or actors.[42] Some of our relationships with other primates (particularly apes), with cetaceans (such as dolphins), and most especially with domesticated companion or work animals (such as dogs and horses) feature reciprocally cognizant compassion grown into moral respect.

Now, typically, those ethicists who champion compassion tend to assume or stress a mentalistic account of empathetic concern (via projective imagination, for example). Diverging from this sort of moral psychology, I have contended that (especially cross-species) moral life is primarily rooted—as a matter of phenomenal fact—in corporal symphysis rather than entirely mental maneuvers in the direction of sympathy. As I have used it, *symphysis* is meant to designate the felt sense of sharing with somebody else a live nexus as experienced in a somatic setting of direct or systemic (inter)relationship.[43] (Some human examples may help illustrate the sort of phenomena to which I refer: they range from negative feelings of sympathy pain to positive ones of sexual intimacy; pregnancy and nursing are particularly thick instances, while sensing tools or enclosures as extensions of one's body are relatively thinner ones.) I believe that speaking of symphysis is the best way to describe the protoethical feeling that assures us of another animal being's moral considerability. Inferential reasoning by analogy may rationally *justify* that assurance, and appealing to psychological theory of imagination may scientifically *explain* it via empathic projection, but only somatologies as it were of genus-being and of alien specificity can properly articulate the actual experience of conviviality at stake.[44] From this last perspective, then, an ethos sculpted somatically by symphysical encounters would inform a character or culture morally sensitive to the being-in-the-world or existential element of flesh, including that carnal vulnerability shared with any live body as such. (See Figure 6.2.)[45] Such sensitivity is made appreciative and appreciable by our own bodily participation *as animals ourselves* in the corporal lifeworld.[46]

FIGURE 6.2: This orangutan's posture and visage can awaken in the witness a symphysical process of corporal compassion, which may then lead to ethical inquiry: Whose neighbor is he or she? To which community does he or she belong? Photo by Britta Jaschinski.

Continental approaches to animal ethics do not necessarily emphasize embodiment of interspecific encounter. Some recent efforts have concentrated instead on personal, soulful, quasi-spiritual, or otherwise primarily mental phenomena of interaction. A common theme in these accounts is the attempt to articulate an existential phenomenology or hermeneutic of ethical address as such, showing that the latter's scope can encompass other-than-human beings. Such an inquiry promises to describe or interpret the moral psychology of intersubjective or social categories like *neighbor* or *community.*

Take the former category first. It bespeaks the second-person voice of ethical address, as in the locution, "it is to you, my neighbor, that I am obliged." Stereotypically, by anthropocentric default, it is assumed by many that a neighbor in this sense must be human. However, it has been suggested lately by some that there are or can be nonhuman neighbors in the sense of that term developed by the twentieth-century French philosopher and rabbi, Emmanuel Levinas, for whom the face as such is a primordial marker of moral importunity. Indeed, for Levinas, the ego does not preexist encounter with the other's face—"I" exist only as recognition of the other's claim on me arrives, as a potential agent of responsibility to someone else emerges, through facial mediation. The question then arises, in the context of animal ethics, could the face of my neighbor be that of a nonhuman creature? It certainly seems that Levinas countenances such a possibility when he refers to a particularly convivial dog outside his WWII prison camp as "the last Kantian in Nazi Germany" (because the canine bore witness to the dignity of the prisoners).[47] In fact, he explicitly encourages biocentric readings of morality when he admits, "It is clear that ... the ethical extends to all living beings."[48]

Something similar is afoot—on the level of first-person plural address—when James Hart interprets Husserl's transcendental phenomenology so that "human beings can say 'we' of the 'biotic community' and, even more so, of nonhuman animal persons in ways analogous to how human beings say 'we' in reference to one another."[49] This sort of talk may sound nonsensical, especially to ears trained by and into humanist discourse, but it is justified when "there is awareness that the good of each is bound up with the good of all and that humans willy-nilly act in such a way that the well-being of the other members of the biotic community is affected."[50] Moreover, the communal significance of saying "we" thickens when the others so collected under that mode of address are themselves plausibly considered subjects of intentional consciousness. "For example, with my cats and dogs," Hart illustrates, "I have confidence that I know their intentions from observing their behavior in the third-person as well as from our mutual efforts at communication."[51]

The approaches just sketched are not without their shortcomings, and these flaws are acknowledged by the propounding thinkers themselves. The chief problem, as we saw with analytic treatments before, is that approaches rooted in mentalistic personhood have a built-in bias placing mature humans at the head of a moral hierarchy (unless we rate cetacean subjectivity above our own or include suprahuman, say extraterrestrial or divine, entities into our picture of ethics). So, for Levinas, though "one cannot entirely refuse the face of an animal ... yet the priority here is not found in the animal, but in the human face"—indeed, "the human face is completely different, and only afterwards do we discover the face of an animal."[52] And Hart's attempt at an Husserlian animal phenomenology continually appeals to analogies from so-called marginal cases of humanity, for example, infants and the mentally handicapped, positioning mature humans in the parental role of species stewards or guardian demigods over the interests of other animals.[53] Such a scenario, it has been charged, constitutes benign patronage at best or backhanded degradation at worst. "The parent is aware of and responsible for the interests of the [infantile or retarded] child in a way the child is not aware of them," Hart remarks.[54] If one substitutes *human* for *parent* and *animal* for *child* here, the flavor of the analogical situation can be sampled and may become distasteful.

It is clear, then, that animal ethics today is no more settled than any other branch of applied moral philosophy. Utilitarian and deontological, hermeneutic and phenomenological, analytic and existential—all these approaches have their strengths and weaknesses, proponents and detractors. And those accounts surveyed above do not represent the full range of theory comprehensively: there are also approaches informed by virtue ethics, pragmatism, and so forth.[55] By and large theoretical dissensus is the field's rule, with perhaps general agreement only on the minimal proposition that nonhuman animals (should) count or matter in moral terms, which implies a loose practical convergence on the notion that the animal kingdom (should) be tread upon (maybe much) more lightly than is the wont of modern civilization.[56]

METAPHYSICS

From the perspective of generic philosophy, animal ethics has been undergoing an evolution not dissimilar from that evident in the more established specialties of biomedical and ecological ethics. Medical ethics has developed from a field devoted fairly strictly to issues about the (im)propriety of high-technology usage into a broader philosophic enterprise that also asks more general questions beyond the scope of morality per se, questions about the nature of health, human identity, and life as such—what might be called the metaphysics of medicine and biology. Likewise, environmental ethics has grown from an earlier predominance of reflection on a relatively narrow set of issues dealing with the rectitude (or turpitude) of our treatment of nature into a wider endeavor that also considers philosophy of nature broadly construed and generates worldviews under the rubric of *ecosophy*. Animal ethics, too, is now transforming into a comparatively more comprehensive field, one that goes beyond an earlier preoccupation with the right and wrong of this or that action, practice, or policy affecting nonhumans and now takes up also matters concerning the ontology of animality. This is not surprising, as much moral philosophy has shown an historical tendency to beg more metaphysical questions germane to the original region of ethical interest—it helps, in other words, to know *what* we are *ultimately* confronted with if we want to reflect on *how* we *ought* to deal with it. So animal philosophy of the period under discussion comes to encompass more than animal ethics; it also includes what can be referred to as philosophical zoology (resemblant to, though more capacious and not necessarily modeled after, the field of thought known as philosophical anthropology). This development is not an entirely new phenomenon—as we shall see, an undercurrent of theoretical biology was already taking form early in the twentieth century outside the mainstreams of Western philosophy and science; nevertheless, current projects of zoontological inquiry are distinctive in attracting greater notice and bearing greater influence than ever before.[57]

Taking these animal ontologies in roughly chronological order, first comes the work of the little-known and underappreciated philosophical biologist Jakob von Uexküll. (See Figure 6.3.)[58] Courageously speculative, he bucked his time's tide of mechanico-behavioral reductionism, creating in its stead an imaginative yet empirical portrayal of animal being:

> We who still hold that our sense organs serve our perceptions, and our motor organs our actions, see in animals as well not only the mechanical structure, but also the operator, who is built into their organs, as we are into our bodies. *We no longer regard animals as mere machines, but as subjects whose essential activity consists of perceiving and acting. We thus unlock the gates that lead to other realms,* for all that a subject perceives becomes his perceptual world and all that he does, his effector world. Perceptual and effector worlds together form a closed unit, the *Umwelt. These different worlds,* which *are as manifold as the animals themselves,* present to all nature lovers new lands of such wealth and beauty that a walk through them is well worth while.[59]

Uexküll thus issued a veritable declaration of phenomenological independence from the entire Cartesian tradition of automated animality (and its by-product, ghost-in-the-machine humanity). Yet the epistemological price he paid for this maneuver was steep, for his approach essentially amounts to a biologically reoriented Kantianism in which each (kind of) creature's phenomenal world filters, frames, and alters raw reality.[60] Indeed, the "world bubbles" posited

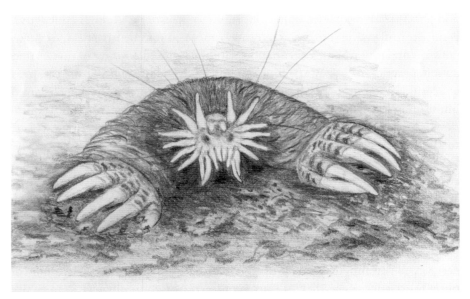

FIGURE 6.3: Jakob von Uexküll conceived of other organisms' worlds (fields of experi-ence) as based on their distinctive sensory modalities. Alien animals can be understood, he thought, by scientifically grounded and phenomenologically guided efforts of imagination. A contemporary example is Craig Holdrege's account of the star-nosed mole. "So [due to high density of nerve tissue] we have to imagine an extremely fine sense of touch con-centrated in the star. In imagining the tactile world of the mole, we must strip away what is so familiar to us—our colorful and airy world of sight and hearing. We can picture ourselves in a dark, quiet, enclosed space where the surface of our body touches myriad objects. Since our sense of touch is most refined in fingertips and tongue, we can imagine concentrating our perceptions of weight, texture, and temperature through these organs. In this way we can begin to acquaint ourselves with a tactile world [such as the mole's], which normally stands in the shadows of our more dominant and focal visual and audi-tory experiences." Sketch of a star-nosed mole (*Condylura cristata*) by Craig Holdrege (after a photo by Kenneth Catania); published in: "How Does a Mole View the World?" *In Context* #9 (Spring 2003).

by Uexküll constitute a veritable monadology (à la Leibniz), only zoologically variegated across species and coordinated within them:

> There are, then, purely subjective realities in the *Umwelten;* and even the things that exist objectively in the environment never appear there as their objective selves. ... Thus we ultimately reach the conclusion that each subject [qua species member] lives in a world composed of subjective realities alone, and that even the *Umwelten* themselves represent only subjective realities.[61]

Martin Heidegger was one of the thinkers influenced by Uexküll, at least regarding the former's treatment of animality. Originally, in his masterpiece *Being and Time* (1927), he articulated an account of being that had little space for animals as such.

Briefly put, three basic terms are operative in the earlier Heidegger's fundamental ontology: being-there (*Dasein*), readiness-to-hand (*Zuhandensein*), and presence-at-hand (*Vorhandensein*). How shall we regard the animal, given this division? Strictly speaking, unless an organism is ontologically oriented (that is, unless the organism cares about the question of the meaning of being), it cannot be properly *Dasein*. In other words, it does not exist in the special way that Heidegger appears to think that humanity (alone) does in terms of having care as a fundamental aspect of its being or in terms of having a fundamental experience as being-in-the-world that is the condition for the possibility of all other experience. But if that is so, then all (or at least most) nonhuman animals must be deemed either ready-to-hand or present-at-hand—which relegates them to the status of tools for use or objects of observation (either of which denies them experience a priori).

Hence, drawing on yet contesting Uexküll, Heidegger eventually reassessed the nature of animality in his Freiburg lectures of 1929–1930.[62] Here he endeavors to carve out an intermediate status for animals as "world-poor" beings occupying some ontological interzone between the "world-forming" human and the "worldless" stone.[63] The idea is that animals have, as it were, a dim awareness of their environment that does not yet attain the full disclosure of true *Dasein*'s "open clearing" of consciousness. Still, this somewhat more subtle description retains a degree of anthropocentrism. For example, Heidegger establishes a sharp distinction between human comportment and animal behavior: "The behaviour of the animal is not a *doing and acting*, as in human comportment, but a *driven performing* [Treiben]."[64] In fact, this portrayal of animal activity as essentially instinctual is at the root of animality's deprivation in the sense of world poverty. The animal is deprived of genuine world, according to Heidegger, because it is captivated by its instinctive drives: "Captivation is the condition of possibility for the fact that, in accordance with its essence, the animal *behaves within an environment* [Umwelt] *but never within a world* [Welt]."[65]

Of course, one may yet wonder whether even this kind of account is adequate. The operative term in the citation just given is *Benommenheit*, but translating it as *captivation* carries too much connotation of lively entrancement (as in fascination); it is more literally equivalent to *benumbedness*. In this sense, closer to the original, it would appear that Heidegger is underestimating the flexibility of at least some or many animals' actions (e.g., relationships that comprise animal communities such as porpoise pods, elephant herds, and primate bands are difficult to read solely in terms of instinctual or rote behavior). In developing an allergic reaction to vitalism, then, he has overcompensated hermeneutically too much back in the direction of mechanism. Take, for instance, the following passage:

> This manner of being [*Benommenheit*] announces itself in the case of the animal in the familiar terms of seeing, hearing, seizing, hunting, fleeing,

devouring, digesting, and all the other organic processes. It is not as if the beating of the animal's heart were a process different from the animal's seizing and seeing, the one analogous to the case of human beings, the other to a chemical process. Rather the entirety of its being, the being as a whole in its unity, must be comprehended as [non-worldly] behaviour.[66]

Here it seems that Heidegger misses (and so can lead his readers to ignore) a crucial difference between automatic functions and relatively flexible actions.

Looking now at the middle of the twentieth century, we do not see much new work in the way of animal ontology, at least not in Western philosophy. In the past two or three decades, however, a great deal of philosophic and interdisciplinary thought has gone into the area. Straddling or pushing the bounds of philosophy, a pair of European thinkers—Gilles Deleuze and Félix Guattari—has instigated an upsurge of reflection on phenomena of animality. They have done this by challenging the very premise of (most prior) animal ontology, namely that different kinds of organisms have substantial essences or existential structures that are the proper objects of such study, so that there is or are animal being(s). What Deleuze and Guattari propose is to concentrate rather on historically contingent and profluently variable processes of animal *becoming,* or in their parlance "becoming-animal." The notion of becoming-animal is part of a larger program of theirs to destabilize certain concepts of reality that they believe yoke us into psychopolitically oppressive modes of thinking and living. Chief among these concepts are the twin ideas that true reality (the "really real" of classical philosophy) is or should be characterized by identity and stasis and that what phenomena of diversity or change must be admitted are best understood according to an "arborescent" paradigm of dualistic branching.[67] As one commentator puts it, "Flux, change, and relation are, for them, more real than permanence, stability, and identity."[68] The model for such an outlook is not the sturdy, dualizing tree trunk but instead the amorphous, self-differential rhizome—which image also connotes meanings of radicalism fully endorsed by Deleuze and Guattari. (See Figure 6.4.)

How does all this rather abstract, somewhat flighty musing redound upon animality? It is sometimes said of the late Alfred North Whitehead's process philosophy of organismic cosmology that it resembles dialectical metaphysics minus any Hegelian absolutism; one could say of rhizomatic proliferation that it resembles Whiteheadian ontology minus the organicism. Applied to animality, this means that "Deleuze and Guattari seek to establish the derivative ontological status ... of the classificatory systems and theoretical concepts of the biological sciences insofar as these rest upon notions such as organism, species identification, evolutionary filiation, teleology, etc."[69] Standard conceptions of organicity portray life-forms as coherent systems of functional parts that subserve the dictates of overarching totalities (organisms). Deleuzo–Guattarian becomings-animal, by contrast, are never finished or determinate entities—rather,

FIGURE 6.4: Becoming-animal, according to Deleuze and Guattari, is constituted as activity in flux—roaring or growling makes the lion or tiger, not vice versa. Photo by Britta Jaschinski.

they are more like radically incomplete pulsions of force moving in between plateaus of impermanent conditions.[70] Lest one think this leaves us adrift in a purely anarchic chaos, it should be noted that Deleuze and Guattari do sketch a threefold typology according to which we can distinguish Oedipal, state, and demonic animalities. These states respectively track domesticated, taxonomized or mythologized, and pack or ferine forms of becoming-animal. The last pattern is valorized because it is felt to release and multiply energies of creativity kept at bay by Oedipal discipline or statist regimes.[71]

About the same time Deleuze and Guattari were generating the views just surveyed (the mid- to late-1980s), a very different zoontology was formulated by the American theorist Edward Reed. Basing his outlook on the ecological psychology of James Gibson, this thinker purports to delineate an actual essence of animality. Animacy, as he terms the phenomenon that includes (yet may be broader than) animal nature, can be characterized—perhaps indeed defined—by appeal to a cluster of manifest aspects: most important is autonomous action or the capacity to move oneself (a factor that has a venerable history going back at least to Aristotle); most distinctive is the display of nonrepetitive motion (newly stressed to distinguish animals from machines); and finally, growth in size or alteration in form is mentioned as well.[72] This account is the foundation for a subtle position that resists being pigeonholed as, say, simply scientific or purely phenomenological. Unlike most scholars and the public at large, who take animals and their terrestrial contexts to be pretty much whatever the physical and life sciences say they are, Reed (following Gibson) bucks the worldview of contemporary materialist science and "treats the environment not as a world made up of physical elements and properties, but as the habitation of animate creatures—as an [already] meaningful environment" that provides organisms a constellation of *affordances* "for locomotion, shelter, manipulation, and other important activities."[73] Despite the rejection of positivism operative here, Reed insists that these affordances are real features of an objective world; in fact, they structure preexisting ecological niches whose common denominators constitute a shared, multispecies environment—in contrast to the species-subjective *Umwelten* described by Uexküll.[74]

Perhaps the most striking facet of Reed's stance is its reliance on (and defense of) direct perception, prior to and thus unmediated by cultural constructions.[75] Most social scientists and many in the humanities refuse such an appeal and hence tend to view animal ontology as relative to culture.[76] One of the more notable examples of constructionism in this area is that of Carol Adams, a feminist critic at the crossroads of literary theory and religious studies. Her analysis aims to demonstrate how, in the dominant society of patriarchal carnivory, "real animals" become "absent referents" through a variety of discursive practices and other cultural conventions.[77]

According to Adams, this process is inaugurated by the institutions of husbandry, slaughter, butchery, marketing, and cuisine—together, they transmogrify the integrity of live organisms into inanimate parcels of commodity fit for consumption. The ways in which participants talk about each stage conceal for them, yet reveal under critical scrutiny, the absence of reference constituted throughout the transformation "at steak." Objectification and fragmentation of animals thus occurs on parallel tracks, materially and linguistically. Just as they are literally used up in being rendered edible, they are digested into and disappear from discourse as well. In the remote routines of factory farming largely removed now from public awareness, animals are treated and referred to as "food-producing units" that are then subjected to the original (dis)assembly line.[78] Via this machinic ritual and diction, a secular form of transubstantiation takes place—*flesh* becomes *meat*. Then, Adams continues, there is further processing in grocery stores and eating establishments: "After being butchered, fragmented body parts must be renamed to obscure the fact that these were once animals. After death cows become roast beef, steak, hamburger; pigs become pork, bacon, sausage." Finally, at home in kitchens and dining rooms, "We opt for less disquieting reference points not only by changing names from animals to meat, but also by cooking, seasoning, and covering the animals with sauces, disguising their original nature." (See Figure 6.5.)[79]

Now the status of this account as zoontology is not exactly clear, for it seems more to tell us about certain treatments of animals than about animals

FIGURE 6.5: Sue Coe's "Modern Man Followed by the Ghosts of His Meat ..." (1990) may be seen as an illustration of how the "absent referent" of Carol Adams' zoontology returns to haunt the consciousness and conscience of patriarchal carnivory. Credit: Sue Coe.

themselves. That is to say, Adams does not ever appear to doubt the independent existence of actual animals (in fact, the real animal is the hidden anchor for her diagnosis of absent referent); rather, she is more interested to examine the ways some humans (those of us enculturated into patriarchal carnivory) work over and talk about other animals (particularly those seen as edible). Thus, to be fair, it may be said that, because Adams emphasizes the ontology of animals as livestock and food, her constructionism does not necessarily apply to animals as such and is not meant to give an account of their outright ontic nature (essence of being).

By century's end one of philosophy's preeminent thinkers, Jacques Derrida, was also deconstructing our discourse of animal being (or what he calls the *animot*). In lectures of the late 1990s, he questioned the term animality used in reference to "an immense group, a single and fundamentally homogeneous set that one has [presumed] the right, the theoretical or philosophical right, to distinguish and mark as opposite" to humanity.[80] Nor, for Derrida, is this usage limited to abstruse corners of science or philosophy—indeed, challenge converts to condemnation when he excoriates the concept at stake thus: "this agreement concerning philosophical sense and common sense that allows one to speak blithely of the Animal in the general singular is perhaps one of the greatest and most symptomatic idiocies of those who call themselves human."[81] Can we develop alternative discourses about or conceptions of animals? According to Derrida, "we have to envisage the existence of 'living creatures' whose plurality cannot be assembled within the single figure of an animality that is simply opposed to humanity"; stated again in another lecture, "that means refraining from reducing [life-forms'] differentiated and multiple difference in a similarly massive and homogenizing manner."[82]

CONCLUSION

So whither animal philosophy in the future? In terms of ethics, theoretical tensions between abstract principlism (of the liberation and rights paradigms) and embodied caring models (generated by feminists and Continental thinkers) could be brought together into new syntheses. More likely, though, would be the spread of pluralistic tendencies according to which different ethical vocabularies will be brought to bear upon different kinds of issues as the field grows and diversifies. Similarly, the divide in practical animal advocacy between alignment with environmentalism or with civil and social rights causes (which tends to track concern with wild and domestic animals, respectively) might be mediated by following the exemplary confluence of inspiration and activism that the ecological justice movement has represented since the 1990s. Or, as I think will be the case for a while at least, political action on behalf of animals may resort to a multiplicity of tactics across a varied range of circumstances at the grassroots level—without there necessarily being any overarching strategy or grand banner.

With respect to ontology, some think the future belongs to Deleuzo–Guattarian rhizomatics of becoming-animal.[83] I am not sure of that myself, since at the meso-level we inhabit during everyday life with other animals there is a good deal more stability (of being or essence) than some queer states of affairs at microscopic and cosmic levels might suggest to the partisans of unlimited flux. One trend that I do think will continue to intensify is a growing interest in the relation of technology to animality. Consider Richard Bulliet's recent warning:

> Urbanism, with its unavoidable isolation from animals, will remain a fact of postdomestic life. And most postdomestic people will continue to draw upon print and electronic media for animal experiences that extend beyond owning a pet or engaging in birdwatching. What those media will deliver will be but a pale substitute for the direct contact with animals that the human species has known for tens of thousands of years.[84]

Although I am unconvinced that species apartheid is inevitable even for urbanites, I agree that techno-organic hybrid experiences will take on a greater profile.[85] In this regard the theorist to watch would be Donna Haraway, the influential essayist of "Manifesto for Cyborgs" who has most recently re-contextualized her biotechnological reflections within a relational process ontology of transpecifically significant otherness, in a pamphlet entitled *The Companion Species Manifesto*.[86] In this latter work Haraway also points in the direction of what is most sorely needed now and into the foreseeable future of animal philosophy, namely a coalescence or cross-fertilization of zoontology and animal ethics.

CHAPTER SEVEN

Animals in Visual Art from 1900 to the Present[1]

JONATHAN BURT

Sometimes there's nothing to say about a line, but there's always something to say about an elephant.

—Martin Herbert[2]

And so if in a painting I cut off the head of a cow, if I put the head upside down, if I have sometimes worked my paintings the wrong way up, it is not to make literature. It is to give my picture a psychic shock that is always motivated by plastic reasons ... If finally, one nevertheless discovers a symbol in my picture, it was strictly unintentional on my part.

—Marc Chagall[3]

Here are two conditions of response to the animal figure in art: something to say and nothing to say. Taking both these statements at face value, and disregarding any disingenuity in the second, we can approach the question here—how do we address the animal figure; how do we speak from it and of it?—not just as a problem for animal art but as a central problem in the articulation, and therefore expressive understanding, of the relations between humans and animals. Questions of speaking to, with, and for animals are an unavoidable preoccupation for all who are engaged with them at any level: from the level of representational rhetoric, Chagall's "literature" (metonyms, metaphors, symbols), to communication via action. This also parallels an issue in art itself. How do we speak of art and how do we meet the challenge of the inadequacy of language before or in the artwork?[4] Here the animal and the artwork offer the same challenge. There is also the question of the artist who at times seeks identification with the animal for all manner of reasons: ritual, aesthetic, psychological, sexual, escapist, or political. Apollinaire's words to the effect that "artists are above all men who want to become inhuman" seem pertinent here, but the fact that the word is *inhuman* and not *animal* already opens up a discourse around art, language, and identity that pushes toward the edges of (human) expression.[5] Evident in all these questions is a particular and profound intertwining of the animal with the aesthetic, which in turn involves a problematic relation to language not just in the critical literature but also in the statements of artists themselves. This awkward and unstable triad of animal, art, and language is a significant feature of twentieth-century animal art. Ultimately, the animal aesthetic extends beyond the artwork: it is integral to the structuring of human–animal relations as themselves an expressive and figured exchange across species.

THE ANIMAL OF ART AND AS ART

There is as yet no overall map for the animal in the art of the twentieth century, nor is there much of a conceptual framework by which such a map may be provided with a scale or even read at all. This is not for lack of examples—topographical features, landmarks, large settlements; there are plenty of these. Despite Steve Baker's pessimistic view of a lack in animal art between the nineteenth century and what he terms postmodern art there exists a huge, yet fragmented, grouping of artworks of every possible kind.[6] They can also be found as scattered examples across numerous discussions in books, articles, and exhibition catalogs, from every part of the world. The lack of a history of animal art is something of a puzzle. As Joshua Taylor notes, "to reconstruct the history of religion, philosophy, or art without reference to the animal image would be impossible."[7] However, to date, animals do not appear to have been considered important enough subjects to constitute key elements in an art history. Alternatively, it may be that the extraordinary diversity of animal art in the twentieth century presents such a multitudinous chaos that there is no sense to be made of it beyond the presentation of a disjointed inventory of genres and examples.

   The animal figure must be the center of gravity for any analysis. In other words, we must weave the history of twentieth-century animal art around the animal figure and pay attention to the detail of how it operates within artworks, rather than restricting ourselves to narrating a sequence of genres in different media, or presenting a catalog of artists. To begin with, the animal figure is split by a tension between signification and designification, between looking *at* the animal and looking *through* the animal to something else, whether these are abstract concepts, metaphorical meanings, or expressions of inner psychic states. To some extent this replays the oscillation between reverence and exploitation that characterizes a split attitude to animals, one manifestation of a Western logic of sacrifice (though how such a logic is mediated by the impact of technology and modernity generally is yet to be properly thought through).[8] The double meaning of *taste* as aesthetic and, in this instance, as carnivorous resonates with this split. More importantly, however, the animal figure embodies a tension without resolution. In the interplay between the opacity and the transparency of the meanings of animals, the inalienable or resistant aspect of the animal (animal as animal and not human, bucket, tree, nation, divinity, or anything else) renders any looking through only ever partial, so that we are left shuttling back and forth across the various divides. Furthermore, for some genres of art, especially more experimental ones, the alien nature or otherness of the animal parallels the open-ended otherness of the artwork: one form of alienating difficulty mutually reinforces the other. This parallel eventually invites a conceptual collapse because it is in fact a short step from animals in art to animals as art. Mark Wallinger's *A Real Work of Art* (1993), for example, depicts a racehorse of the same name, which the artist had bought and raced (though it only managed one race). (Also see Figure 7.1.) As a thoroughbred the horse was already an artwork, though Wallinger well understands that this notion of the aesthetic is made up of many strands: "the thoroughbred is itself an

FIGURE 7.1: Mark Wallinger, *Half-Brother (Exit to Nowhere—Machiavellian)* (1994–1995). Copyright of the artist, Courtesy Anthony Reynolds Gallery. Tate Collection.

ambivalence … [it is] instinct become eugenic theory become economics … they [i.e., the horses] question their own construction as painting/bloodstock/trophy and reflect the desires of the viewer to fill out their missing dimensions."[9] The animal has the potential to do the work of art before it is ever an object for art; is always already an inhabitant within a domain of aesthetics.[10] This is a significant reason why it cannot but be a central, even formative, element in key areas of twentieth-century art.

It might be argued that the animal is still something outside art that is brought in to be used by virtue of the fact that art is a thoroughly human activity that freely turns to selected objects and media as it chooses. According to this view, art epitomizes what it is to be human. Paul Crowther has argued that art objects are expressions of "freedom," available for recognition by others and creating a reciprocal relation between "our sense of freedom and our *species identity* [*emphasis mine*]."[11] Crowther believes that while animals share in rudimentary form many of the capacities by which we humans are self-conscious (attention, comprehension, projection), mere animal consciousness lacks a sense of species identity, personal freedom, and reversibility.[12] However, twentieth-century animal art complicates this picture. At every stage of the century the animal is exhibited as a complex and divided object and challenges the very coherence of species identity.

Taking a very preliminary and canonical overview of Western art, the animal shapes the work of key painters such as Marc, Chagall, Miró, Picasso, Toledo, and Rego; saturates the imagery and the discourses of surrealism; provides totemic identities for major artists (Ernst, Leonora Carrington, Kahlo, and Beuys); is manipulated in all kinds of ways in the modernist sculptures of Epstein, Gaudier-Brzeska, Skeaping, Brancusi, Duchamp-Villon, and later Marini and Moore; contributes to the expressive politics of the COBRA collective after World War II and the South African artists Legae and Alexander; gives up its slaughtered body for painters like Soutine, Bacon, and Durrant, and its flesh to the art of Brugeura, Hirst, Schneemann, Nitsch, and Kulik; finds itself alive in memorable installations by environmental artists and Arte Povera; dead and alive in performances by Beuys; is a pop cultural toy in the work of Messager, Koons, Fritsch and Kelley; and is recreated by the transgenic art of Eduardo Kac and the virtual evolutionary systems of computer art. That is just the beginning of a much longer list of names and artworks. To this plethora of artworks we can also add the significance of the animal for decorative arts (especially art deco), taxidermy, mobiliary art (medals, jewelry), watercolorists and nature painters, the animalier tradition in sculpture, not to mention artists working outside the West, as well as powerful depictions of the animal in influential exhibitions of ethnic art throughout the century. One begins to wonder why the animal seems in the general art historical literature to be such a blindspot—much exemplified, rarely theorized.

This challenges Paul Crowther's speciesist notion of art because the animal inhabits art as a figure that is already fundamentally *of* art. The integrity of human freedom and identity is thus compromised.[13] The freedom to look at the art of others or exchange artifacts does not mean that the viewer is psychically free. Animals are of central importance in art's expression of doubt about identity (whether of the individual, the species, or the body), challenging the coherence or connectedness of commonplace ideas, and standards of human behavior. If anything, it is the animal figure and not the human that brings these instabilities into play. Taking a cue from Deleuze and Guattari, Baker describes the consequences of the collapsing of categories around the figure of the animal: "art's work—moving the human away from anthropocentric meaning and subjective identity—is presented as much the same thing as the animal's work. It is the work of figuring out how to operate other-than-in-identity ... Art, it seems, consists in letting fearsome things fly."[14] In certain contexts, unlike nature writ large with its connotations of sublimity, the animal operates a dialectic between the sublime and an antisublime, forever setting grandeur or vitality against death, fragmentation or, to use Baker's word, botchedness. The love of hunting that haunts the spectacular nature paintings of the Swedish painter Bruno Liljefors or the interplay between beauty and death in Jordan Baseman's skinned animals, *The Cat and the Dog* (1995), for instance, are cases in point. To illustrate the aforementioned ideas in more detail, I initially structure this narrative around five well-known artworks.[15] Then I balance this in the later sections with an account of other genres and media (nature painting, mobiliary art, the animalier tradition, and so forth). The five works are Franz Marc's *Fate of the Animals* (1913), Max Ernst's *The Master's Bedroom* (1920), Picasso's *Guernica* (1937), Joseph Beuys's *I Like America and America Likes Me* (1974), and finally Damien Hirst's *A Thousand Years* (1990).

FIVE ANIMAL ARTWORKS

Franz Marc wrote in 1908 that he wished to animalize art: "I can see no more successful means toward an 'animalisation' of art ... than the painting of animals. That is why I have taken it up."[16] The idea of the animalization of art collapses the borders between art and animal. In his essay "How Does a Horse See the World?" Marc shifts the notion of painting animals as objects seen out in a landscape to a type of seeing *with* the animal. We need to "divine its [i.e., the animal's] way of sight."[17] The animal art object becomes the animal art subject: "the predicate is the most important part of a thoughtful sentence ... the object is a negligible echo."[18] Marc contrasts the attempt to paint liveness and the inner world of the animal with a previous tendency to avoid living subject matter and devote itself to the "predicate of the still-life"—*nature morte*. At one level Marc's engagement with animals is an intensive one. He spent a great deal of time studying animals such as deer and hares, as well as agricultural and zoo animals. In 1908 for his large Lengriess Horse Painting he followed horses for months in the village of Lengriess near the Austrian border.[19] As a number of critics note, the absence of riders in his horse paintings indicates a suspicion of humans, whose corruption contrasts with the purity of animals.[20] At one level Marc's empathetic intentions place the animal at the center of his work and are used to articulate a superior notion of being. The innate goodness of animals, which awakened the sense of good in Marc, was directly contrasted with the impiety of humans. However, there is a considered move away from animals per se in his later work to something much more abstract in which notions of empathy and the animal subject are sacrificed to a greater sense of apocalypse and rebirth.[21] Mark Rosenthal has noted that there is a shift in Marc's treatment of animals around 1912–1913 in which they become less heroic and more symbolic. Certainly there is a greater violence to some of the pictures, as in the huntsman on horseback in *Saint Julian L'Hospitalier* (1913) and *The Wolves (Balkan War)* (1913). During World War I, not long before Marc was killed, he tempered his view of animals further by noting that his move to abstraction was motivated by the fact that there was indeed something "ugly and unfeeling" in animals.[22] Thus, he comes increasingly to render animal bodies partially visible by camouflaging, burying, or fragmenting them within the rhythms and abstract patterns of his painting. Yet, this abstraction is only partial. At another level the animal in its reconfiguration becomes essential to the dynamics of movement and change. This theme appears in other works of the period such as Giacomo Balla's *Dynamism of Dog on a Leash* (1912). Furthermore, even though the animals are, in both color and shape, highly artificial, they make the eye work to delineate them in their half-concealed state, to seek them out in the explosions of color and form that they inhabit. To bury animals in painting is also to force the issue of their finding.

The original title for *Fate of the Animals* was "The Trees Show Their Rings, The Animals Show Their Veins" (see Figure 7.2). On the reverse of the canvas Marc wrote, "And all being is flaming suffering."[23] Marc came to see the painting as a premonition of war and as a manifestation of the necessity to paint constructive pictures for a better future. In this painting the notion of apocalypse is split to mean both conflagration and renewal as embodied by the animal. In some senses Marc should have kept to his original title because in the picture the animal ruptures fate and opens the world to a new beginning. Frederick Levine interprets the tree as the giant ash tree Yggdrasil ("horse of god"), central to ancient Nordic mythology, and the deer on the left as a new quality of earthly life. One might compare this painting to Paul Nash's *The Mule Track* (1918), which depicts at its center a track zigzagging across the war-torn landscape like a spike of lightning, with the mules as tiny figures. This is at least one painterly answer to Marc's apocalyptic optimism.

FIGURE 7.2: Franz Marc, *Fate of the Animals* (1913).

Marc's split idea of using the animal to represent a higher order (looking through, beyond, or beside the animal), and yet at the same time implying that nothing else will do but an animal figure, does not so much ground or embody his metaphysics but rather fragments it. Hence, its entanglement in the fissures of Marc's painting. Yet, as a principle of otherness or difference the animal figure becomes generative rather than something that resolves, substitutes for, or sublates. In surrealism this is foregrounded even more strongly.

In Rosalind Krauss's outline of the history of modernism, she identifies a counterhistory that she places under the heading of the "optical unconscious" described as "a refusal of the optical logic of mainstream modernism." This occurs initially toward the end of the 1910s.[24] She identifies as the significant ideas in this refusal "concepts like *informe,* mimicry [which would have derived from Roger Caillois's notions of insect mimicry published in *Minotaure* in the mid-1930s], the uncanny ... figures like the acéphale, the minotaure, the praying mantis."[25] In fact, the surrealist bestiary contains a further profusion of creatures such as birds, fish, elephants, giraffes, butterflies and so on, plus a range of scarcely identifiable quasi-organic forms. A fish with *Surréalisme* written the length of its body illustrates the inside front cover of the first number of *La Révolution Surréaliste* published in 1924.[26] In the promotion of psychic automatism as a manner of producing words and images outside the control of reason, along with the celebration of the dream and the bringing together of random associations, surrealism in many ways cuts the animal figure loose and realigns it as a figure of mystery and surprise. "In my wake I raise up monsters that are lying in wait; they are not yet too ill-disposed towards me, and I am not lost, since I fear them. Here are the elephants with the heads of women and the flying lions ... am I not the soluble fish, I was born under the sign of Pisces, and man is soluble in his thought! The flora and fauna of Surrealism is unacknowledgeable [*inavouable*]."[27] A year earlier André Breton had written in 1923, "to escape, as much as possible, from the human species to which we all belong—that is all that seems worthwhile to me."[28]

In my next main example, *The Master's Bedroom* (1920) (see Figure 7.3), Max Ernst took a page from a teaching aid that depicted an array of objects including humans, animals, birds, flora, and household objects, and erased them by painting over them the picture of a room, leaving just a handful of objects exposed. There are many different ways of reading the animal figures, both in terms of their individual reference, and in terms of interconnected references via the bed, the windowlike wardrobe, and the tree, to Freud's *Wolf Man*. As Werner Spies notes in his study of Ernst's bird totem Loplop, the artist has left those figures that carry erotic connotations in Freud: fish and snake as the male sexual organ, the table as woman, and the bed as marriage.[29] However, the disruption of perspective, the manner in which the animals carry different, even opposing types of significance (the erotic, the pedagogical), indicate a tension across a set of meanings that are best understood as split horizontally rather than as vertically analyzable (that is by peeling the layers off down to a fixed core). For Spies, the figures in Ernst are not intended, as he claims they are in Freud, to settle an interpretation but rather to resist and disperse it.

The figure of Loplop, Ernst's bird totem and alter ego, appeared for the first time at the end of the 1920s, though birds figure throughout his work from 1920. Loplop, "a private phantom very much attached and devoted to me,"

FIGURE 7.3: Max Ernst, *The Master's Bedroom* (1920). ADAGP Paris and DACS, London, 2007.

expressed a split within Ernst's own creative identity.[30] Birds are central to Ernst's description of key moments in his life. His birth is described as an emergence from an egg, and the bird haunts key stages of his emergent familial and sexual identity. The coincidence of the birth of his sister Loni with the death of his pet cockatoo puts the bird at the center of his creativity. "In his imagination he connected both events and charged the baby with the extinction of the bird's life. A series of mystical crises, fits of hysteria, exaltations and depressions followed. A dangerous confusion between birds and humans became encrusted in his mind and asserted itself in his drawings and paintings."[31] The important thing about Loplop and other animal figures is that paradoxically while they act as signposts for the sexual unconscious they do not, ultimately, map anything specific. As Hal Foster notes, "the surrealist image is patterned upon the symptom as an enigmatic signifier of a psychosexual trauma."[32] Thus the animal is central to the economy of desire and draws the eye to that area of the artwork that trades on an opacity that motivates repeated attention. In other words, the animal is that which forces one to look and look again without a sense of resolution, part siren, part black hole.

The animal does not matter as such in surrealist art and yet among the free-floating figures, opaque and disjunctive associations, and novel hybrid formations, artists turn to the animal again and again, though for many different reasons ranging from the absurd to the mystifying. In 1920 Francis Picabia exhibited a *Tableau Vivant* in which he glued a stuffed toy monkey onto a canvas surrounded by inscriptions: "Portrait of Cézanne," "Portrait of Rembrandt," "Portrait of Renoir." The premises of the Bureau of Surrealist Research, which opened in 1924, contained a headless plaster statue of a boar.

In the early 1920s Ernst included a number of animals in his paintings such as the ambiguous horned head that is both birdlike and cowlike in *Oedipus Rex* (1921), and the abstract elephant figure of *L'Éléphant Célèbes* (1921). Paintings by Joan Miró such as *Le Carneval de l'Arlequin* (1924–1925) and *Terra llaurada* (1923) contain all manner of toylike and distorted living forms bearing varying degrees of resemblance to animals. In fact, *Carneval* was made up of a number of drawings in which Miró recorded the hallucinations caused by the hunger from which he frequently suffered.[33]

Another strand of surrealist art used animal bodies, anticipating a practice that would become more commonplace toward the end of the century. Some of these works, especially from 1930 onward, expressed an increasing interest in the idea of the surrealist object. Examples include Élisa Breton's *Il coud son ciel* (n.d.), which has a dead bird perched on an old blue sewing machine and, if one can temporarily include him with the surrealists, Picasso's *Composition au papillon* (1932), in which a butterfly is fixed along with other objects to a pale canvas. More memorable still are Meret Oppenheim's *Déjeuner en fourrure* (1935), in which a teacup, saucer, and spoon are covered with the fur of a Chinese gazelle, and Salvador Dalí's hybrid of lobster and telephone, *Téléphone blanc aphrodisique* (1936). In surrealist film the abjection implicit in using corpses appears for the first time. In Dalí and Buñuel's *Un Chien Andalou* (1928), dead donkeys placed in a piano are stuffed with rotting fish, while their eyes ooze wax. More significantly the film contains a sequence that could be taken as a key symbol of twentieth-century animal art: the eyeball cut by the razor, with a calf's eyeball standing in for the human one. Buñuel and Dalí continued to use animal symbolism in *L'Age d'Or* (1930) where the killing of a rat by a scorpion was considered by one critic as analogous to the eye-cutting sequence in *Chien Andalou*.[34]

The reason for choosing *Guernica* as a key example of twentieth-century animal art is that the painting is an example of how animals render meaning opaque, while at the same time holding resonances of intense personal and cultural significance. *Guernica* is in any case a highly ambiguous work, open to many political, religious, and humanist interpretations. However, its animals are among the primary figures with which Picasso initially expressed his artistic response to the bombing of Guernica. They thus provided a means of confronting the issue of war and massacre while at the same time, in ways not dissimilar to the animals in Marc's apocalyptic work, setting it at one remove.[35]

The background to *Guernica* has been well documented. Initially requested to do a painting for the Spanish Pavilion for the Paris World's Fair in 1937, Picasso did little until the impact of the bombing, which occurred on April 26, made itself felt around the world. On May 1 more than one million people marched for the May Day parade, the biggest such demonstration in the history of Paris. The march was dominated by outrage over the bombing and appeals

FIGURE 7.4: Pablo Picasso, preliminary sketch for *Guernica* (May 1937). Courtesy of Succession Picasso/DACS (2007).

for aid for the victims.[36] That same afternoon Picasso made an initial, very abstract, sketch, which contained three figures: a horse, a bull, and a woman (see Figure 7.4). Herschel Chipp suggests that this indicates an intimacy to Picasso's response to Guernica, not just in the figure of the woman, who was already present well prior to May 1 in some preliminary sketches for a mural depicting the theme of artist and model, but in the animals too. Since Picasso was young he had been a fan of the bullfight, having been taken by his father, who was himself an amateur painter of pigeons and doves.[37] In fact, Picasso's first painting at the age of eight was of a picador on his horse.[38] "'The bulls are in his very soul,' Picasso's friend Hélène Parmelin has written. 'The bullfighters are his cousins, the bullring is his home.' He equated the family with the corrida."[39]

At one level the association between bull and horse is fundamental in evoking the notion of Spanish culture in one of its most distinctive expressions: the bullfight (*corrida*). In terms of the ritual of the *corrida*, the horse and bull come into conflict after an initial interaction between the matador and the bull. The mounted *picadores* encourage the bull onto the horse so that they can weaken it by driving a pike into the hump on its back. Prior to 1928, when the horses were not protected by padding, they would frequently be killed.[40] Picasso himself was critical of the protective padding of the horse, feeling that it inhibited the bull's combative spirit.[41] There are a number of dimensions to Picasso's treatments of this pairing, most of which indicate a fascination with this fundamental violence of one sort or another. At times he depicts the horse and bull as sexualized and engaged in an erotic conflict with the bull as the masculine penetrating figure and the horse as (even if portrayed with male genitalia) receptive or violated. There is a triangular version of this with horse, bull, and naked women intertwined, the bull and woman kissing, in his *Femme Torero* etchings of 1934 (see Figure 7.5). Picasso also used the animals to satirical political effect in his sequence of etchings *The Dream and Lie of Franco* (1937). Elsewhere in Picasso's work his focus on, and apparent identification with, the bull also finds expression in his many depictions of the minotaur, another fundamentally split figure that in many instances is also sexualized. That Picasso seems to have approached *Guernica* initially through the figure of the animal is further confirmed by the fact that on the second day of working, May 2, he drew a series of sketches of the screaming horse. This marked one of the main continuities that ran right through the various versions of *Guernica* up to the completion of the painting.

The question that *Guernica* presents for an animal-centered-perspective art is how the animal figure opens out the possibilities of expression through by

FIGURE 7.5: Pablo Picasso, *Femme Torero I* (1934). Courtesy of Succession Picasso/ DACS (2007).

generating an excess of the meanings, while also signaling at the same time a fundamental opacity and resistance to such meanings. The opacity of the animal drives this excess and this overdetermination with multiple meanings is not a saturation of the animal with meaning but the acknowledgment of an inexplicable deficit. Thus, one can list all manner of possible meanings for the bull, such as Spain itself, cruelty (i.e., fascism), hope for the survival of Spain, or even the wavering policy of France in the face of the Civil War. In response to this, it can then be equally argued that no reading of the bull is possible because it can always be made to "to stand for something else."[42] The split animal (in the case of *Guernica* a split represented by the two animals) then becomes the very principle of splitting. Parallels to this can be found in the double-edged symbolism of animals in Paula Rego's work, such as in *Wife Cuts Off Red Monkey's Tail* (1981) and her women and dog paintings. These animals also reflect an enigmatic and overdetermined interplay between the politics of her Portuguese background, domestic gender politics, and a general ambience of violence (see Figure 7.6).[43]

Picasso's few and much-quoted statements on the animals in *Guernica* at least have the advantage of summarizing this complexity quite neatly. In one response, related at second hand, Picasso denied that the animals in *Guernica* were symbolic as he painted them: "this bull is a bull and this horse is a horse." It is up to the public to see as it wishes. For Picasso himself, "there are animals: these are massacred animals. That is all for me."[44] This abrogation of meaning is slightly disingenuous; the "all" that could be a nothing or an everything. In another context Picasso does offer meanings for the bull, suggesting that it represents darkness and brutality, thus admitting a symbolic, or rather allegorical, function for *Guernica*.[45] Whatever Picasso intended by these remarks, whether he was driven to make them unwillingly or not, they do at least point to a principle of denial that appears like a blind spot in the context of animal representation.

Although animals introduce an opacity into the politics of an art work they do so in part because they embody the dynamics of transformation. For example, the artists who banded briefly under the name of COBRA between 1948 and 1951 (named after the cities where the artists came from, Copenhagen, Brussels, and Amsterdam) were largely Marxist and rejected contemporary Western culture in favor of the art forms of prehistory, the Middle Ages, Eastern calligraphy, and primitivism. They painted in bold, brightly colored styles and frequently depicted animals, as well as imaginary hybrid figures that looked like a combination of human, animal, and plant. This represented for them a desire for a different world and a different artistic practice.[46] When animal imagery is used as a deliberate and avowedly political metaphor, its dynamics of transformation are never lost sight of. This is even true outside the west. The South African artist Ezrom Legae, for instance, used chickens and

FIGURE 7.6: Paula Rego, *Red Monkey Drawing* (1981). Copyright of artist.

other bird forms in drawings in the late 1970s and early 1980s as a comment on the massacre of child demonstrators in Soweto and the death of the activist Steve Biko. The chicken, a common sacrificial animal whose blood symbolizes renewal, does a lot of conceptual work here, cutting across a variety of religious and secular ideas.[47] "Chickens and goats are the ultimate sacrificial animals of Africa, and yet they represent resistance and eternal life, because no matter how many are tortured, killed, or sacrificed, there will always be others."[48] Legae's use of the "resurrectionist theme drawn from Christian and traditionalist iconographic sources" also draws on the common ordinariness of the chicken to represent the impossibility of destroying the spirit of popular protest. In Legae's *Jail Series II* (1981) the human body in a prison cell is in part a bird figure and, as a becoming other, points toward the possibility of freedom. However, the political possibilities implicit in hybrid animal figures follow a logic of change that is only ever uncertain and ambivalent. Another South African artist, Jane Alexander, made a gruesome set of figures entitled *The Butcher Boys* (1985–1986) as a comment on apartheid, violence, and the unspoken. The piece comprises three life-size male human bodies with horned heads, indeterminate foreshortened faces without mouths (ram, dog, pig, bull?), and a cut down the center of their torsos from the neck to the navel.[49] Animals lend themselves readily to figuring the suspension of codes at the scene of political violence.

Joseph Beuys's address to the animal, whether dead or alive, appears in some ways to construct a very different animal art object than has been described so far. In the example discussed herein, the elements of totemism and mysticism are enacted performatively in strikingly original ways and yet point back to many of the themes we have seen worked through in earlier animal art. However, Beuys's split is complicated not just by the ways in which ritual structures his difference from the animal, but also in the ways in which it separates him from the human as well. Beuys had used animals in a number of pieces prior to *I Like America and America Likes Me* (1974). In 1966 he had founded the Political Party for Animals and he had co-opted a number of animals as totem figures from his earliest work onward. He identified with the hare in works like *Being an Animal* (*Essere un Animal*, 1948) and later gave a lecture on painting to a dead hare. The stag was also important to him.[50] "'I am the hare,' as Joseph Beuys is given to say when put on the spot."[51] He also used a live horse in his performance piece *Iphigenia/Titus Andronicus* (1969). For Beuys, animals are a source of energy since he believes that behind the power of each species stands the spirit of group consciousness or soul; the human is a fundamentally spiritual being, though one who has lost contact with the invisible energies with which he or she needs to become reacquainted.[52]

In the interaction with the coyote in *I Like America and America Likes Me* (1974) a number of factors were in play ranging from shamanistic contact with animal spirits to consideration of the plight of Native Americans and the war in Vietnam.[53] This performance took place over three days at the opening of René Block's gallery in New York. During the time Beuys spent in the gallery with the coyote, Little John, he repeatedly enacted a ritual that involved pulling a length of gray felt over himself and poking a walking stick out of the top of his shrouded body as if he was a statue; then he would take up a sequence of positions before falling on the floor. Finally, he would suddenly spring up, casting off the felt, and strike three notes on a triangle tied to his waist; a twenty-second sound of turbine engines from a tape recorder concluded the cycle. The coyote, on the other hand, responded in a variety of ways ranging from apathy to a nervous excitement. Sometimes he would attempt to lie down with the prone Beuys and crawl under the felt. For Beuys the actions were partly a reparation for the denigration of the coyote by White Americans, and partly a reenactment of their veneration by Native Americans, for whom the coyote was an important figure of power and transformation, a trickster figure with a strong sexual prowess and even an ability to turn itself inside out through its anus.[54] Beuys said, "I believe I made contact with the psychological trauma of the United States' energy constellation: the whole American trauma with the Indian, the Red Man ... you could say that reckoning has been made with the coyote and only then can this trauma be lifted."[55] However, significantly, Beuys felt that animals were restricted to their group souls and were not free like humans to develop new specializations and patterns of thought. Yet, despite this, he also hoped that his interaction with the coyote would remind the creature "that he too has possibilities in the direction of freedom, and that we need him as an important cooperator in the production of freedom."[56]

Beuys's address is *through,* as much as it is *to,* the animal. His concern is with both the worlds of human and animal spirit: the traumatic racial division of the United States and the freedom of the animal. Nature and politics are inseparable. However, the structures of power between artist and animal within the performance itself limit the inclusiveness of this politics. Beuys remarked that his actions were dependent on those of the coyote yet grand claims of reparation are threatened by a prosaic ordinariness underlying the event. On abandoning the animal at the end of the performance Beuys transforms Little John into the very opposite of a free spirit: "suddenly finding himself without the man's presence, Little John behaved for the first time like a caged and captive animal, padding up and down with the true wolf's swinging gait, back and forth, sniffing, searching, whining and scenting the air with fear."[57]

Beuys's work reminds us that in a great many canonical artworks using animals the landscape itself is rarely of significance. When Beuys invokes nature it is as an abstraction. However, there are exceptions to this such as the work of wildlife artists and, more recently, Olly & Suzi and, to some extent, Mark Dion. Of course, there is also much recent landscape art that denudes the environment of animals, such as the work of Richard Long and Andy Goldsworthy. Part of the reason for this is the influence of minimalism and process art on landscape and environmental art, especially from the 1960s onward.[58] Some of these works, such as Robert Smithson's *Spiral Jetty* (1970), imposed abstract forms on the landscape or reworked existing landforms. Those which did involve animals either recreated living ecosystems in gallery spaces or used animals in performance statements. For *Ten Turtles Set Free* (1970), Hans Haacke purchased turtles from a pet shop and released them in a forest in southern France as part of an art exhibition. Bonnie Sherk, in *Public Lunch* (1971), ate and slept in a cage with animals at the San Francisco Zoo. Haacke's *Rhinewater Purification Plant* (1972) contained fish in a tank of recycled, purified water drawn from the polluted river. Comparable works operating as miniature ecosystems in art galleries included Newton Harrison and Helen Meyer's *Notation on the Eco-system of the Western Salt Works with the Inclusion of Brine Shrimp* (1971) and Alan Sonfist's *Colony of Army Ants* (1972), which included video monitors featuring people rushing from a subway and ants forging a stream in their native habitat.[59] The emphasis in these works is on movement and ecology so that the animal is not figured as something separable from its context but operates more collectively as a plural subject, without necessarily being singled out to carry the symbolic burdens of totemism, difference, or an ambivalent anthropomorphism.

Mark Dion takes these ideas much further in a reconfiguration of the artist himself or herself in relation to animals and environment. Beuys is an important figure for Dion, along with artists such as Marcel Bloodthaers and Robert Smithson. Dion's interest in the categorization of knowledge and animals in museum contexts involves varying degrees of playfulness and seriousness, as in *The Desks of Mickey Cuvier* (1990), in which, among other things, four animated Mickey Mouse figures lecture humorously on, and use quotations from, the work of the nineteenth-century naturalist and zoologist Georges Cuvier. But in Dion's work involving living creatures the line between scientist, artist, and museum curator becomes blurred. Just as artists used small, culturally insignificant creatures in the 1970s installations described previously, Dion is interested in the apparently insignificant underside of fauna. In *A Yard of Jungle* (1992) he exhibits a cubic yard of soil from a rainforest park at the mouth of the Amazon. His concern for the protection of species is expressed in the proposition that we need to preserve and manage the ecosystem at all levels of life and not simply focus on the attractive species.[60] Dion is in fact critical of a conservation movement that bases too much of its argument on "charismatic megafauna" and fails to provide a more systematic critique of the environmental impact of capitalism.[61] Dion's notion that the artist involves a fusion of roles reflects the fact that he wishes to see a dissolution of the boundary, as far as possible, between the gallery and the world outside.[62]

The British artists Olly & Suzi also claim to be strongly influenced by Joseph Beuys in their own interactive work with animals. Their mantra, "no experience, no art," describes the importance they attribute to direct interaction with animals.[63] As with Beuys, though with a much less developed and idiosyncratic philosophy than their mentor, Olly & Suzi see their role as confronting a world that is losing itself. They echo Beuys's work with Little

John by "interacting with a white wolf in Canada's Ellesmere Island … We wanted to take the animal–human and artistic interaction that stage further, to feel its spirit. We wanted to co-exist."[64] Their need to work rapidly to capture moments with intensity and the heightened emotions (especially fear) that they describe as important carry the traces of a rhetoric of human–animal interaction familiar from nineteenth-century hunting and expedition literature. In addition to their proanimal and environmental values there is an exotic grandeur, even a sense of privilege, to their project that is highlighted by the documentation of their work in spectacular travelogue-style photography. The art work made by an anaconda slithering across a sheet of paper requires photography as an integral part of the witness of an animal that may one day completely disappear as a species.[65] Olly & Suzi represent a very important moment in the history of animal art because of the scale and ambition of their project. As with Beuys, their attempt to register a closeness to animals is highly mediated and is achieved by bringing together a variety of methods of representation (text, painting, photography, animal marks) so that the animal or event is a composite. Furthermore, as in some sense a doubled artist, there is no singularity to their interaction with the animal; the animal is always multiply watched. "[W]e attempt to integrate clarity and ambiguity into the same painting."[66] Like Beuys's ritual, the grandeur of the claims about interaction, something one might describe as a quest for the animal sublime, in fact incorporates its own antisublime, as the animal ignores, eats, defecates on, or walks across the artwork that it is cocreating.[67]

Seen through these examples, one could characterize the trajectory of animal art through the twentieth century as one of an increasing engagement with the animal as an embodied being that in turn raises questions through art about the nature of species, questions of extinction, and human identity. However, one has to be careful of setting this as a benchmark from which earlier animal art might be judged as somehow lacking in its degree of address to the animal. There is no categorical imperative in animal art. The metaphysics behind Marc's or Brancusi's animal figures may appear a world away from more viscerally expressed versions found in later twentieth-century examples, but in all cases the animal has a rupturing effect. Thus, we might compare Max Ernst's use of animals to explore his sexual and artistic identity with, say, Carolee Schneemann's *Eye Body* (1963) in which at one point the artist lies naked with snakes crawling on her body, a line painted down the center of her face. The presence of a real animal does not necessarily entail more or less of an address to the animal than an abstract one. In fact, although the seriousness with which Marc sought to express a coherent philosophy for an ideal future through his animal art contrasts with Damien Hirst's more anarchic pronouncements concerning his use of animals, both artists, in their different ways, raise important questions about thinking through death and its consequences via the interplay of human and animal identity. "Death leads us back into normal being," as Marc noted.[68] Hirst puts it more viscerally: "the less I feel like an artist, the better I feel, like a shark. Its great to go get a shark. Anything like that. Go to an abattoir."[69]

Damien Hirst's youthful taste for pathology text books, trips to the morgue, and his admiration for the work of Francis Bacon are well documented. *A Thousand Years* (1990), one of his favorite works, was first exhibited at a show entitled "The Gambler." Containing in one half of a glass case a real cow's head with a fly electrocution device, and in the other a source of flies in a box, it encapsulates the animal sublime–antisublime dialectic as well as any work in the late twentieth century. Confronting the viewer with an artwork that becomes increasingly abject while referencing the central significance of the cycle of death in life, the initial version of the work became literally unapproachable. When the smell of the rotting cow's head drove viewers away, Hirst had to remove it—it was seething with maggots underneath the skin—and burn it. For that first exhibition he returned the charred skull to its glass box, though for later exhibitions he would use a prosthetic head covered in dog food, ketchup, blood, and mayonnaise.[70] Hirst also produced an infamous series of related works, many of which also articulate an idea of splitting in their presentation: the pig that is cut down the center in *This Little Piggy Went to Market, This Little Piggy Stayed at Home* (1996); the pregnant cow divided into twelve sections, *Some Comfort Gained from the Inherent Lies in Everything* (1996); and the tryptichlike subdivision by its vertical bars of the tank containing the tiger shark in formaldehyde, *The Physical Impossibility of Death in the Mind of Someone Living* (1991). The confrontation with death here is staged in both senses of the word: first, provocatively in the theatricality of Hirst's art, and second, in the sense that the stage of death is approached by degrees through that of life or vice versa. As Hirst once said, "you kill things to look at them. You expect it to look back at you. I hope at first glance it will look alive."[71] In *In and Out of Love* (1991) the full life cycle of the butterfly from chrysalis to death was exhibited in one room of a gallery, while their bodies were painted onto brightly colored canvases in another.[72] We might compare this work with Marc Dion's *Library for the Birds of Antwerp* (1993), which included eighteen African finches, bought in Antwerp's Vogelmarkt, flying in the gallery space round a tree.[73] More recently, the Russian artist Oleg Kulik presented an exhibition in which visitors were placed in a cage to observe live leopards, borrowed from a circus, roaming the gallery.[74]

For some critics contemporary art has replaced a sacred relationship with the animals with one based on horror and disgust: the mutilated and skinned lambs of Wols, Eli Lotar's photographs of slaughterhouses, and the 1970's performance art of Stuart Brisley are examples of this. For instance, the latter's *And for Today ... Nothing* involved the artist lying for hours in a bath of water, blood, and entrails.[75] There are numerous gruesome stories of dealing with animal corpses in the service of contemporary art. Paco Mesa's *Hacia La Isla* (2000) installed the corpse of a donkey on a sofa that was then half covered in a blanket of peat. Mesa had brought the donkey straight from the slaughterhouse to the taxidermist wrapped in plastic in a box dripping with blood, only to find on arrival that the creature was still alive.[76] There are precedents for this. Chaim Soutine's repeated painting of beef carcasses in the 1920s, inspired by Rembrandt's *The Slaughtered Ox* (1655) that hung in the Louvre, expressed a complicated relationship the artist had with food. One carcass rotted in his studio; he would pay someone to brush away the flies as he painted. In a complex recreation of the hunger he suffered in his youth and his physiological inability to eat meat, he would fast before painting. As a friend noted, "he buys a piece of raw meat and fasts in front of it, as it rots, for two days before he starts to paint it. Look at that red: hasn't he put all his cannibal appetite into it?"[77]

The increasingly intensive use of carcasses and raw meat from the mid-1960s onward to produce a more transgressive form of animal art, one that is even at times opulent and indulgent (Carolee Schneemann's *Meat Joy*, 1964, Tania Bruguera's *El cuerpo de silencio*, 1998), needs to be set in the context of a changing visual economy of both animal life and death. Earlier in the century in the West the slaughter of animals for meat would have been a more visible and far less centralized practice. Privations including meat would have been very familiar to generations who lived through two world wars, as well as other conflicts prior to the 1950s, and the day-to-day routine familiarity with animals, whether in transport, the military, or agriculture, would have made animals an improbable resource for the notion of striking excess that is requisite for transgressive thinking.[78] At one level this issue of visibility is straightforward. For contemporary artists interested in the ethics of animal slaughter, such as Sue Coe, making visible is key to attacking the meat industry precisely because it is now invisible: "if we could see it, we would certainly call a halt to it."[79] However, the relation between art, modernity, and slaughter is made up of too many strands for us to suggest that there is a dominant form of response to changing configurations of animal death through the century. In the work of Coe the address to slaughter is quite direct, whereas for other artists it is less so. Herman Nitsch's performances and film recordings of dramatic rituals, which include things like the disemboweling of dead animals and the adorning of humans on crucifixes with entrails and blood, highlight the sexualization of the human association with animal death.[80] Sexuality and ritual also haunt Tania Bruguera's *El peso de la culpa* (1997) where she covers the front of her naked body with the torso of a sheep split open to reveal the spine and the ribs (see Figure 7.7).[81] Francis Bacon links his own attitudes about meat to issues of religion, mortality, and aesthetics. Slaughterhouse pictures put him in mind of the crucifixion, but for him meat is also a matter of painterly pleasure: "one has got to

FIGURE 7.7: Tania Bruguera, *El peso de la culpa* (1997).
Copyright the artist.

remember as a painter that there is this great beauty of the colour of meat."[82]
Bacon's ambivalence about meat turns on the association of beauty and horror,
the beautiful carcass in the butcher's shop that puts one in mind of "the whole
horror of life."[83] Deleuze sees Bacon's paintings as a *"zone of indiscernibility or
undecidability* between man and animal" with meat as their common ground.
Here the art is grounded in both the glory and suffering of the flesh: "meat is
not dead flesh; it retains all the sufferings and assumes all the colours of living
flesh. It manifests such convulsive pain and vulnerability, but also such delight-
ful invention, colour, and acrobatics."[84] For Bacon the animal points toward a
virtually faceless crisis of suffering in the living being.

SCULPTURE, MOBILIARY ART, AND WILDLIFE PAINTING

Although it might seem that the previous discussion positions a narrative
of canonical Western animal art as central to any account of the twentieth

century, the materials discussed next are of equal importance in understanding the complexity of animal imagery. Some of these art forms also raise a different set of questions about the relationship of artists to animals or the impact of animal imagery across national boundaries. The animalier sculpture tradition, and what might best be termed nature painting, provide something of a counterweight to the transformations of animals effected by the high art genres discussed previously. Indeed, the more realist genres of animal art have often been considered by many art critics as peripheral genres and have certainly been of little theoretical interest. While the realistic depiction of animals may appear to tell us less about the problematics of human–animal identity, much of this art arises both from a working interaction or a deep familiarity with animals, which in many instances give rise to a different set of issues around, for example, domestication, sport, killing, hunting, and conservation.

The animalier tradition began as very much a nineteenth-century phenomenon, taking its name from a disparaging epithet applied to Antoine-Louis Barye's work in the early 1830s. The animaliers' emphasis was on the realistic modeling of animals as well as on the attempt to convey the emotions and mental states of their subjects without anthropomorphism. As with nature painting, there was a strong commercial dimension to this work seen especially in the sculpture of horses with hunting and racing themes, mostly exported from France to Britain and the United States.[85] Many of the more high-profile animaliers who continued this tradition in the twentieth century had artistic family backgrounds as well as contact with animals from an early age. Even though working on animal sculpture in this particular style did not always bring wealth, its history is surrounded by the feel of prestige and privilege, as can be attested by those working in the early part of the century. William Hunt Dietrich, for instance, had a father who raised horses for the Prussian cavalry, while his grandfather, William Morris Hunt, introduced the Barbican school of landscape painting to the United States. Dietrich enjoyed fox and stag hunting and this was reflected in his subject matter: bullfights, hounds, and stags, and, for classical themes, the huntress Diana. Herbert Heseltine, whose father was a landscape watercolorist, was likewise an accomplished rider who, from an early age, was interested in polo and hunting. Later, he went to Spain to study bullfighting. Anne Vaughan Hyatt Huntington's mother was an amateur painter, and her father was a distinguished professor of paleontology and zoology. She was also an expert rider and trainer of horses.[86] Later in the century the American sculptor Harry Jackson spent his late teens working in Wyoming wrangling horses and working the cattle ranches, while the British animalier Jonathan Kenworthy visited Africa annually from 1963 onward to work on animal anatomy and travel on safari.

The realist tradition would suggest that there is less ambiguity in the depiction of the animal so that it is less of a divided object. If this were the case the tension between looking at and looking through, as discussed earlier, would be less marked. However, in this art, notions of ideal form or capturing the essence of movement are crucial in the animalier tradition and lock directly into the idea of the animal as already a work of art in life. A good example of this is Herbert Heseltine's quest to sculpt the ideal horse, which he began in 1912. He extended the idea in 1921 when he conceived the project of using as models a series of outstanding animals that had won prizes at British agricultural shows.[87] However, for *The Thoroughbred Horse* (1925), he could find no animal "either in my memory or actually alive, that came up to the ideal" so he ended up creating a composite.[88] The idea of animal pedigree was matched by the opulence of his materials. Influenced by Egyptian sculpture and Assyrian bas-reliefs, he decorated his bronze of *Sudbourne Premier* (1922), a stallion, with gold, lapis lazuli, ivory, and onyx. His *Black Knight of Aucterarder* (1933), an Aberdeen Angus bull, was powerfully rendered in a deep black Belgian marble, while in his sheep he exploited the rough surfaces of Burgundy limestone.

The sculpture of animals in twentieth-century art moves from the animalier tradition at one end of the figural spectrum to the more abstract forms of say, Brancusi, or Bernard Meadows's *The Black Crab* (1953) at the other, with for example, at various points in between, the animals of François Pompon, Jacob Epstein's *Doves* (1914–1915), or, more recently, the works of Maureen Quinn. Jan and Joël Martel, for instance, produced many animal sculptures that expressed a stylized response to the animalier tradition by streamlining the animal, smoothing its shape and surfaces.[89] Many sculptors were fascinated by animals even if they worked them in a very abstract manner. When Gaudier-Brzeska was in London he spent a great deal of time at the zoo as well as studying the deer in Richmond Park. For Henry Moore sheep were a particular source of interest, and he would watch them from his studio window. He also had a special affection for crows.[90] Moore's engagement with animals was extensive, producing fifty-eight sculptures and scores of drawings between 1921 and 1982. Baker has argued that Moore's work treats the animal as an object very much separate from the artist: "it is a thing to be addressed and presented ... by means of the authority and expertise of the artist, who surrenders nothing to it."[91] However, Moore's work also pulls in another direction because he was bound by a deep fascination with animals from childhood onward, to the extent that he claimed to derive the same feelings from animals as from people.[92] At the same time animals were more liberatory for him, as far as the production of sculptural form was concerned, than other types of figure, and led him on a quest for different sorts of ideal abstractions. For example, he remarked of the elephant skull he was given by Julian Huxley in 1968 that he hoped to "isolate an idea found in the skull and to dissociate it from the skull's entity ... to reveal forms contained in [the skull] that most people would simply not be able to see."[93] The relation to the animal here is characterized by a revelation that also signals a move away from it. Given that Heseltine and Moore were working with very different ideas of the sculptural animal in mind it may seem surprising to compare them. Yet they both demonstrate in sculptural terms the split between looking at and looking through, whether in the working out of the perfect example (the template of the pedigree) or in the imagining of new shapes within existent animal forms.

Artists such as Heseltine and Moore figure the animal as universal, timeless, figure. There is, however, a sculptor who embeds his animals in historical change. The progression of Marino Marini's horse sculptures after the end of World War II, which expressed his pessimistic response to the difficulties of postwar political developments, derives from a recognition of the fact that the horse is itself a profoundly historical object. Marini, who was a friend of Moore, linked the changes in development of the horse in art via a trajectory that ran from Géricault through to Degas and Dufy, and then Redon, Picasso, and de Chirico, to the changing contexts of technology, sport, and military life. According to him the unreal world of Redon's work marks the horse's change of status as it is replaced by machines and becomes part of a world of myths and dreams. Inspired in part by the sight of homeless crowds fleeing the advancing Allies, some on horseback, and a brief image of a rearing horse seen from a train window, his configurations of horse and rider can be seen as straightforward metaphors for what he saw as the crisis of the age. The clash between horse and modern urban industrialism had been a theme for other artists too, such as in Umberto Boccioni's painting *The City Rises* (1910). Over time, Marini's horses become increasingly restive, more abstract and fragmented, and the riders slowly lose their dominion over their animals, become more and more dehumanized at the same time. He describes the rider as it falls from the rearing horse in *Miracle* (1951–1952) as being like Icarus: "my aim is to render palpable the last stages in the dissolution of a myth, the myth of the heroic and victorious individual, the humanists' *uomo di virtù*."[94] Marini saw his work as going from "representing a horse as part of the fauna of the objective world to suggesting it as a visionary monster arisen from a subjective bestiary."[95] The increasing abstraction and fragmentation of his horses express not just the state of human affairs but the fate of the horse, too. In Marini's work human and animal fates are interconnected.

Turning to naturalistic wildlife painting, the changing status of the Swede Bruno Liljefors, one of the most impressive wildlife painters of the late nineteenth and early twentieth centuries, tells us much about the marginal status of wildlife art when compared to the major genres of canonical art (see Figure 7.8). Seen very much as a painter for hunters and zoologists, he reemerged as a popular figure in part due to the environmentalism of the 1980s and a consequent nostalgic desire for Swedish landscape painting.[96] Liljefors also represented a strand of wildlife art dependent on a deep knowledge of animals gleaned through

FIGURE 7.8: Bruno Liljefors, *Hawk and Black Game* (1884). Courtesy of DACS (2007).

observation and hunting. The key feature of Liljefors' work arose when he came to appreciate the significance of color and camouflage in situating creatures in the landscape. As a result he actively engaged the viewer to search more carefully for the outlines of animals in his canvases.[97] Liljefors himself had no patience with sentimental animal lovers who were opposed to hunting, though he abhorred wasteful slaughter. At the same time his engagement with the animal world was profound. In 1908 he bought an estate, Bullerö, which was an archipelago in the Nandö region, where he spent the summers observing, painting and hunting. Liljefors is not the only painter either to hunt, or to use hunted animals as models. Carl Rungius, Wilhelm Kuhnert, George Lodge, who was also a keen falconer, Louis Aggasiz Fuertes, and Peter Scott are notable examples of a very long list.[98] And although artists such as Archibald Thorburn and Keith Shackleton gave up shooting, Thorburn, for instance, still painted gamebirds for a lucrative market among sportsmen.[99]

Wildlife art operates under different conditions from other forms of animal art, being necessarily more commercially dependent on public taste and demand, which in turn influences the choices of subject matter.[100] However, the challenges to drawing and painting wildlife in the field have been tackled in different ways by different artists. Carl Rungius would draw from shot animals strung up on a framework of poles and arranged into lifelike postures; Peter Scott would often rely on his memory rather than on field sketches or paintings. Taxidermy, photographs, and zoo animals all provide source models for wildlife art, though artists have markedly different attitudes in how they should be used. Charles Tunnicliffe would use dead specimens for the detail of plumage or pelage, but was well aware of how color could change after death. The Canadian artist Robert Bateman uses frozen and stuffed bodies of birds but not mammals because he feels taxidermy distorts their shape. The challenge of capturing movement can require holding on to the most fleeting perceptions, while also bearing in mind the influences of time of day and changing qualities of light on the coloring of animals. As Eric Ennion put it, you need the ability to draw quickly and develop a retentive memory. "After I have been watching, say, a flock of birds I would probably come home with anything between 50 and 100 sketches, most of them no more than a slant of a wing or tilt of a beak. As soon as your memory runs out (or the bird has flown) never go on with the sketch."[101] Although many artists depend on photography, that has not prevented a longstanding debate among wildlife artists on the degrees to which photorealism is a requirement of this genre and the role of expressive license in rendering animals. Certainly George Lodge felt that a preoccupation with the standards of scientific book illustration actually drew him into mistakes and that an overdependency on photography does not necessarily match the advantages of a trained eye.[102]

Wildlife art in the twentieth century has been an important indicator of the changing engagement of people with their wild landscape, in relation to both national and exotic fauna. The dissemination of modes of bird identification, which had been heavily dependent on the work of artists from the second half of the nineteenth century onward was continued and popularized in the twentieth. Thorburn's *British Birds,* published between 1915 and 1916, and then his *British Mammals,* serialized in 1920, were important in the popularization of animal observation as a pastime. Key field guides were published in the 1920s and 1930s such as Edmund Sandars's *A Bird Book for the Pocket* (1927), W. B. Alexander's *Birds of the Ocean* (1928), and Roger Tory Peterson's *A Field Guide to Birds* (1934). Furthermore, from 1899 onward, Thorburn painted for Christmas cards to be published as fundraisers by the British conservation organization, the Royal Society for Protection of Birds. The popularization of animal imagery on cards and stamps, which also enabled members of the public to see species for the first time, benefited many wildlife artists, especially Peter Scott. Scott founded his own conservation organization in 1946. The institutionalization of wildlife art has been very much a feature of the later twentieth century, reflecting the impact of environmental awareness. Societies of wildlife artists were founded in Britain in 1964, in America in 1968, and later in Australia, and the journal *Wildlife Art News* was started in 1981. Specialist wildlife art museums were founded in England in 1979, and in America in 1976. In 1987 the National Museum of Wildlife Art was opened in Jackson Hole, Wyoming. In 1990, the Artists for Nature Foundation, which

organizes both trips to threatened areas and exhibitions to create public interest, was founded.[103] However, as with all genres of animal art, wildlife painting
is no exception to the variability of address to the animal. Thus, the impact of
environmentalism provides important and relevant contexts for wildlife art, but
that does not necessarily delimit the public taste for dramatic depictions of animal combat and a continued appreciation of sporting and hunting art. In other
words, wildlife art as a genre does not resolve the tension between the celebration of animal life and its haunting by death any more than any other genre.

Looking at animals in the decorative arts is like examining the marginalia
of medieval manuscripts. Once you start to look animals are ubiquitous, or-
namenting everything from special editions of books, homes, buildings, public
spaces, and clothing. At the high end of the market in, say, art deco and crafts
of the early decades of the century, favored animals included snakes, peacocks,
fish, butterflies, horses, parrots, doves, and polar bears, and they were rendered in everything from glass to precious metals and stones, fabrics, ceramics,
lacquer, bronze, marble, and so on. They readily lent themselves to an opulent
exoticism both as objects and, in some instances, as materials. The fan maker
Georges Bastard, for instance, used ivory, mother-of-pearl, tortoiseshell, and
coral.[104] Animal skins were used in room design. Special editions of decorated
books exploited the opulence of leather, such as François Schmied's edition of
the *Jungle Book,* bound in Morocco leather with a lacquered inset of a reclin-
ing Mowgli in front of a stylized panther.[105]

Animal jewelry in the nineteenth century had been influenced in its themes
by a number of factors such as new archaeological discoveries. The influence
of Japanese art in the 1860s led to the popularity of insects, especially the
dragonfly and the grasshopper. Hunting in India inspired many pieces set with
tiger claws, whereas insects and aquatic creatures in art nouveau encouraged
an interest in transformation.[106] Here the distinction between the animal of
art and the animal as art is marked by a very thin dividing line. Although the
coloration that marks camouflage or sexual display is used for design purposes
(and of course human display), the fluidity represented by the very principle of
camouflage, and the changeable outlines of the animal body in relation to light
or landscape, also become a working principle of the art work. In Louis Tiffany's famous peacock lamp, for example, exhibited at the 1901 Pan-American
exhibition, the overall shape of the lamp is that of an anthropomorphic figure
wearing a dress. The dress is decorated with the eyes of the male peacock
feather and is hung with scarab beetles around the top. Two peacock necks
instead of arms support the head of the lamp. This taste for fluidity also favored the use of creatures like the jellyfish.[107] Some of the most famous pieces
of twentieth-century jewelry are of course purely opulent and still reference
hunting and imperial privilege. The Cartier panther, commissioned in 1949
by the Duke and Duchess of Windsor, depicted a diamond and sapphire cat

on a sapphire ball, which led to a series of what became trademark pieces for Cartier—their "great cat menagerie."[108]

NON-WESTERN ART AND THE FUTURE

Although there are identifiable trends in twentieth-century animal art, their historical trajectory depends in part on how inclusive one wants the category of animal art to be. A standard art history that looks at canonical movements as outlined in the recent *Art Since 1900* compilation, for instance, would inscribe the animal as undergoing particular transformations depending on art practices of the time.[109] So we could track the animal through the abstract object of modernism, the found object of surrealism, the bricolage of postmodernism, and so on. But clearly with the parallel currents of more realist imagery in various media and the manner in which artworks bring together different kinds of styles or materials, for example the combination of abstraction and photography in the images of Olly & Suzi, it also makes sense to look at animal art as something that is made up of many different strands at any point in the century. However, it remains the case that one striking shift, from Rauschenberg's use of an angora goat in *Monogram* (1955–1959) and in performance art especially from the 1970s onward, is the increasing use of actual animal bodies, whether dead or alive.[110] But artists who work with the animal body do not all do so for ethical or proanimal reasons, so that even in contemporary art we cannot assume a direct address to the animal. It is tempting to attribute a greater awareness of animal issues to recent artists, either overtly or less consciously, because of the political visibility of environmentalism and animal rights, particularly in the last quarter of the century.[111] However, this is tacitly to suggest that are implicit ethical imperatives in animal art, or that there should be, and to underestimate the range of the engagement with animals in less critically scrutinized genres like nature painting, realist sculpture, or even very marginal works such as animal war memorials. Tensions around life and death and the contradictory ethics of conservation, welfare, and animal use resonate just as much in these latter areas of work.

The impact of African art on Western art has been well documented, although problems of establishing a history for African art, as well as issues of authenticity and ethnocentrism, are very much part of a lively ongoing debate among African art historians.[112] While African animal imagery may not seem to be an integral part of twentieth-century modernity, and has certainly not registered any notice among those writing on animal art, the fact that it has circulated widely in the West especially from the 1920s onward and the fact that African artists, such as members of the École de Dakar, have used wild and imaginary animal imagery in their work, means that it is long overdue for attention.[113] In 1995, the book written to accompany an exhibition of animal art at the Museum for African Art in New York noted that animals "all remarkable for how they look or act—are ultimately not the subjects here." Animals are "useful metaphors for people's predicaments and, as such, mirror human qualities."[114] "In Africa, as everywhere, people use animals as mirrors of humanity."[115] That this long familiar rhetoric of the metaphor and the mirror appears even here is not surprising, though it needs to be emphasized that the African animal image, in its making and its context, is central not just in reflecting the human world but is actively involved in creating or maintaining a human world that is integrally interlocked with the nonhuman world writ large.

This transformative importance is reflected in the fact that the commonly chosen animals of African imagery are frequently not so much those that more usually attract Western interest, such as zebra, lions, giraffes, and rhinos, but those that are held to have an anomalous status for particular reasons, depending how they are seen by different regional cultures. Buffalo, for instance, are seen as divided animals by the Tabwa of southeastern Zaire. They can be docile or aggressive, visible and invisible, in and out of water, and active at dusk and dawn and are associated with chiefs and cultural heroes.[116] The leopard, likewise, is a key figure in the representation of authority, but both its physical features and its behavior show how richly constituted this association is. The configuration of its spotted coats may represent the alternation of day and night, and the Igbo of Nigeria have leopard images in their houses because they see the creature as both beautiful and fearful at the same time.[117] Although the particular ritual significance or context of African animal imagery may be lost by the time it reaches the gallery spaces of London, Paris, or New York, animals still embody, in their strangeness, a principle of opacity and splitting or doubling that I've noted in other contexts. Animals mirror not so much humanity but rather generate the very principle of division on which mirroring so paradoxically depends. This does not means, incidentally, that we should in any way reject a metaphorical reading of the animal image out of hand. When Chris Ofili, the British artist, rests his paintings on balls of elephant dung they can indeed be seen as grounding his work, a principle of earthiness. But the placing of elephant dung on the breast of Mary, depicted as an African, in his painting *The Holy Virgin Mary* (1996), intensifies a multitude of connotations around race, religion, and shock that if anything exemplifies a de-earthing; the animal antisublime at work again.[118]

Many of these issues similarly arise in contemporary Chinese art. A couple of years after the African animal art exhibition in New York, the Chinese artist Zhou Chunya painted his *Green Dog* series, which depicted a large green dog with erotic figures in the background in a somewhat expressionist style. Zhou himself made the point that for the Chinese the most important question concerns relations between people, and thus his dog figure was expressive of such.[119] Similarly, Zhang Huan in his performance piece *Pilgrimage—Wind and Water in New York* (1998) used the presence of dogs (and their owners) to symbolize a spiritual deficit in the West. In his performance in New York, enacting a confrontation between Eastern asceticism and Western corporeality, the artist lay naked on an ice mattress placed on a Chinese bed, with dogs attached by their leads to the bed and the owners standing by.[120] At one level the increased use of animals, both living and dead, in recent Chinese art reflects exchanges between Eastern and Western art and a mingling of traditions of Oriental animal symbolism with a more general exploration of the human and animal condition. The artist Xu Bing embodies this very neatly but takes it to another level by incorporating the problem of language as a mediating element in rethinking the human. In his *A Case Study of Transference* (1994–1995), two pigs that were to be mated were painted with script, the female with Chinese characters and the male with Roman ones. Both scripts were meaningless. Some shocked critics referred to this as a form of cultural rape, and by doing so interestingly conflated animal sex and human codes just, one suspects, as Bing intended.[121] Bing played further on animals and texts with his exhibit *Net and Leash* (1997) for the Finnish exhibition *Animal. Anima. Animus.* (1998) in which a live sheep was installed in a wire cage of text, tied by a leash shaped in the form of a verse from John Berger's proanimal poem "They Are the Last."[122]

The use of animals and meat in contemporary Chinese art parallels most of the modes found in the West: provocative, metaphorical, conceptual, questioning. A chair was stuffed with rotting meat at the 2000 Shanghai Biennale. Gu Zhenquing's *Man and Animal* exhibition, which toured cities in China in 2000, had the intention of provoking public argument about ethics, art, and the relationship between human and animal.[123] Zhenquing invoked the cause of animal protection in an effort to counter the trend in Chinese art of using animals only as a means of expression, and occasionally with violence. However, many of the artists' performances were not particularly addressed to the goal of the exhibition with regard to animals per se but certainly tested public criteria for what might count as art. For example, Cheng Guang's *Zero Plus Zero* involved the naked artist covering himself in dirt and breathing on a block of ice in which he'd frozen a cow kidney and intestines. In a sense the significant point here is not how important this art may in retrospect turn out to be with regard to the history of animal art or whether it provokes lasting responses about art and identity. Rather, it is that at the very end of the century across the world, the animal is still exemplary as an operative, and intensifying, principle of difference and a mark of change, as it was at the beginning of the century.

The shift from the depiction of animals to the use of animals, from Marc to, say, Beuys, can be contextualized in many ways, some of which have as much to do with the changing aesthetics of the human body. However, in purely animal art terms the use of live and dead animals, or the killing of animals for artistic purposes, during a period which in the West has seen considerable cultural space given to animal issues, continues the principle of an, at times anarchic, operative difference. A philosophical version of this is expressed by Steve Baker in his discussion of Eduardo Kac's *GFP Bunny* project (2000). This was a work in which a transgenic animal was created in a laboratory, in this instance a rabbit whose DNA had a fluorescent jellyfish protein added to it. The intention was to raise it as a domestic pet in the home of the artist. For various reasons the rabbit was not released from the laboratory, and the subsequent controversy around both genetic engineering and this use of animals for artworks opened up an important debate.[124] For Baker, the failure of the project reinforced its claim as a significant artwork, its botchedness: "getting things wrong is one model of what art quite properly does. It calls for an experimental attitude; one that is prepared (to borrow the words of Gillian Rose) 'to go on getting it all more or less wrong, more or less all of the time.'"[125] It is interesting that this comment should be made in the context of art's confrontation with science, a confrontation ignored by animal art for pretty much most of the century. Not only does it reinforce the sense of art's need for indeterminacy, or incompleteness, but also it establishes a principle by which artistic practice distinguishes itself from a science that is also involved in the making of animals. This is highlighted in Catherine Chalmers's photograph of a transgenic mouse, *Rhino* (2000), which is indistinguishable either as an artwork (it was commissioned for the *New York Times Magazine*) or as an illustration in a scientific magazine.[126] It is important to note here that in areas that mark out the twentieth century as distinctive, especially regarding science and technology, animal art has never acted as a barometer or even as particularly prophetic in regard to human–animal relations. The manufacture of animals for science, and manipulations of form and body color, have been going on since the beginning of the century.[127]

The manipulation of living creatures, as in the work of Kac, or the creation of virtual life systems in computer art, does not envisage life forms as isolated but situates them in interacting networks in which codes of various kinds, such as Morse code in Kac's *Genesis* (2000), or artificial-life art software, are key in structuring the interaction between audience and artwork.[128] If we follow the changes in the presentation of the animal body in the last thirty years of the twentieth century they almost comprise a minihistory of their own in which the codes that mediate or surround the animal artwork become increasingly complex even if no more nor less opaque. We can see this from the ritual dramas of performance art (the animal as coactor), to the simple mechanics of landscape installations (the animal as an ecological unit) and the live, dead, or dying animals in the gallery space (the animal body as art), to science art (the animal as biological system).

This fragmentation of the animal, and the collapse of art into science, is best exemplified by the MEART project (from 2001).[129] This was a collaboration between scientists in Australia and the United States. Neurons from an embryonic rat cortex were grown over a multielectrode array. This was then connected to a computer that fed stimuli to the neurons from information converted from a Web cam filming visitors in an art gallery. A recording was made from the reactions of the neurons that in turn drove a robotic arm to make images. The rat neurons were in a laboratory in Atlanta, Georgia, and the robotic arm was in Perth, western Australia.[130] At one level this seems a fitting point of closure for twentieth-century animal art: the final disarticulation of the animal and its integration into a global, computerized, network. MEART encapsulates the domination of modernity by science. Although the tension between looking at animals and looking through animals is never resolved, the rich and varied tradition of animal art offers enough of a resource to enable what Baker calls "a seeing-through-to-animals"—provided, ironically, that it is also made the center of a nonartistic (i.e., linguistic) critical tradition.[131]

NOTES

Introduction

1. John Berger, *About Looking* (New York: Vintage, 1980), p. 13.
2. Bjorn Lomborg, *The Skeptical Environmentalist: Measuring the Real State of the World* (Cambridge: Cambridge University Press, 2001).
3. My formulation, not Lomborg's, lifted from W. H. Auden's "Musée de Beaux Arts."
4. Claude Lévi-Strauss, *Totemism,* trans. Rodney Needham (Boston, Beacon, 1963), p. 89.
5. Peter Singer, *Animal Liberation* (New York: Random House, 1975).
6. The image was first published in Britta Jaschinski, *Zoo* (London: Phaidon, 1996).
7. www.fsinet.or.jp/~sokaisha/rabbit/rabbit.htm (accessed May 30, 2007).
8. Gilles Deleuze and Félix Guattari, *A Thousand Plateaus,* trans. Brian Massumi (Minneapolis: University of Minnesota Press, 1987), pp. 239–240.
9. www.infinitecat.com (accessed May 30, 2007).
10. Animal Planet's homepage is at http://animal.discovery.com/ (accessed May 30, 2007).
11. http://www.newsbackup.com/about1208659.html (accessed May 30, 2007).
12. http://www.nbc11.com/news/5288960/detail.html (accessed May 30, 2007).
13. www.cbc.ca/cp/world/051201/w120168.html (accessed May 30, 2007).
14. W. Broad, "It's Sensitive. Really. The Storied Narwhal Begins to Yield the Secrets of Its Tusk," *New York Times,* December 13, 2005, D1, D4.
15. Thomas Nagel, "What is it Like to Be a Bat?" *Philosophical Review* 83, no. 4 (October, 1974): 435–450.
16. Deleuze and Guittari, *A Thousand Plateaus,* p. 237.
17. Ibid., p. 240.
18. Steve Baker, *Postmodern Animal* (London: Reaktion, 2000), p. 139.
19. "Chris Rock: Never Scared," HBO, April 2004.
20. Will Self, *Great Apes* (London: Penguin, 1998).

21. Patrick Neate, *The London Pigeon Wars* (New York: Farrar, Straus and Giroux, 2004).

22. José Emilio Pacheco, *An Ark for the Next Millennium,* trans. Margaret Sayers Peden (Austin: University of Texas Press, 1993).

23. Britta Jaschinski, *Zoo,* and Britta Jaschinski, *Wild Things* (London: powerHouse, 2003).

24 Barry Commoner, *The Closing Circle: Nature, Man, and Technology* (New York: Random House, 1971).

Chapter 1

1. At about the same time the same discovery was made independently by Geoffrey Parnell, a former archivist employed by the Tower of London.

2. Boria Sax, "Medievalism, Paganism and the Tower Ravens." *The Pomegranate: The International Journal of Pagan Studies.* 9, no. 1 (2007): 62–77.

3. Hae Won Choi, "Koreans Honor Dead Lab Animals (Who Knows—They May Return," *Wall Street Journal,* November 10, 1998, 1.

4. Apollodorus, *The Library of Greek Mythology,* trans. Robin Hard (New York: Oxford University Press, 1997).

5. Hesiod, *Theogony, Works and Days,* trans. M. L.West (New York: Oxford University Press, 1991).

6. Apollodorus, *The Library of Greek Mythology.*

7. Rudolf Otto, *The Idea of Holy* (New York: Oxford University Press, 1958).

8. Boria Sax, *The Mythical Zoo: An Encyclopedia of Animals in World Myth, Legend, and Literature* (Santa Barbara, CA: ABC-CLIO, 2002).

9. James George Frazer, *The* New *Golden Bough: A New Abridgement of the Classic Work,* ed. Theodore H. Gaster (New York: Criterion, 1959).

10. Walter Burkert, *Creation of the Sacred: Tracks of Biology in Early Religion* (Cambridge, MA: Harvard University Press, 1996).

11. Roberto Marchesini, *Post-human: Verso nuovi modelli di esistenza* (Turin, Italy: Bollati Boringhieri, 2002).

12. Wilhelm Heinrich Riehl, *Von deutschem Land und Volk: Eine Auswahl,* ed. Paul Zaunert (Jena, Germany: Eugen Diedrichs, 1922).

13. Boria Sax, *The Frog King: On Fables, Fairy Tales, Legends and Anecdotes of Animals* (New York: Pace University Press/University Press of America, 1990).

14. Boria Sax, *Animals in the Third Reich: Pets, Scapegoats and the Holocaust* (New York: Continuum, 2001).

15. Donald Worster, *Nature's Economy: A History of Ecological Ideas,* 2nd ed. (New York: Cambridge University Press, 1994).

16. Aldo Leopold, "Thinking Like a Mountain," in *A Sand County Almanac: And Sketches Here and There* (New York: Oxford University Press, 1968), p. 130.

17. Worster, *Nature's Economy.*

18. David Aftandilian, Marion W. Copeland, and David Scofield Wilson, eds., *What Are the Animals to Us? Approaches from Science, Religion, Folklore, Literature, and Art* (Knoxville: University of Tennessee Press, 2006).

19. Francis Fukuyama, *Our Posthuman Future: Consequences of the Biotechnology Revolution* (New York: Picador, 2002).

20. Jeremy Rifkin, *The Biotech Century: Harnessing the Gene and Remaking the World* (New York: Jeremy P. Tarcher/Putnam, 1998).

21. Steven Johnson, *Emergence: The Connected Lives of Ants, Brains, Cities and Software* (New York: Simon and Schuster, 2002).

22. Fukuyama, *Our Posthuman Future*; Johnson, *Emergence*.

23. Marchesini, *Post-human: Verso nuovi modelli di esistenza*.

24. Sax, *Animals in the Third Reich*.

25. Fukuyama, *Our Posthuman Future*.

26. Boria Sax, *The Serpent and the Swan: Animal Brides in Literature and Folklore* (Austin: McDonald and Woodward/University of Tennessee Press, 1998).

27. E. Schochet, *Animal Life in Jewish Tradition: Attitudes and Relationships* (New York: Ktav, 1984).

Chapter 2

1. There is no space here to elaborate on the complexity of dress codes. There are other people who are significantly marked out by red coats.

2. The huntsman, who can either be a professional or an amateur, is responsible for the actual processes of hunting with the hounds. There will only be one in each hunt.

3. My research into foxhunting has consisted, in large part, in a long-term engagement with the lived social worlds of several Hunts. I have been trusted and welcomed into those worlds and been given access to all the information I asked for because, I believe, it was understood that I wished to explore foxhunting as a social and cultural event from the perspectives of the participants. Foxhunting is a hugely contested event morally and politically but I have adopted the position of not engaging directly with those issues, although this is, in itself, a moral and political stance. In keeping with this particular personal and anthropological position I do not here deal with the legitimacy or illegitimacy of foxhunting or with foxhunting as a contested performance.

4. E. Schieffelin, "Problematizing Performance," in *Ritual, Performance and Media,* ed. F. Hughes-Freeland (London: Routledge, 1998), p. 194.

5. The field master, who can be male or female, is the person responsible, on a hunting day, for maintaining the discipline of the mounted riders. The field master must ensure that the riders do not interfere with the huntsman, hounds, and the processes of hunting and that the riders move across the countryside in a considerate manner. Of particular concern here is to make sure that there is minimal damage to hedges, fences, and agricultural land, minimal disturbance to livestock, and minimal inconvenience to other people if they are on roads.

6. Any hunt is likely to develop in much more complex ways, and there are rules and regulations about what may or may not be done should a fox seek refuge in particular places.

7. Foxhunting also takes place in Wales, Scotland, and Northern Ireland but for the sake of simplicity here I have referred only to England. Hunt with a capital *H* refers to the foxhunt as a social entity rather than to the practice of hunting itself.

8. There will be exceptions to this. Many Hunts will have members and supporters who live in urban areas.

9. M. Bell, *Childerley: Nature and Morality in a Country Village* (Chicago: University of Chicago Press, 1994), p. 170.

10. G. Marvin, "Natural Instincts and Cultural Passions: Transformations and Performances in Foxhunting," *Performance Research* 5, no. 2 (2000): 109–110.

11. In some ways this is a simplified exposition. There could be a fleeting audience for any hunt—for example, the people who see it while driving across the countryside. On some occasions—for example, on Boxing Day—Hunts deliberately engage in display and pageantry. There is another potential audience for the foxhunt—the antihunting protesters. It is impossible to engage here with the complexity of this issue but they, too, constitute a body of engaged (although, from the perspective of the Hunt, unwelcomed) participants in the event. They are not present merely to observe but actively to disrupt it. One could certainly explore, in terms of their dress codes, language, and practices, the performative quality of their interjections into the performance of hunting.

12. R. Schechner, *Performance Theory* (London: Routledge, 1988), pp. 193–196.

13. Ibid., p. 195.

14. J. Ortega y Gasset, *La Caza y Los Toros* (Madrid: Revista de Occidente, 1968), p. 48.

15. E. Fromm, *The Anatomy of Human Destructiveness* (Harmondsworth, UK: Penguin Books, 1990), p. 185.

16. A. Franklin, "Neo-Darwinian Leisures, the Body and Nature: Hunting and Angling in Modernity," *Body and Society* 7, no. 4 (2001): 67

17. David Mamet, *The Village* (London: Faber and Faber, 1994), p. 194.

18. Ibid., p. 194.

19. Ibid., p. 195.

20. Ibid., p. 196.

21. Ibid., p. 196.

22. J. Dizard, *Mortal Stakes: Hunters and Hunting in Contemporary America* (Amherst: University of Massachusetts Press, 2003), p. 107.

23. C. McLeod, "Pondering Nature: An Ethnography of Duck Hunting in Southern New Zealand" (Ph.D. diss., University of Otaga, Dunedin, New Zealand), p. 310.

24. Ibid., p. 311.

25. Portions of this chapter are excerpted from my previous essays: "A Passionate Pursuit: Foxhunting as Performance," *Sociological Review* 51 (October 2003): 46–60, and "Sensing Nature: Encountering the World in Hunting," *Etnofoor* 18, no. 1 (2005): 15–26.

Chapter 3

1. For my purposes, domestication is defined as the process of maintaining animals in captivity, selectively breeding them for human purposes, and controlling their food supply, reproduction, and other aspects of life, thus creating a dependency on humans for survival, and a marked alteration in appearance and behavior. See Juliet Clutton-Brock, *A Natural History of Domesticated Mammals* (Cambridge: Cambridge University Press, 1987), for a more detailed definition.

2. Ibid. See also Jared Diamond, *Guns, Germs and Steel: The Fate of Human Societies* (New York: W.W. Norton, 1999); Frederick Zeuner, *A History of Domesticated Animals* (New York: Harper and Row, 1963).

3. A true history of domesticated animals would not be complete without looking at working animals. However, because most of the working animals' jobs (hunting, pulling a plow or carriage, etc.) are largely unchanged in the modern period (with the exception of relatively recent jobs like search and rescue, police and military

work, or service dogs), I have omitted a discussion of working animals from this chapter.

4. Stephen Budiansky, *The Covenant of the Wild: Why Animals Chose Domestication* (New Haven: Yale University Press, 1992), and J. Clutton-Brock, *A Natural History of Domesticated Mammals.*

5. Diamond, *Guns, Germs and Steel.*

6. Tim Ingold, "From Trust to Domination: An Alternative History of Human-Animal Relations," in *Animals and Human Society: Changing Perspectives,* ed. A. Manning and J. Serpell (London: Routledge, 1994).

7. Budiansky, *The Covenant of the Wild*; Clutton-Brock, *A Natural History of Domesticated Mammals.*

8. J. Clutton-Brock, "The Unnatural World: Behavioral Aspects of Humans and Animals in the Process of Domestication," in *Animals and Human Society: Changing Perspectives,* ed. A. Manning and J. Serpell (New York: Routledge, 1994).

9. Budiansky, *The Covenant of the Wild*; Zeuner, *A History of Domesticated Animals.*

10. Laurie Winn Carlson, *Cattle: An Information Social History* (Chicago: Ivan R Dee, 2001).

11. Adrian Franklin, *Animals and Modern Cultures: A Sociology of Human–Animal Relations in Modernity* (London: Sage Publications, 1999).

12. Ibid.

13. Barbara Noske, *Beyond Boundaries: Humans and Animals* (Montreal: Black Rose Books, 1997).

14. Susan E. Davis and Margo DeMello, *Stories Rabbits Tell: A Natural and Cultural History of a Misunderstood Creature* (New York: Lantern Press, 2003).

15. Until 1997, cows, pigs, chickens, and other animals were routinely fed the rendered remains of other livestock; since the advent of mad cow disease, however, cows are no longer fed other cows.

16. Clutton-Brock, "The Unnatural World," p. 34.

17. G. Gorman, "Down on the Pharm: Agribusiness in the 21st Century," *Nutrition Health Review* (Winter 2002), http://www.encyclopedia.com/doc/1G1-99292185.html (accessed 31 May 2007).

18. J. Raloff, "Hormones: 'Here's the Beef,' Environmental Concerns Reemerge over Steroids Given to Livestock," *Science News Online* 161, no. 1 (January 5, 2002): 10.

19. V. Pursel, and others, "Genetic Engineering of Livestock," Beltsville, MD: U.S. Department of Agriculture.

20. R. Weiss, "Cloned Cows' Milk, Beef Up to Standard: Researchers Find No Significant Differences with Products of Conventionally Raised Cattle," *Washington Post,* April 12, 2005, A3.

21. K. Kiley, "Copy This: Livestock Cloning Faces an Uneasy Public," *Consumer Markets Insider,* November 14, 2005.

22. J. Motavalli, "The Case Against Meat," *E Magazine* XIII, no. 1, January/February 2002.

23. C. DeHaan and others, eds. *Livestock Development: Implications for Rural Poverty, the Environment, and Global Food Security* (Washington, DC: World Bank Publications, 2001).

24. Franklin, *Animals and Modern Cultures.*

25. Noske, *Beyond Boundaries.*

26. S. Gura, "Losing Livestock, Losing Livelihoods," *Seedling Magazine,* January 2003.

27. Ibid.

28. According to a scientist at North Carolina State University, the "transfer efficiency rate" for cloned cattle is 10 percent while for pigs it is 8–9 percent. I. Oransky, "First Dog Cloned," *The Scientist Daily News,* August 3, 2005.

29. BBC News, "Produce from Cloned Cattle 'Safe'," April 12, 2005.

30. Paul Robbins notes that India's national meat industry is growing rapidly thanks to a growing demand for meat in the country; he also notes that with that growth comes a radical transformation in the relationship between domesticated animals, particularly the India's sacred cattle and the people. P. Robbins, "Shrines and Butchers: Animals as Deities, Capital and Meat in Contemporary North India," In *Animal Geographies: Place, Politics, and Identity in the Nature-Culture Borderlands,* ed. J. Wolch and J. Emel (London: Verso, 1998).

31. Vegetarian Resource Group, "Roper Poll," *Vegetarian Journal* 16, no. 5 (September/October 1997): 21–22.

32. Agricultural Marketing Service, "Organic Food Standards and Labels: The Facts," The National Organic Program, United States Department of Agriculture, April 2002.

33. M. Colin, "Elite Meat," *Christian Science Monitor,* July 14, 2003.

34. E. Weise, "Organic Chicken May Not Be All It's Cut Out To Be," *USA Today,* February 26, 2003.

35. Ufkes, F. "Building a Better Pig: Fat Profits in Lean Meat," in *Animal Geographies: Place, Politics, and Identity in the Nature-Culture Borderlands,* ed. J. Wolch and J. Emel (London: Verso, 1998).

36. This trend is in marked contrast to the popularity in recent years of Kobe beef, which is raised in Japan, fed beer, and hand massaged to produce the most tender, fatty product available.

37. USDA Agricultural Research Service National Program Annual Report, 1998.

38. American Pet Product Manufacturing Association, 2005–2006 National Pet Owners' Survey.

39. James Serpell, *In the Company of Animals: A Study of Human-Animal Relationships* (Cambridge: Cambridge University Press, 1986).

40. Ibid.

41. Paul Shepard, *The Others: How Animals Made Us Human* (Washington: Island Press, 1996).

42. Ibid. Chilla Bulbeck, in her discussion of ecotourism in Australia, discusses how tourists who visit wildlife parks often want to get close to and cuddle the wild koalas, dolphins and kangaroos seen on such tours, even while they realize that this experience is hardly an authentic wildlife experience. Chilla Bulbeck, *Facing the Wild: Ecotourism, Conservation and Animal Encounters* (London: Earthscan, 2005).

43. Grier, K., "'The Eden of Home': Changing Understandings of Cruelty and Kindness to Animals in Middle-Class American Households, 1820–1900," in *Animals in Human Histories,* ed. M. Henninger-Voss (Rochester, NY: University of Rochester Press, 2002).

44. Franklin, *Animals and Modern Cultures.*

45. But not the first widespread pets: according to Katherine Grier, goldfish were the first mass-produced and distributed pet. Grier, "Eden of Home."

46. Davis and DeMello, *Stories Rabbits Tell.*

47. The raising and selling of captive birds is a very different operation from the raising of mammals like dogs or cats, and a discussion of this important subject is
beyond the scope of this chapter, since even domestically raised parrots and other
birds commonly kept as companions are not truly domesticated, but simply captive
raised (and often captive caught as well).

48. While culling is commonplace in the world of show and pet breeding, certain breed
standards *demand* the killing of unwanted babies. For instance, the American Boxer
Club's code of ethics prohibits the sale by a club member of a boxer with a coat
color not conforming to breed standards. Because white boxers are born with regu-
larity (up to 20% of all boxers are born white), this has led to the routine killing
of a huge number of white babies (although some members now give them away, a
practice that used to be prohibited as well). Other breeds have similar defects such
as Australian shepherds: the Australian Shepherd Club of America recommends
immediate killing for the 25 percent of all puppies born white, because some may
be blind or deaf.

49. From the AKC's position statement on ear cropping, tail docking, and dew claw
removal: http://www.akc.org/canine_legislation/position_statements.cfm#earcrop
ping (accessed May 30, 2007).

50. R. Wansborough, "Cosmetic Tail Docking of Dogs' Tails," *Australian Veterinary
Journal* 74, no. 1, July 1996.

51. "Sales of Cloned Cattle Multiply," *Houston Chronicle,* November 3, 2003.

52. S. McHugh, "Bitches from Brazil: Cloning and Owning Dogs through the Missyplicity Project," in *Representing Animals,* ed. N. Rothfels (Bloomington: Indiana
University Press, 2002).

53. The Delta Society is one organization that tracks the various studies of the benefits
of pet ownership on human health, and a perusal of back issues of *Society and
Animals* will also show readers a wide variety of such studies. Another example of
the widespread acknowledgement of the positive role animals play in human lives
is the rapidly growing field of animal-assisted therapy.

54. Shepard, *The Others.*

55. Leslie Irvine, *If You Tame Me: Understanding Our Connection with Animals* (Philadelphia: Temple University Press, 2004).

56. See J. Serpell and E. Paul, "Pets and the Development of Positive Attitudes to
Animals," in *Animals and Human Society: Changing Perspectives,* ed. A. Manning
and J. Serpell (London: Routledge, 1994). Also Paul, E. "Love of Pets and Love
of People," in *Companion Animals and Us: Exploring the Relationships between
People and Pets,* ed. A. Podberscek, E. Paul, and J. Serpell (Cambridge: Cambridge
University Press, 2000).

57. F. Ascione, "Enhancing Children's Attitudes about the Humane Treatment of Ani-
mals: Generalization to Human-Directed Empathy," *Anthrozoos* 5 (1992); also
G. Melson, "Studying Children's Attachment to Their Pets: A Conceptual and
Methodological Review," *Anthrozoos* 4 (1991).

58. B. Daly and L. Morton, "Children with Pets Do Not Show A Higher Empathy:
A Challenge to Current Views," *Anthrozoos* 16, no. 4 (2003).

59. The practice of keeping exotic animals as pets is beyond the scope of this chapter
as exotic animals are not, by any definition, domesticated. However, it should be
noted that the capture, trafficking, and sale of exotic animals as pets is a multimil-
lion dollar growth industry.

60. See J. Serpell and E. Paul, "Pets and the Development of Positive Attitudes to Animals," in *Animals and Human Society: Changing Perspectives*, ed. A. Manning and J. Serpell (London: Routledge, 1994).

61. Marinell Harriman, *House Rabbit Handbook* (Alameda: Drollery Press, 1985).

62. A. Arluke and C. Luke, "Physical Cruelty towards Animals in Massachusetts, 1975–1996," in *Society and Animals* 5 (1997): 95–204. See also F. Ascione, "Children Who are Cruel to Animals: A Review of Research and Implications for Developmental Psychopathology," *Anthrozoos* 6 (1993): 226–247.

63. F. Ascione, "Domestic Violence and Cruelty to Animals." Paper presented at the Fourth International Conference on Family Violence, Durham, NH, July 21–24, 1995; F. Ascione, C. Weber, and D. Wood, "The Abuse of Animals and Domestic Violence: A National Survey of Shelters for Women Who Are Battered," *Society and Animals* 5 (1997): 205–218; F. Ascione, "Battered Women's Reports of Their Partners' and Their Children's Cruelty to Animals," *Journal of Emotional Abuse* 1 (1998): 119–133.

64. C. Adams, "Woman-Battering and Harm to Animals," in *Animals and Women, Feminist Theoretical Explorations*, ed. C. Adams and J. Donovan (Durham, NC: Duke University Press, 1999).

65. A. Beetz, "Bestiality and Zoophilia: Associations with Violence and Sex Offending," in *Bestiality and Zoophilia: Sexual Relations with Animals*, ed. A. Beetz and A. Podberscek (Lafeyette, IN: Purdue University Press, 2005).

66. Mary Elizabeth Thurston, *The Lost History of the Canine Race* (New York: Andrews McMeel Publishing, 1996).

67. Paul Hamlyn, *African Mythology* (London: Geogffrey Parrinder, 1967).

68. See especially Budiansky, *The Covenant of the Wild*, for the most extreme version of this argument.

69. Shepard, *The Others*, p. 267

70. Clearly we are also dependent on the role animals play, necessary or not, in the fields of medical science and product testing, issues dealt with in chapter 5, this volume.

71. American Animal Humane Association.

72. Yi-Fu Tuan, *Dominance and Affection: The Making of Pets* (New Haven: Yale University Press, 1984).

73. Shepard, *The Others*, p. 141.

Chapter 4

1. C. Tudge, *The Day Before Yesterday: Five Million Years of Human History* (London: Cape, 1995), pp. 282–289.

2. J. Fisher, *Zoos of the World* (London: Aldus, 1966), p. 24.

3. D. Hancocks, *Animals and Architecture* (London: Evelyn, 1971).

4. H. Reichenbach, "A Tale of Two Zoos: The Hamburg Zoological Garden and Carl Hagenebeck's Tierpark," in *New Worlds, New Animals: From Menagerie to Zoological Park in the Nineteenth Century*, ed. R. J. Hoage and W. A. Deiss (Baltimore: Johns Hopkins University Press, 1996).

5. J. S. Curl, *Oxford Dictionary of Architecture* (Oxford: Oxford University Press, 1999), p. 298.

6. T. Pratchett, *Men at Arms: Discworld Book 15* (New York: Harper, 1993), p. 71.

7. C. Hagenbeck, *Beasts and Men*, trans. H. Elliott and A. Thacker (London: Longmans, Green, 1910), p. 40.

8. H. Strehlow, "Zoos and Aquariums of Berlin," in *New Worlds, New Animals: From Menagerie to Zoological Park in the Nineteenth Century*, ed. R. J. Hoage and W. A. Deiss (Baltimore: Johns Hopkins University Press, 1996), p. 69.

9. W. Bridges, *Gathering of Animals: An Unconventional History of the New York Zoological Society* (New York: Harper and Row, 1974).

10. P. Guillery, *The Buildings of London Zoo* (London: Royal Commission on the Historical Monuments of England, 1993), p. 15.

11. P. Heyer, *American Architecture: Ideas and Ideologies in the Late Twentieth Century* (New York: Wiley, 1993), p. 198.

12. H. Hediger, *Wild Animals in Captivity: An Outline of the Biology of Zoological Gardens*, trans. G. Sircom (London: Butterworth, 1950); H. Hediger, *Studies of the Psychology and Behaviour of Captive Animals in Zoos and Circuses*, trans. G. Sircom (London: Butterworth, 1995).

13. Hancocks, *Animals and Architecture*, 1971.

14. N. Walter, "What Sort of Man Designs a Penguin House That Children Can't Even See Into?" *The Observer* (London), September 22, 1996, 9.

15. J. Glancey, "Waddling Off: Penguins Moved from Listed Pool," *The Guardian* (London), July 3, 2004, 10.

16. C. Blackstock, "Tea Party over for PG Tips Chimps," *The Guardian* (London), December 1, 2001. A. Sherwin, "Single Birds End the Tea Party for PG Chimps," *The Sunday Times* (London), December 1, 2001.

17. Guillery, *The Buildings of London Zoo*, p. 10.

18. L. R. Brightwell, *The Zoo Story* (London: Museum Press, 1952), p. 197.

19. S. Zuckerman, *The Social Life of Monkeys and Apes* (London: Routledge and Kegan Paul), 1932.

20. Brightwell, *The Zoo Story*, p. 198.

21. Zuckerman, *The Social Life of Monkeys and Apes*, 1932.

22. J. Seidensticker and J. Doherty, "Integrating Animal Behavior and Exhibit Design," in *Wild Mammals in Captivity: Principles and Techniques*, ed. D. Kleiman and others (Chicago: University of Chicago Press, 1996), p. 181.

23. E. Wilson and C. Michener, "Alfred Edwards Emerson," in *Biographical Memoirs* (Washington, DC: National Academy of Sciences, 1982), p. 164.

24. W. Rybczynski, *The Look of Architecture* (Oxford: Oxford University Press, 2001), p. xi.

25. Rybczynski, *The Look of Architecture*, 2001.

26. P. Crowcroft, *The Zoo* (Milson's Point, New South Wales: Mathews/Hutchinson), 1978.

27. B. Mullan and G. Marvin, *Zoo Culture* (Urbana: University of Illinois Press, 1987), p. 52.

28. W. Conway, Promotional statement for *A Different Nature*, David Hancocks, 2001.

29. D. Streatfield, "Regionalism in Landscape Design," in *Jones & Jones: Ideas Migrate, Places Resonate*, ed. K. Kobayashi (Tokyo: Process Architecture, 126, 1995), p. 20.

30. A. Powell, "Breaking the Mold," *Landscape Architecture*, October 1997, 127.

31. Jones and Jones, *Woodland Park Zoo: Long Range Plan, Development Guidelines and Exhibit Scenarios* (Seattle: Department of Parks and Recreation, 1976).

32. D. Hancocks, *A Different Nature: The Paradoxical World of Zoos and their Uncertain Future* (Berkeley: University of California Press, 2001).

33. M. Akeley, *Carl Akeley's Africa* (New York: Blue Ribbon, 1929).

34 T. Maple, "Strategic Collection Planning and Individual Animal Welfare," *Journal of the American Veterinary Medical Association* 223, no. 7 (October 2003): 967.

35. W. Hornaday, *The Minds and Manners of Wild Animals: A Book of Personal Observation* (New York: Kessinger, 1922), p. 45.

36. P. Barker, "Setting the Stage," in *AZA Communiqué* (Silver Spring, MD: American Zoo Association, August 2002), pp. 42–43.

37. D. Hancocks, "Zoological Gardens, Arboreta, Botanical Gardens: A Trilogy of Failure?" Paper presented at the National Conference of the American Association of Botanical Gardens and Arboreta, Pasadena, California, June 15–19, 1994.

38. E. McToldridge, personal communication with the author, March 27, 1992.

39. J. Ogden, C. Vernon, and K. Wagner, "Measuring our Impact," in *AZA Communiqué* (Silver Spring, MD: American Zoo Association, September 2002), pp. 23–24.

40. AZA, "AZA Elephant Care and Conservation Speak Louder than Extremist Hype," in *U.S. News Wire* (Silver Spring, MD: American Zoo Association, 2006) http://www.elephant-news.com/index.php?id=841 (accessed June 1, 2007).

41. L. Dierking, K. Burtnyk, K. Buchner, and J. Falk, *Visitor Learning in Zoos and Aquariums: Executive Summary* (Silver Spring, MD: American Zoo Association, 2006).

42. L. Margulis and C. Sagan, *Microcosmos: Four Billion Years of Microbial Evolution* (New York: Touchstone, 1991), pp. 11–14.

Chapter 5

1. The best source for general information on the *Pinky and the Brain* series is the Internet Movie Database (www.imdb.com; accessed February 15, 2006).

2. Quotes and plots, respectively, from title sequence and "Brinky" episode (aired February 1997). A comprehensive *Pinky and the Brain* episode guide can be found at www.ladyofthecake.com/pinkyandbrain/ (accessed February 15, 2006).

3. See 2004 Animal Welfare Act report, published by the U.S. Dept. of Agriculture at www.aphis.usda.gov/ac/awreports/awreport2004.pdf (accessed February 5, 2006).

4. Estimating total mouse use (especially relative to other animals) is complicated. Andrew Rowan (*Of Mice, Models, and Men,* New York: SUNY Press, 1984) estimated that in 1965, a total of nearly thirty-seven million mice were consumed in U.S. laboratories, and by 1984, that figure had risen to an estimated forty-five million—or 63 percent of the total number of (counted) animals used by U.S. scientists. But Rowan's sources are unclear and he does not break down the kinds of mice included in that percentage (namely, percentage of inbreds versus outbreds). Still the best statistics on animal use at the U.S. National Institutes of Health (cf. "Office of Technology Assessment: Report on Lab Animal Use," Bethesda, MD: NIH, 1990) confirm his conclusions; mice and rats together, for example, accounted in 1991 for 60–70 percent of all animals used, and approximately 90 percent of all mammals used. An additional problem is one of general scientific animal accounting: who, for example, is compiling numbers for every use of a *Drosophila* fly in a test tube? The existence of such recordings would drastically change animal use estimates.

5. See Karen Rader, *Making Mice: Standardizing Animals for Biomedical Research, 1900–1955* (Princeton: Princeton University Press, 2004), pp. 5, 19.

6. Though biologically inaccurate, throughout this chapter I am using the conventional parlance of "animals" to represent the more precise (but too wordy) concept "nonhuman animals."

7. Tim Birkhead, *A Brand New Bird: How Two Amateur Scientists Created the First Genetically Engineered Animal* (New York: Basic, 2003).

8. Robert Kohler, *Lords of The Fly: Drosophila Genetics and the Experimental Life* (Chicago: University of Chicago Press, 1994).

9. Stephen Budiansky, *The Covenant of the Wild: Why Animals Chose Domestication* (New Haven: Yale University Press, 1992).

10. Kohler, *Lords*, p. 19.

11. H. J. Muller, "The Measurement of Gene Mutation Rate in Drosophila, Its High Variability, and Its Dependence Upon Temperature," *Genetics* 13 (July 1928): 279–357.

12. Clyde Keeler, "In Quest of Apollo's Sacred White Mice," *Scientific Monthly* 34 (January 1932): 48–53; see also Clyde Keeler, *The Laboratory Mouse: Its Origin, Heredity and Culture* (Cambridge, MA: Harvard University Press, 1931), chaps. 1 and 2. Cf. Josef Grohmann, *Apollo Smintheus und die bedeutung der mause in der mythologie der Indogermanen* (Prague: J.C. Calve, 1862); Angelo de Gubermatis, *Zoological Mythology, or the Legends of the Animals* (1872; repr., Detroit: Singing Tree Press, 1968); Bjarne Beckman, *Von Mäusen und Menschen: die hoch- und spätmittelalterlichen Mäusesagen mit Kommentar und Anmerkungen* (Bremgarten, Switzerland: Beckman, 1974); Pierre Malriey, *Le Bestiare Insolite: L'Animal dans la Tradition, le Mythe, le Rêve* (Realmont, France: Editions la Duralie, 1987).

13. Keeler, "Apollo's Sacred White Mice."

14. A search of the *Reader's Guide to Periodical Literature* for the years 1927 to 1939 turns up the following accounts to illustrate the point: "House Mice Indicated as Nerve Disease Carriers," *Science News Letter* 35 (1939): 329; "Rodent Control in Food Establishments," *American Journal of Public Health* 27 (1937): 62–66. Rhea Kimberly Johnson, "White Mice," *Nature Magazine* 13 (1929): 48–50; "Mice as Disease Carriers," *Science* 69, supp. 14 (1929): 1631; "Are Mice Smarter Than Men?," *Popular Mechanic* 49 (1928): 519; F. T. Humphrey, "Serious Plague of Mice in California," *Scientific American* 136 (1927): 330–331. For a more exhaustive analysis of a similar cultural phenomenon with rats, see Robert Hendrickson, *More Cunning than Man: A Social History of Rats and Men* (New York: Dorset Press, 1988).

15. Interestingly, Disney's original choice for a new character that year was not a mouse but a rabbit. When contract disputes forced him to quit his original company, which owned all of his extant work, he needed to develop a new figure and he supposedly drew Mickey from his own experiences with mice: "He liked mice; in fact, he had sheltered some wild mice in his office in Kansas." Qtd. in *Walt Disney: An American Original* (Mankato, Minnesota: Creative Education, 1974), p. 18. See also David Bain and Bruce Harris, *Mickey Mouse: Fifty Happy Years* (New York: Harmony Books, 1977), pp. 10–16. Cf. "Mickey Mouse Is Eight Years Old," *Literary Digest* 122 (1936):18–19 and "Mickey Mouse's Miraculous Movie Monkey-Shines," *The Literary Digest* 6 (1930): 36–37.

16. Johnson, "White Mice."

17. "Mice Beautiful," *Time* 30, July 19, 1937, 50. Other scientific pursuits also benefited from the culture of the animal fancy in the nineteenth century, most famously in attempts by Charles Darwin to apply the concepts and methods of artificial selection to understand and influence the biology of natural selection: see James Secord, "Nature's Fancy: Charles Darwin and the Breeding of Pigeons," *Isis* 72 (June 2, 1991): 163–186.

18. "The English Craze for Mice," *Reader's Digest* 30 (March 1937): 19.

19. "Mouse Show," *Newsweek* 9, January 23, 1937, 40.

20. Lathrop's contributions to the historical development of the inbred mouse are acknowledged in the second edition of *The Biology of the Laboratory Mouse* (by the Staff of the Jackson Lab, New York: McGraw Hill, 1966); in M. Potter and R. Lieberman, "Genetics of Immunoglobulins in the Mouse," *Advances in Immunology* 7 (1967): 91; in Herbert S. Morse, ed., *The Origins of Inbred Mice: Proceedings of an NIH Workshop in Bethesda, Maryland* (New York: Academic Press, 1978); and Jan Klein, *The Biology of the Histocompatibility-2 Complex of the Mouse* (New York: Springer-Verlag, 1975).

21. For a more detailed discussion of the uses of mice in scientific research during this period see Rader, *Making Mice*, chapter 1.

22. Karen Rader, "Of Mice, Medicine, and Genetics: C.C. Little's Creation of the Inbred Laboratory Mouse, 1909–1918," *Studies in the History and Philosophy of Biology and the Biomedical Sciences* 30, no. 3 (Spring 1999): 319–343.

23. Keeler, "Apollo's Sacred Mice," quotes on pp. 51, 53.

24. Clarence Cook Little, "A New Deal For Mice: Why Mice Are Used in Research on Human Diseases," *Scientific American* 152 (1937): 16–18.

25. Cf. Mary Midgley, *Animals and Why They Matter* (Athens: University of Georgia Press, 1983), chaps. 9, 10; see also Harriet Ritvo, *The Animal Estate: The English and Other Creatures in Victorian England* (Cambridge, MA: Harvard University Press, 1989).

26. "New Breed of Mouse Aids Alzheimer's Work," *New York Times,* October 4, 1996, A22. Nicholas Wade, "Of Mice, Men, and a Gene that Jump-Starts Follicles," *New York Times,* October 5. 1999, F1. Sharon Begley, "The Mice That Roared," *Newsweek,* December 4, 1995, 76; Gina Kolata, "Studies on a Mouse Hormone Bear On Fatness in Humans," *New York Times,* April 2, 2004, 1.

27. Nicholas Wade, "Of Smart Mice and an Even Smarter Man," *New York Times,* Science Times, September 7, 1999; Michael D. Lemonick, "Smart Genes?" *Time* 154, no. 11, September 13, 1999, 54–59 plus cover photo. On possible drug applications of smart mouse research, see also Catherine Arnst, "Building a Smarter Mouse," *Business Week* 3646, September 13, 1999, 103.

28. Cf. Donna Haraway, *Modest Witness @ Second_Millenium.FemaleMan©Meets OncomouseTM: Feminism and Technoscience* (New York: Routledge, 1997).

29. K. T. Paige, L. G. Clima, M. J. Yaremchuk, J. P. Vacanti, and C. A. Vacanti, "Injectable Cartilage," *Plastic and Reconstructive Surgery* 96 (1995): 1390–1400.

30. Dashka Slater, "Humouse™," Legal Affairs, November/December 2002, pp. 1; Aaron Zitner, "Patently Provoking a Debate," *Los Angeles Times,* May 12, 2002, A1.

31. On 1999 NSF Science and Engineering Indicators Report, see Jon D. Miller and Linda Kimmel, *Biomedical Communications* (San Diego: Academic Press, 2001), chaps. 2, 12, and appendix for questionnaires. Meredith Wadman, "U.S. Lab Animals May Win in Lawsuit," *Nature,* 407 (2000): 549. Cf. "Mighty Mice," at www.fastcompany.com/online/47/agendaitems.html (accessed August 2002).

32. Hershkowitz qtd. in "The Mouse Sequence: A Rosetta Stone," *The Genes We Share*, Howard Hughes Medical Institute, at www.hhmi.org/genesweshare (accessed February 2003); on Baudrillard and mice, see Marc Holthof, "To the Realm of Fables: The Animal Fables from Mesopotamia to Disneyland, trans. by Milt Papatheophanes, in *Zoology on (Post) Modern Animals*, ed. Bart Verschaffel and Marc Vermick (Dublin: Liliput Press 1993), pp. 37–55, quote p. 55.

33. Anita Guerrini, *Experimenting with Humans and Animals: From Galen to Animal Rights* (Baltimore: Johns Hopkins University Press, 2003), pp. 38–39.

34. Anita Guerrini, "The Ethics of Animal Experimentation in Seventeenth-Century England," *Journal of the History of Ideas*, 50, no. 3 (1989): 391–407; Christopher Lawrence, "Cinema Vérité? The Image of William Harvey's Experiments in 1928," in *Vivisection in Historical Perspective*, ed. Nicholaas Rupke (London: Routledge, 1990), pp. 295–313.

35. Bert Hansen, "American's First Medical Breakthrough: How Popular Excitement about a French Rabies Cure in 1885 Raised New Expectations for Medical Progress," *American Historical Review*, 103, no. 2 (April 1998): 373–418; quote from 1884 *Harper's Weekly* article, qtd. in Guerrini, *Experimenting with Humans and Animals*, p. 101.

36. Cf. Guerrini, *Experimenting with Humans and Animals*, pp. 75–82, and Hansen, "America's First Medical Breakthrough" for various British and American images of dogs; Nicholaas Rupke, "Pro-vivisection in England in the Early 1880s: Arguments and Motives," in *Vivisection in Historical Perspective*, ed. Nicholaas Rupke (London: Routledge, 1990), pp. 188–208, with Tompkins' painting reproduced on p. 211.

37. Susan E. Lederer, "The Controversy over Animal Experimentation in American, 1880–1914," in *Vivisection in Historical Perspective*, ed. Nicholaas Rupke (London: Routledge, 1990), pp. 236–258, and Susan E. Lederer, "Political Animals: The Shaping of Biomedical Research Literature in Twentieth Century America," *Isis* 83 (1992): 61–79, esp. pp. 62–63.

38. Whipple to J. L. Whitley, qtd. in Lederer, "Political Animals," p. 65.

39. Adele Clarke, "Research Materials and Reproductive Science in the United States, 1910–1940," in *Physiology in the American Context, 1850–1940*, ed. Gerald Geison (Bethesda, MD: American Physiological Society, 1987), pp. 323–350.

40. Lederer, "Political Animals," pp. 65–66.

41. Lederer, "Political Animals," pp. 68–74.

42. Cf. A. Saul Benison, Clifford Barger, and Elin L. Wolfe, *Walter B. Cannon* (Cambridge, MA: Harvard University Press, 1987).

43. Daniel P. Todes, "Pavlov's Physiology Factory," *Isis* 88 (1997): 205–246, quote p. 221.

44. Daniel P. Todes, *Pavlov's Physiology Factory: Experiment, Interpretation, Laboratory Enterprise* (Baltimore: Johns Hopkins University Press, 2002), p. 94.

45. Cf. Larry Carbone, *What Animals Want: Expertise and Advocacy in Laboratory Animal Welfare Policy* (New York, Oxford, 2004).

46. Todes, *Pavlov's Physiology Factory*, chap. 3.

47. Diane B. Paul, "The Rockefeller Foundation and the Origins of Behavior Genetics," in *The Expansion of American Biology*, ed. Keith Benson, Jane Maienschein, and Ronald Rainger (New Brunswick, NJ: Rutgers University Press, 1991), pp. 262–283, quote from Gregg on p. 275.

48. John Paul Scott and John L. Fuller, *Genetics and the Social Behavior of the Dog* (Chicago: University of Chicago Press, 1965), p. 416. Quote from Robert Morrison

of the Rockefeller Foundation in Paul, "Rockefeller Foundation and Genetics," p. 283, n. 58.

49. See Jasper Rine's "Dog Genome Manifesto," http://mendel.berkeley.edu/dog/manifesto.html (accessed March 18, 2006)

50. "Dog Genome," *The Osgood File,* CBS Radio Network, August 27, 2002, at www.acfnewsource.org/science/dog_genome.html (accessed March 18, 2006).

51. Donna Haraway, "Alpha Bitches On-Line: The Dog Genome for the Next Genderation" (lecture presented at the IV European Feminist Research Conference Body Gender Subjectivity: Crossing Borders of Disciplines and Institutions, Bologna, Italy, September 28–October 1, 2000). At www.women.it/cyberarchive/files/haraway.html (accessed March 18, 2006). See also Donna Haraway, "Cloning Mutts, Saving Tigers: Ethical Emergents in Technocultural Dog Worlds," in *Remaking Life and Death: Toward an Anthropology of the Biosciences,* ed. Sarah Franklin and Margaret Lock (Sante Fe, NM: School of American Research Press, 2003), pp. 293–328.

52. Sarah Franklin, *Embodied Progress: A Cultural Account of Assisted Reproduction* (New York: Routledge, 1997); also, Sarah Franklin, "Ethical Biocapital: New Strategies of Cell Culture," in *Remaking Life and Death: Towards an Anthropology of the Biosciences,* ed. Sarah Franklin and Margaret Lock (Sante Fe, NM: School of American Research Press, 2003), pp. 97–128. Cf. Charis Thompson, "Strategic Naturalizing: Kinship in an Infertility Clinic," in *Relative Values: Reconfiguring Kinship Studies,* ed. Sarah Franklin and Susan McKinnon (Durham, NC: Duke University Press, 2001), pp. 175–202.

53. Ian Wilmut and others, "Viable Offspring Derived from Fetal and Adult Mammalian Cells," *Nature* 385 (February 27, 1997): 810. Cf. Ian Wilmut, Keith Campbell, and Colin Tudge, *Second Creation: Dolly and the Age of Biological Control* (New York: Farrar, Strauss, and Giroux, 2000), pp. 20–21, 30–32.

54. For analysis of contemporary reactions to Dolly, see essays by Nelkin and Lindee, and Klotzko, in *The Cloning Sourcebook,* ed. A. Klotzko (New York: Oxford University, 2001). These same reactions extended to subsequent policy discussions—see, for example, coverage of the NAS Panel on Human Cloning, in John Travis, "Cloning Hearing Creates Media Frenzy," *Science News* 160, no. 7 (August 18, 2001): 105.

55. On Dolly's death, see BBC News Coverage ("Dolly the Sheep Clone Dies Young") beginning in February 2003, http://news.bbc.co.uk/1/hi/sci/tech/2764039.stm (accessed February 25, 2006); Lee Silver, "Thinking Twice, or Thrice, About Cloning," in *The Cloning Sourcebook,* ed. A. Klotzko (New York: Oxford University, 2001), pp. 60–63, quote p. 63.

56. Will Knight, "Dolly the Sheep Dies Young," *New Scientist* 17 (February 14, 2003): 56. For subsequent scientific study of premature aging in cloned mice, see Narumi Ogonuki and others, "Early Death of Mice Cloned from Somatic Cells," *Nature Genetics* 30 (February 11, 2002): 253–254; for a refutation of this hypothesis in cattle, see R. P. Lanza and others, "Cloned Cattle Can Be Healthy and Normal," *Science* 294, no. 5546 (November 16, 2001): 1459–1462.

57. Sarah Franklin, "Life Itself: Global Nature and the Genetics Imaginary," in *Global Nature, Global Culture,* ed. Sarah Franklin, Celia Lury, and Jackie Stacey (London: SAGE, 2000), pp. 188–227, quote p. 203. Cf. Franklin's "Dolly Mixtures: Capitalisation of the Germplasm," in *Genetic Nature-Culture,* ed. A. Goodman, D. Heath, and S. Lindee (Berkeley: University of California Press, 2003), pp. 221–245.

58. Franklin, "Life Itself," p. 188.

59. Leslie Pray, "Missyplicity Goes Commercial," *The Scientist* (November 27, 2002), www.the-scientist.com/news/20021127/03 (accessed December 5, 2005). "First Pet Clone is a Cat," *BBC News Online*, February 15, 2002, http://news.bbc.co.uk/1/hi/sci/tech/1820749.stm (accessed September 9, 2003).

60. Cf. Susan McHugh, "Bitches from Brazil: Cloning and Owning Dogs through The Missyplicity Project," in *Representing Animals,* ed. Nigel Rothfels (Bloomington: Indiana University Press, 2002), pp. 180–198.

61. See various articles by scientists and science writers (including Gretchen Vogel of *Science*) on ANDi at the home laboratory's Web site: www.grg.org/OHSUmonkey.htm (accessed March 18, 2006).

62. Linda Bren, "Cloning: Revolution of Evolution in Animal Production," *FDA Consumer,* May–June 2003, www.fda.gov/fdac/features/2003/303_clone.html (accessed March 18, 2006).

63. Q. Zhou and others, "Generation of Fertile Cloned Rats Using Controlled Timing of Oocyte Activation," *Sciencexpress* (2003): http://doi:10.1126/science.1088313 (accessed September 30, 2005).

64. Gordon L. Woods and others, "A Mule Cloned from Fetal Cells by Nuclear Transfer," *Science* 301, no. 5636 (August 22, 2003): 1063.

65. Elizabeth Pennis, "Cut-Rate Genetics on the Horizon?" *Science* 309, no. 5736 (August 5, 2005): 862.

66. Edward Winstead, "Endangered Wild Sheep Clone Reported to be Healthy," *Genome News Network,* October 12, 2001, www.genomenewsnetwork.org/articles/10_01/cloned_sheep.shtml (accessed March 18, 2006); Robert P. Lanza, Betsy L. Dresser, and Philip Damiani, "Cloning Noah's Ark," *Scientific American,* November 2000; Julie Grisham, "Pigs Cloned for First Time," *Nature Biotechnology* 18, no. 4 (2000): 365; Natasha McDowell, "Mini-Pig Clone Raises Transplant Hope," *New Scientist* 16, no. 35 (January 13, 2003).

67. Cf. Mark Westhusin: "This is just an assisted reproductive technology. We're not trying to resurrect animals or get animals back." Qtd. in Bren, "Cloning: Revolution or Evolution." Cf. National Academy of Sciences, "Animal Biotechnology: Science-Based Concerns," Committee on Defining Science-Based Concerns Associated with Products of Animal Biotechnology, Committee on Agricultural Biotechnology, Health, and the Environment, National Research Council (Washington, DC: National Academy of Sciences Press, 2002).

68. Cloned animals and transgenic animals are sometimes mistaken to be the same, but they are different. Transgenic animals are produced by adding or removing genes, or by altering the expression of their existing gene; this process can involve genetic information taken from different species or created in DNA synthesizing machines. Cloned animals are produced using bioengineering techniques (primarily, somatic cell nuclear transfer [SCNT]) but are intended to be biological copies of existing animals. For more on transgenic animals see Donna Haraway, *Modest Witness*, and Carol Lewis, "A New Kind of Fish Food: The Coming of Biotech Animals," *FDA Consumer,* January–February 2001, www.fda.gov/fdac/features/2001/101_fish.html (accessed March 18, 2006).

69. Carol Tucker Foreman, "Animal Cloning: New Issues in Public Policy" (remarks at the FDA/PIFB Workshop on Animal Cloning and Production of Food Products, Dallas, September 26, 2002).

70. M. C. Nisbet and Bruce Lewenstein, "Biotechnology and the American Media: The Policy Process and the Elite Press, 1970 to 1999," *Science Communication* 23, no. 4 (2002): 359–391.

71. Institute of Medicine, "Xenotransplantation: Science, Ethics, and Public Policy" (Washington, DC: National Academy Press, 1996), especially chapter 4, which discusses ethics in terms of patient-informed consent and fairness of animal organ allocation systems.

72. Arnold Arluke, "'We Build a Better Beagle': Fantastic Creatures in Lab Animal Ads," *Qualitative Sociology* 17, no. 2 (1994): 143–158, quote p. 156. Cf. also Arnold Arluke, "Sacrificial Symbolism in Animal Experimentation: Object or Pet?" *Anthrozoos* 4 (1988): 88–112.

73. Donna Haraway, *Modest Witness*.

74. Aldous Huxley, *Brave New World: A Novel* (New York: Harpers, 1932); On the history of eugenic sterilization laws in America, see Paul Lombardo, "Eugenic Sterilization Laws," Essay for the Human Genome Project Eugenics Archive, 2003, www.eugenicsarchive.org/html/eugenics/essay8text.html (accessed December 19, 2003); see also "Miscegenation, Eugenics and Racism: Historical Footnotes to Loving v. Virginia," *University of California Davis Law Review* 21 (1988): 421–452.

75. Zadie Smith, *White Teeth* (New York: Random House, 2000).

76. Smith, *White Teeth*, quotes p. 401 and p. 357, respectively.

Chapter 6

1. Indeed he is the towering exception to the otherwise accurate observation that "the first half of the twentieth century witnessed a lull in both philosophical thought and political activism involving animals." Helena Silverstein, *Unleashing Rights: Law, Meaning, and the Animal Rights Movement* (Ann Arbor: University of Michigan Press, 1996), p. 43.

2. "Man and Creature," in *The Teaching of Reverence for Life*, trans. R. and C. Winston (New York: Holt, Rinehart and Winston, 1965), p. 50.

3. C. R. Joy, trans. and ed., "Philosophy and the Movement for the Protection of Animals," in *The Animal World of Albert Schweitzer: Jungle Insights into Reverence for Life* (Hopewell, NJ: Ecco, 1996), chap. 15, p. 185.

4. As excerpted at http://www.schweitzer.org/english/ase/aseref.htm from *The Philosophy of Civilization*, 1926, chap. 26, and "The Ethics of Reverence for Life," *Christendom* (Winter 1936).

5. Ibid.

6. Joy, "Philosophy and Protection", p. 183. Cf. Rod Preece's revisionist correction: "From the perspective of the animal, there is much to be welcomed in the philosophies of the Orient. It is unfortunate, however, that those who write to praise Eastern thought systems rarely recognize the worth of their Western counterparts and fail to notice the negative aspects of the Eastern traditions." From "Aboriginal and Oriental Harmony with Nature," in *Animals and Nature: Cultural Myths, Cultural Realities* (Vancouver: University of British Columbia Press, 1999), chap. 7, p. 214.

7. Joy, "Philosophy and Protection," p. 186.

8. Ibid., pp. 184–185.

9. Ibid., p. 187.

10. "An Absolute Ethic," in *The Animal World of Albert Schweitzer,* trans. and ed. Charles R. Joy (Hopwell, NJ: Ecco Press, 1950) p. 189 (emphasis added).

11. This phenomenon did not appear entirely *de novo;* it was more a reemergence, with precursors ranging from Plutarch and Porphyry in antiquity to Henry Salt in the nineteenth century.

12. See Lisa Mighetto's *Wild Animals and American Environmental Ethics* (Tucson: University of Arizona Press, 1991), esp. chaps. 6, 7.

13. Adrian Franklin, *Animals and Modern Cultures: A Sociology of Human-Animal Relations in Modernity* (London: Sage, 1999), chap. 3.

14. Richard Bulliet, *Hunters, Herders, and Hamburgers: The Past and Future of Human-Animal Relationships* (New York: Columbia University Press, 2005), p. 35.

15. Peter Singer, *Animal Liberation: A New Ethics for Our Treatment of Animals* (New York: Avon Books, 1975), chap. 1.

16. Ibid., chap. 6.

17. Ibid., chaps. 2, 3.

18. In the aforementioned cases, it is not economically feasible at full-scale supermarket provision of meat or dairy to manage livestock according to strictly humane standards, and different species' variability from each other much more often than not make research extrapolation or therapeutic consumption of nonhuman data or bodies scientifically suspect.

19. This remark may sound odd to nonphilosophers (and vaguely insulting to at least some philosophers)—it is not that professional philosophers are necessarily disbelievers in the dignity of humankind, rather that many of them find conceptual flaws in the very notion of "right" itself.

20. Tom Regan, *The Case for Animal Rights* (Berkeley: University of California, 1983), chaps. 7, 8.

21. Ibid., p. 243.

22. Some anthropocentrist critics will charge that this is not enough, because the story at stake must be (able to be) told *by the being herself*—namely, subjectivity must entail *auto*biographical capacity. Such a definition may be deemed too narrow, however, since it would rule out many marginal humans (e.g., the severely senile or intellectually challenged) whom most would not want to discount as subjects-of-a-life.

23. Singer, *Animal Rights*, chaps. 1, 2.

24. Ibid., chap. 9.

25. For defense of such, see Val Plumwood's critical discussion of the "use exclusion assumption" in her *Environmental Culture: The Ecological Crisis of Reason* (London: Routledge, 2002), pp. 156–159.

26. Obviously, invitation and encouragement of this sort begs for rhetorical tact on the part of any dominant-culture academics or activists involved; ideally, too, such exhortations would come *from within* communities of primal peoples or First Nations themselves.

27. The rest of this paragraph, as well as the next, derive largely from chapter 4 of my book, *Corporal Compassion: Animal Ethics and Philosophy of Body* (Pittsburgh: University of Pittsburgh Press, 2006).

28. As Silverstein notes, "The 1970s and 1980s witnessed a move away from the discourse of compassion that had been the primary mode of conversation concerning animals for more than a century." *Unleashing Rights*, pp. 27–28.

29. Ibid., p. 46.

30. *Perception, Empathy, and Judgment* (State College, PA: Pennsylvania State University Press, 1994), pp. 210–216.

31. Josephine Donovan, "Attention to Suffering," in *Beyond Animal Rights,* ed. J. Donovan and C. J. Adams (New York: Continuum, 1996), p. 158.

32. Carol Gilligan, *In a Different Voice* (Cambridge, MA: Harvard University Press, 1982).

33. Nel Noddings, *Caring: A Feminine Approach to Ethics and Moral Education* (Berkeley: University of California Press, 1984).

34. Josephine Donovan, "Animal Rights and Feminist Theory," in *Beyond Animal Rights: A Feminist Caring Ethic for the Treatment of Animals,* ed. J. Donovan and C. Adams (1990; repr., New York: Continuum, 1996), p. 40.

35. D. Slicer, "Your Daughter or Your Dog?" in *Ecological Feminist Philosophies,* ed. K. Warren (1991; repr., Bloomington: Indiana University Press, 1996), p. 102.

36. Slicer, "Daughter or Dog?" p. 100.

37. Val Plumwood, "The Ethics of Commodification," in *Environmental Culture: The Ecological Crisis of Reason* (London: Routledge, 2002), chap. 2, p. 147. It is not clear that this objection stands up to scrutiny, because Singer and Regan do not use humanity as a moral standard first and then go out looking for humanoids to protect—rather they start out from sentience or subjectivity as a standard for moral considerability and point out that such a criterion happens to include (most) humans and a good number of nonhumans as well. Even if these theorists or their followers do harbor underlying speciesist inclinations, there does not appear to be anything about the theories themselves that logically assumes or entails speciesism.

38. Ibid., p. 101. No *good* reason—that is, aside from a minimalism that "is not able to recognize consciousness as just one among many relevant differences among species, differences which are largely incommensurable as to value rather than hierarchically ordered along the lines of resemblance to the human" (Plumwood, p. 148).

39. Donovan, "Animal Rights and Feminist Theory," p. 52.

40. The following passage is derived from portions of my essay, "The Problematic Situation of Post-Humanism and the Task of Recreating a Symphysical Ethos," *Between the Species* 11, nos. 1/2 (Winter/Spring 1995): 25–28. For commentary, see in that journal's same issue Kenneth Shapiro's "The Lived-Bodily Basis of an Animal-Friendly Ethic," pp. 29–32.

41. Edith Wyschogrod, "Does Continental Ethics Have a Future?" in *Ethics and Danger,* ed. A. Dallery and others (Albany: State University of New York Press, 1992), p. 236.

42. Mental factors (e.g., second-order consciousness of each other's mutual recognition) must also come into play for respect in this sense to emerge fully as a moral phenomenon.

43. David Seamon uses the word in his "Different Worlds Coming Together: A Phenomenology of Relationship," in *Dwelling, Seeing, and Designing: Toward a Phenomenological Ecology* (Albany: State University of New York Press, 1993); as he notes, it originated in medical usage and means in ancient Greek "the state of growing together" (p. 230).

44. European philosophy from Aristotle to Hegel and Marx has evolved a tradition of philosophical anthropology on the premise of studying the *human* animal's species-being strictly; the posthumanist task before us late moderns is to go beyond that tradition's homoexclusive bounds into the ontology both of generic animality (if there be such) and of nonhuman speciations (to whatever extent accessible).

45. Compare Sue Cataldi's *Emotion, Depth, and Flesh: A Study of Sensitive Space* (Albany: State University of New York Press, 1993), and the neo-Confucian ideal of "forming One Body" with all other corporeal beings (as per Wang Yang-ming, in

Tu Weiming's "The Ecological Turn in New Confucian Humanism," Tasan Lecture no. 1, South Korea, November 2001, http://smedia.vermotion.com/media/12002/resources/TuEcology.pdf [accessed June 1, 2007]).

46. The "carnosphere" to which I refer is akin to what the late Maurice Merleau-Ponty called "flesh-of-the-world;" cf. David Abram's "Merleau-Ponty and the Voice of the Earth," *Environmental Ethics* 10, no. 2 (Summer 1988): 101–120, and Elizabeth Behnke's "From Merleau-Ponty's Concept of Nature to an Interspecies Practice of Peace," in *Animal Others: On Ethics, Ontology, and Animal Life*, ed. H. Peter Steeves (Albany: State University of New York Press, 1999), chap. 5, esp. pp. 100–111.

47. Emmanuel Levinas, "The Name of a Dog, or Natural Rights," in *Animal Philosophy: Ethics and Identity*, ed. P. Atterton and M. Calarco (London: Continuum, 2004), p. 49; from Levinas' *Difficult Freedom*, trans. S. Hand (Baltimore: Johns Hopkins University Press, 1990), p. 153.

48. Emmanuel Levinas, "Interview," in *Animal Philosophy*, p. 50; from "The Paradox of Morality," trans. A. Benjamin and T. Wright, in *The Provocation of Levinas*, ed. R. Bernasconi and D. Wood (London: Routledge, 1988), p. 172.

49. James Hart, "Transcendental Phenomenology and the Eco-Community," in *Animal Others: On Ethics, Ontology, and Animal Life*, ed. H. Peter Steeves (Albany: State University of New York Press, 1999), p. 187.

50. Ibid., p. 192. For greater detail on this insight, see these works of Hart's student and colleague, H. Peter Steeves: "The Boundaries of the Phenomenological Community: Non-Human Life and the Extent of Our Moral Enmeshment," in *Becoming Persons*, ed. R. Fisher (Oxford: Applied Theology Press, 1995), pp. 777–797; and H. Peter Steeves, *Founding Community* (Dordrecht: Kluwer, 1998).

51. James Hart, "Transcendental Phenomenology and the Eco-Community," in *Animal Others: On Ethics, Ontology, and Animal Life*, ed. H. Peter Steeves (Albany: State University of New York Press, 1999), p. 190. Here we are not so far from the way in which Regan considers mammals to be subjects-of-a-life.

52. "Name of a Dog," p. 49.

53. At pp. 190ff. of "Eco-Community," for instance.

54. Ibid., p. 191.

55. See Rosalind Hursthouse's *Ethics, Humans and Other Animals* (New York: Routledge, 2000), esp. commentary on Mary Midgley, and *Animal Pragmatism: Rethinking Human-Nonhuman Relationships*, ed. E. McKenna and A. Light (Bloomington: Indiana University Press, 2004).

56. The exceptions to this consensus are far and few between—they include Tibor Machan, *Putting Humans First: Why We Are Nature's Favorite* (Lanham, MD: Rowman and Littlefield, 2004); Michael Leahy, *Against Liberation* (New York: Routledge, 1991); perhaps Jan Narveson, "Animal Rights," *Canadian Journal of Philosophy* 10 (1980): 463–471; and arguably R. G. Frey, "Rights, Interests, Desires and Beliefs," *American Philosophical Quarterly* 79, no. 16 (1979): 233–239. In fact, there is in the published record a rather poignant instance of conversion from the exploitive to the respectful attitude: see Michael Allen Fox's dramatic about-face from *The Case for Animal Experimentation: An Evolutionary and Ethical Perspective* (Berkeley: University of California Press, 1986) to *Deep Vegetarianism* (Philadelphia: Temple University Press, 1999).

57. The next two paragraphs are drawn partially from chapter 1 of my *Corporal Compassion*.

58. Though I refer below to the midcentury translation of his *Streifzüge durch die Umwelten von Tieren und Menschen* (original 1934), there are also earlier works of his on similar themes: *Theoretische Biologie* (1928) and *Umwelt und Innenwelt der Tiere* (1921).

59. Jakob von Uexküll, "A Stroll through the Worlds of Animals and Men," in *Instinctive Behavior: The Development of a Modern Concept,* trans. C. H. Schiller (New York: International Universities Press, 1957), p. 6 (emphasis added). Uexküll and his publishers made creative use of the print technology available during their time, attempting to represent various animals' *Umwelten* through illustrations, diagrams, and photographs (see p. 26); in fact, the paradoxical subtitle of this quaint work is "A Picture Book of Invisible Worlds."

60. On the intersection of animal ontology and post-Kantian epistemology, see my "The Joyful Wisdom of Ecology: From Nietzsche to Rolston on Perspectival and Relational Contact with Nature and Animality," *New Nietzsche Studies* 5, nos. 3/4 and 6, no. 1/2 (Winter 2003/ Spring 2004), pp. 22–34.

61. Jakob von Uexküll, "A Stroll through the Worlds of Animals and Men," p. 72. At the very end of this work (p. 80), Uexküll allows himself to wax quasi-mystical: "And yet all these diverse *Umwelten* are harbored and borne by the One that remains forever barred to all *Umwelten.* Behind all the worlds created by Him, there lies concealed, eternally beyond the reach of knowledge, the subject—Nature."

62. The next two paragraphs derive partially from chapter 2 of my *Corporal Compassion.*

63. See sections 45–48 of Martin Heidegger, *The Fundamental Concepts of Metaphysics: World, Finitude, Solitude,* trans. W. McNeill and N. Walker (Bloomington: Indiana University Press, 1995), pt. 2, chap. 3.

64. Ibid., pp. 38–40.

65. Ibid., p. 40.

66. Ibid., p. ix.

67. Gilles Deleuze and Félix Guattari, *A Thousand Plateaus,* vol. 2 of *Capitalism and Schizophrenia,* trans. B. Massumi (Minneapolis: University of Minnesota Press, 1987).

68. James Urpeth, "Animal Becomings," in *Animal Philosophy,* p. 102.

69. Ibid., p. 104.

70. For an illustration of such animality, see the discourse on rats running through Nick Land's "Spirit and Teeth," in *Of Derrida, Heidegger, and Spirit,* ed. D. Wood (Evanston, IL: Northwestern University Press, 1993).

71. Deleuze and Guattari, *A Thousand Plateaus,* pp. 240–243.

72. Edward S. Reed, "The Affordances of the Animate Environment," in *What Is an Animal?* ed. T. Ingold (London: Unwin Hyman, 1988), pp. 114–115, 117–118.

73. Ibid., p. 113. Or again, at p. 111: "By an environment I mean the surroundings of animals, with the earth below and the sky above, with places filled with useful resources, inanimate and animate objects."

74. Ibid., pp. 122–123. For Reed, it is worth noting, many if not most mammals and birds share a common (at least conspecific) *social* environment in virtue of their capabilities to recognize that they themselves present affordances to others and that others' particular affordances may vary from their own.

75. See Ingold's editorial remark: "Reed holds ... that animacy is an inherent characteristic of environmental objects with the power of autonomous movement, quite independently of the symbolic interpretation that human subjects of one culture or

another might place upon them. Because of their distinctive properties of transformational growth and non-repetitive motion, we *see* animals as such, irrespective of how we might [later] come to describe or classify them" (p. 12).

76. For representatives of this view, see anthropologist Richard Tapper's "Animality, Humanity, Morality, Society," in Ingold (chap. 4), and sociologist Keith Tester's *Animals and Society: The Humanity of Animal Rights* (London: Routledge, 1991).

77. See Carol Adams' major work, *The Sexual Politics of Meat: A Feminist-Vegetarian Critical Theory* (New York: Continuum, 1990).

78. The (dis)assembly-line operation of slaughterhouses and meatpacking plants in Chicago and Cincinnati predate Fordist car factories by half a century or more.

79. Last two quotations from Adams, "The Rape of Animals, The Butchering of Women," in *Sexual Politics of Meat,* pp. 47–48.

80. Jacques Derrida, "The Animal That Therefore I Am (More to Follow)," trans. D. Wills, *Critical Inquiry* 28, no. 2 (Winter 2002): 408.

81. Ibid., 409.

82. Ibid., 415. Second quotation from "And Say the Animal Responded?" trans. D. Wills, in *Zoontologies,* ed. C. Wolfe (Minneapolis: University of Minnesota Press, 2003), p. 128.

83. Such was Adrian Franklin's prognostication, for example, in his concluding speech at the *Animal Arenas* conference sponsored by the International Society for Anthrozoölogy in London (University College, 2002). Cf. Keith Ansell-Pearson's postmodern variant of Bergsonism in *Germinal Life* (London: Routledge, 1999).

84. Bulliet, *Hunters, Herders, and Hamburgers,* p. 207.

85. On the prospects for multispecies urbanization, see the growing literature in animal geography—such as Jennifer Wolch's "*Anima Urbis,*" *Progress in Human Geography* 26, no. 6 (2002): 721–742; on technicized animality, see Ursula Heise's "From Extinction to Electronics: Dead Frogs, Live Dinosaurs, and Electric Sheep," in *Zoontologies,* ed. C. Wolfe (Minneapolis: University of Minnesota Press, 2003), pp. 59–81, and Jami Weinstein's *Returning [to] the Level of the Skin and Beyond: A Techno-Zoontology* (PhD diss., CUNY Graduate School and University Center / L'Ecole des Hautes Etudes en Sciences Sociales, 2005), pt. 2, esp. sec. 7, "The Flight Beyond a Taxidermic Ontology."

86. The former originally appeared in *Socialist Review* 80 (1985): 65–108 and has been revised and reprinted in numerous and various venues; the latter was published in Chicago by Prickly Paradigm Press (2003)—see also her videotaped lecture at McGill University, "We Have Never Been Human" (Montreal, 2004).

Chapter 7

1. The aim of this chapter is twofold. Confronted with a huge amount of material I have attempted to offer something of a general introduction by selecting a number of well-known works that reveal how the animal figure operates in twentieth-century art. At the same time I try to convey the extraordinary diversity of what might be included under the rubric of animal art. Much of this material will doubtless be familiar to art historians but the purpose of the analysis is very much to look at art history through an animal studies lens. This chapter is necessarily full of omissions, but is intended as a preliminary overview, and the works cited in the footnotes contain further references to many more artists and artworks. I have

used terms such as "sublime" and "antisublime," "animal," "human," and "animal art" fairly loosely throughout. Contests over such terminology can be found in many of the works cited herein, though there is not enough space to reproduce such discussions in the main text. This work comes out of a longstanding engagement with the work of Steve Baker to whom this chapter is dedicated in gratitude. My thanks also to Nicky Zeeman.

2. Martin Herbert, "Old Dogs—New Tricks," *Art Review* (June 2000): 36.

3. Monica Bohm-Duchen, *Chagall* (London: Phaidon, 1998), p. 5.

4. Peter de Bolla, *Art Matters* (Cambridge, MA: Harvard University Press, 2001), pp. 4–5.

5. Qtd. in Allen Roberts, *Animals in African Art: From the Familiar to the Marvellous* (New York: Museum of African Art, 1995), p. 14.

6. Steve Baker, *The Postmodern Animal* (London: Reaktion, 2000), pp. 20–21.

7. Michael W. Munroe, *The Animal Image: Contemporary Objects and the Beast* (Washington, DC: Smithsonian Institution Press, 1981), p. 7

8. On theories of sacrifice and their importance for cultural formation see R. G. Hammerton-Kelly, ed., *Violent Origins: Ritual Killing and Cultural Formation* (Stanford: Stanford University Press, 1987); Cary Wolfe, *Animal Rites: American Culture, the Discourse of Species, and Posthumanist Theory* (Chicago: Chicago University Press, 2003), pp. 100–101. For an outline of non-Western sacrifice see Luc de Heusch, *Sacrifice in Africa: A Structuralist Approach* (Manchester: Manchester University Press, 1985).

9. Theodora Vischer, ed., *Mark Wallinger: Lost Horizon* (Basel, Switzerland: Museum für Gegenwartskunst, 2000), p. 20. This split is exemplified by Wallinger in his *Half-Brother* series (1994–1995) in which the paintings of horses are split down the middle so that the back half of the body is a portrait of a different thoroughbred from the front half.

10. On the aestheticization of wild animals in Africa, see V. Y. Mudimbe, "*Reprendre:* Enunciations and Strategies in Contemporary African Arts," in *Reading the Contemporary: African Art from Theory to the Marketplace,* ed. Olu Oguibe and Okwui Enwezor (London: IVA, 1999), pp. 42–43.

11. Paul Crowther, *Art and Embodiment: From Aesthetics to Self-consciousness* (Oxford: Clarendon Press, 1993), p. 166.

12. Ibid., p. 151. Reversibility is the capacity to see oneself as part of a broader phenomenological field.

13. See Steve Baker's discussion of the parallels between becoming-animal in Deleuze and Guattari and the practice of art, *The Postmodern Animal* (London: Reaktion, 2000), pp. 138–140.

14. Steve Baker, "What Does Becoming-Animal Look Like?" in *Representing Animals,* ed. Nigel Rothfels (Bloomington: Indiana University Press, 2002), p. 74.

15. I have confined myself mainly to the plastic arts. Here is a very preliminary list of references for other instances of animal art. On film art, see Jonathan Burt, *Animals in Film* (London: Reaktion, 2002), pp. 50–51, 191–196; Andy Bellows and Marina Macdougall with Brigitte Berg, *Science Is Fiction: The Films of Jean Painlevé* (Cambridge, MA: MIT Press, 2000); Akira Lippit, "The Death of an Animal," *Film Quarterly* 56 (2002): pp. 9–22; Ruth Jones, "Becoming Hysterical—Becoming-Animal—Becoming Woman in *The Horse Impressionists," Journal of Visual Practice* 3 (2004): 123–138; Laura Marks, "Animal Identifications, Animal Appetites," *Parachute* 72 (1993): 26–30. On

photography see Steve Baker, *Postmodern Animal,* for remarks on Britta Jaschinski see especially pp. 145–148; Kitty Hauser, "Coming Apart at the Seams: Taxidermy and Contemporary Photography," *Make* 82 (1998–1999): 8–11; Frank Horvart, *Virtual Zoo* (Washington, DC: Smithsonian Institution Press, 1998); Alexandra Noble, ed., *The Animal in Photography 1843–1985* (London: The Photographer's Gallery, 1986); C. W. Guggisberg, *Early Wildlife Photographers* (New York: Taplinger Publishing Co., 1977). For animals in drama see, for instance, Una Chaudhuri, "Animal Geographies: Zooësis and the Space of Modern Drama," *Modern Drama* 46 (2003): 646–662. On animals in music there is the well known influence of birdsong for composers such as Messaien, and operas such as Janacek's *Cunning Little Vixen* and Peter Greenaway's *Rosa: A Horse Opera.* See De Voy Merry, "Horse Opera," *World Art* 2 (1995): 64–69.

16. John F. Moffit, "Fighting Forms: *The Fate of the Animals.* The Occultist Origins of Franz Marc's 'Farbentheorie,'" *Artibus et Historiae* 6 (1985): 123.

17. Herschel B. Chipp, *Theories of Modern Art: A Source Book by Artists and Critics* (Berkeley: University of California Press, 1968), p. 178.

18. Ibid., p. 179.

19. Mark Rosenthal, *Franz Marc* (Munich: Prestel, 2004), p. 14.

20. Klaus Lankheit, *Franz Marc: Watercolours, Drawings, Writings* (London: Thames and Hudson, 1960). For a detailed study of the animal figures in *Fate of the Animals* and related artworks, see also Andreas Hüneke, *Franz Marc Tierschicksale: kunst als Heilsgeschichte* (Frankfurt: Fischer Taschenbuch Verlag, 1994).

21. As Levine points out there are a number of paintings with apocalyptic themes leading up to *Fate of the Animals* in 1913 and then, as if acting as a watershed, a number of paintings and woodcuts indicating rebirth, all of which depict animals (for example, *The First Animals, The World Cow, Birth of the Wolves, Birth of the Horses*). F. S Levine, *The Apocalyptic Vision: The Art of Franz Marc as German Expressionism* (New York: Harper and Row, 1979), pp. 136–137.

22. Chipp, *Theories of Modern Art,* p. 182.3

23. Frederick S. Levine, "The Iconography of Franz Marc's *Fate of the Animals,*" *The Art Bulletin* 58 (1976): 269. The painting was damaged in a fire in November 1916. Paul Klee reconstructed the right hand side of the painting but didn't attempt to reproduce the coloring.

24. Rosalind Krauss, *The Opticalunconscious* (Cambridge, MA: MIT Press, 1993), p. 21.

25. Ibid.

26. Gérard Durozoi, *History of the Surrealist Movement* (Chicago: University of Chicago Press, 2002), p. 81.

27. André Breton, *Manifestoes of Surrealism* (Ann Arbor: University of Michigan Press, 1972), p. 40. I have used the word "unacknowledgeable" here, rather than "inadmissible," which is in the English translation, to get across a better sense of the ambivalence at work here. The monsters and hybrid animals arise in the context of remarks on surrealism's return to childhood, which may be a return to salvation or perdition. "In the shadow we again see a precious terror." The meaning in French of *inavouable* as referring to something best kept hidden for moral reasons reinforces the links between childhood sexual fantasies, the unconscious, and animals that needs to be kept in mind given the importance of Freud to surrealism. See Hal Foster, *Compulsive Beauty* (Cambridge, MA: MIT Press, 1995), chap. 3. Breton's "Soluble Fish" (1924) is a collection of hallucinatory prose pieces.

28. Durozoi, *History,* p. 53.

29. Werner Spies, *Max Ernst Loplop: The Artist's Other Self* (London: Thames and Hudson, 1983), p. 99.

30. Ibid., p. 79. Note also p. 78 where Spies discusses the difference between Ernst's Loplop and Picasso's minotaur.

31. *Max Ernst: Beyond Painting and Other Writings by the Artist and His Friends* (New York: Wittenborn, Schultz, 1948), p. 28.

32. Hal Foster, *Compulsive Beauty,* pp. 80–81: "Ernst frames an aesthetic discovery in terms of an infantile one, the visual fascinations and (pre)sexual confusions of the primal scene. This association determines not only his definition of collage, 'the coupling of two realities, irreconcilable in appearance, upon a plane which apparently does not suit them' (BP 13), but also his understanding of its purpose: collage disturbs the 'the principle of identity' (BP 19), even 'abolishes' the concept of 'author' (BP20)." BP refers to *Beyond Painting* as referenced in note 31. In relation to identity and trauma it is important to note here the significance of the animal in *Art Brut* and in the work of psychiatric patients. See Lucienne Peiry, *L'Art brut* (Paris: Flammarion, 1997); John M. Macgregor, *The Discovery of the Art of the Insane* (Princeton: Princeton University Press, 1989); D. Maclagan, "Gaston Duf," *Raw Vision* 31 (2000): 65; Carola Long, "Freddie Brice," *Raw Vision* 32 (2000): 62–63.

33. Durozoi, *History,* p. 118.

34. Paul Hammond, *L'Age d'Or* (London: BFI, 1997), p. 9. See also his remarks about Buñuel and insects, pp. 10–12.

35. For a general discussion of animals in Picasso see Neil Cox and Deborah Povey, *A Picasso Bestiary* (London: Academy Editions, 1995).

36. H. B. Chipp, *Picasso's Guernica: History, Transformations, Meanings* (Berkeley: University of California Press, 1988), p. 43. Herschel Chipp has written one of the most convincing texts on *Guernica,* and I largely follow his account here.

37. Cox and Povey, *A Picasso Bestiary,* p. 24.

38. H. B. Chipp, "*Guernica:* Love, War, and the Bullfight," *Art Journal* 33 (1973–1974): 103. Chipp points out that the bull horse encounter has no iconographic or emotional significance during the Blue Period or Cubism.

39. John Richardson, *A Life of Picasso: Volume 1 1881–1906* (London: Pimlico, 1991), p. 31.

40. Garry Marvin, *Bullfight* (Oxford: Blackwell, 1988), p. 22.

41. Chipp, *Picasso's Guernica,* p. 50.

42. Rachel Wischnitzer, "Picasso's *Guernica:* A Matter of Metaphor," *Artibus et Historiae* 6 (1985): 165n.

43. See Maria Manuel Lisboa, *Paula Rego's Map of Memory: National and Sexual Politics* (Aldershot, UK: Ashgate, 2003), pp. 38, 44; John McEwen, *Paula Rego,* 2nd ed. (London: Phaidon, 1997), p. 216.

44. Allen Leepa, *The Challenge of Modern Art* (London: Peter Owen, 1957), p. 235. The wording is a little different from that quoted in Dore Ashton, *Picasso on Art: A Selection of Views* (London: Thames and Hudson, 1972), p. 155, though it does not alter the point. On Picasso's attitudes to animals, especially his dogs, see Cox and Povey, *A Picasso Bestiary,* pp. 112–117.

45. Ashton, *Picasso on Art,* p. 137.

46. Willemijn Stokvis, *Cobra: An International Movement in Art after the Second World War* (New York: Rizzoli, 1988). Asgar Jorn, one of the members, had founded

a review in 1941 named *Helhesten, the Horse of Hell,* a three-legged harbinger of death from Scandinavian mythology. The name was intended as an allusion to the Nazis. In keeping with the idea of distorting animals, this particular figure was in fact a sad creature who wanders around neighing pathetically, unable to find food, p. 10.

47. On the significance of the chicken see Roberts, *Animals in African Art,* pp. 38–42.

48. John Peffer, "Animal Bodies/Absent Bodies: Disfigurement in Art after Soweto," *Third Text* 17 (2003): 74.

49. Ibid., pp. 75–77.

50. Ileana Marcolescou, "'I Am a Transmitter, I Radiate,' Joseph Beuys," *Sculpture* 24 (2005): 53–54.

51. Caroline Tisdall, *Joseph Beuys Coyote* (Munich: Schirmer Mosel, 1976), p. 26. At the 101 Gallery in Copenhagen in 1966 Beuys performed *Eurasia, 34 Movement of the Siberian Symphony,* whereby he manipulated the body of a hare, scattering white powder between its legs and putting a thermometer in its nose. The hare was, for him, a mediating element for a harmonious reunion of Europe and Asia.

52. Ibid., p. 22.

53. Due to his opposition to the Vietnam War, Beuys was transported to the gallery in an ambulance from the airport, wrapped in felt so as not to set foot on American soil outside the gallery.

54. Mark Rosenthal, *Joseph Beuys: Actions, Vitrines, Environments* (Houston: Menil Collection, 2004), p. 24.

55. Tisdall, *Beuys,* p. 24.

56. Ibid., p. 28.

57. Ibid., p. 22.

58. Barbara C. Matilsky, *Fragile Ecologies: Contemporary Artists' Interpretations and Solutions* (New York: Rizzoli, 1992), p. 38. Process art was defined by the use of nonrigid materials that could be scattered, thrown, or poured. The compositions were determined by chance. "By allowing nature itself to determine the form and content of the work, environmental artists share many of the concerns defined by process art."

59. Ibid., pp. 40–53.

60. Miwon Kwon, "Unnatural Tendencies: Scientific Guises of Mark Dion," in *Natural History and Other Fictions—An Exhibition by Mark Dion* (Birmingham, UK: Ikon Gallery, 1997), p. 38.

61. Miwon Kwon, "In Conversation with Mark Dion," in *Mark Dion,* ed. Lisa Corrin, Miwon Kwon, and Norman Bryson (London: Phaidon, 1997), p. 33.

62. On his other related ecological projects such as *Project for Belize Zoo* (1990) and the *Chicago Urban Ecology Action Group* (1993), see Corrin and others, *Dion,* pp. 81–82.

63. Olly & Suzi, *Arctic Desert Ocean Jungle* (New York: Abrams, 2003), p. 176.

64. Ibid., p. 67.

65. Ibid., p. 187.

66. http://www.ollysuzi.com/statement/index.php (accessed April 2006). Their whole statement reinforces the sense that the interaction of animals and artists carries a wide-ranging conceptual responsibility. "The painting is primarily about representation and symbolism. Whether we place the 'animal as icon,' singular, primitive and large upon the paper or paint the landscape, heard, migration, or movements

of the predatory pack we attempt to integrate clarity and ambiguity in the same painting. Conceptually we aim to raise awareness and an understanding of our subject matter. When possible we incorporate the track, print, spoor or bite of the animal in our work, documenting the habitat or the passing of a creature that is here now but may not be for much longer. This interaction can be viewed as evidence to an event, a form of primal investigation; a physical performance of the senses."

67. I use the term *sublime* in the context of considerations of human–animal identity in art mainly inspired by Peter de Bolla's discussion of the development of the sublime in relation to the constitution of the identity of the subject in the eighteenth century. See his *Discourse of the Sublime: Readings in History, Aesthetics and the Subject* (Oxford: Blackwell, 1989).

68. Rosenthal, *Marc*, p. 38.

69. Damien Hirst and Gordon Burn, *On the Way to Work* (London: Faber, 2001), p. 25.

70. Baker, *Postmodern Animal*, pp. 86–87; Hirst and Burn, *On the Way*, p. 181.

71. Qtd. in Julian Stallabrass, *High Art Lite: British Art in the 1990s* (London: Verso, 1999), p. 20.

72. Another artist who links the color of animal beauty with death in contemporary art is Manuel Vilariño. His dead birds are wrapped in velvets or lie on beds of colored spices habitually used for seasoning meat. See M. Rebollar, "Transcendent Flesh," *Lapiz* 23 (2004): 72. This is a very worthwhile special issue of the journal devoted to animal art.

73. Norman Bryson, "Marc Dion and the Birds of Antwerp," in *Marc Dion*, ed. Corrin and others, pp. 91–93.

74. J. Gambrell, "The Best and the Worst of Times," *Art in America* (November 1992): 54. Kulik has done a number of animal performances including acting as a dog and slaughtering a pig in a gallery for invitees to watch on close circuit video. On issues around the use of live and dead animals in art see Steve Baker, "'You Kill Things to Look at Them': Animal Death in Contemporary Art," in *Killing Animals*, ed. Animal Studies Group (Urbana: University of Illinois Press, 2006), pp. 69–98.

75. Piedad Solans, "Horror and Animality," *Lapiz* 23 (2004): 38–40. Although there are few remarks about animals in the text, there is plenty to explore in the images situating animal figures Paul McCarthy's exploration of an abject aesthetic; Ralph Rugoff, Kristine Stiles, and Giacinto di Pietratonio, *Paul McCarthy* (London: Phaidon, 1996).

76. Rebollar, "Transcendent Flesh," p. 82.

77. Richard Leppert, *Art and the Committed Eye: The Cultural Functions of Imagery* (Boulder, CO: Westview Press, 1996), pp. 90, 94. On some of the paintings that influenced paintings of slaughtered animals in the twentieth century see also Nathaniel Wolloch, "Dead Animals and the Beast-Machine: Seventeenth Century Netherlandish Paintings as Anti-Cartesian Statements," *Art History* 22 (1999): 705–727.

78. On problems raised by slaughter and changing patterns of visibility for the animal in public culture, see Jonathan Burt, "The Illumination of the Animal Kingdom: The Role of Light and Electricity in Animal Representation," *Society and Animals* 9 (2001): 203–228; and Ibid., "Slaughter in Modernity," in *Killing Animals*, ed. Animal Studies Group (Urbana: University of Illinois Press, 2006), pp. 120–144.

79. Sue Coe and Mandy Coe, *Meat: Animals and Industry* (Vancouver: Gallerie, 1991), p. 7. See also Daniel Thomas, "Fleshly Moralities: Ivan Durrant in Melbourne,"

Art Monthly Australia 172 (2004): 31–34; and Julie Lavigne, "Helen Chadwick: l'erotisme de la viande," *Espace* 52 (2000): 24–26.

80. Johannes Brantl, "An den Grenzen des guten Geschmacks? Gedanken zum Orgien Mysterion Theater von Hermann Nitsch," *Das Munster* 4 (1997): 368–376.

81. Agar Ledo, "Intimate Traces," *Lapiz* 23 (2004): 48–63.

82. David Sylvester, *Interviews with Francis Bacon 1962–1979* (London: Thames and Hudson, 1980), p. 46. In relation to the question of undercurrents of desire and animal art one might note as an aside that Bacon's father was a racehorse trainer, and although Bacon disliked him, he was sexually attracted to him when young. "It was only later, through the grooms and the people in the stables I had affairs with, that I realised that it was a sexual thing towards my father" (pp. 71–72).

83. Ibid., p. 48.

84. Gilles Deleuze, *Francis Bacon: The Logic of Sensation* (New York: Continuum, 2005), pp. 16–17.

85. James Mackay, *The Animaliers: The Animal Sculptors of the 19th and 20th Centuries* (London: Ward Lock, 1973), p. 7.

86. For accounts of these artists see Janis Conner and Joel Rosenkranz, *Rediscoveries in American Scultpure: Studio Works 1893–1939* (Austin: University of Texas Press, 1989). Mackay notes that this tradition has produced a number of women sculptors in the twentieth century including Elizabeth Frink, Lorna Mckean, Gillian Wiles, and Jean Walwyn. See Mackay, pp. 133–134, 138.

87. Malcolm Cormack, *Champion Animals: Sculptures by Herbert Heseltine* (Richmond: Virginia Museum of Fine Arts, 1996), p. 1.

88. Ibid., p. 46.

89. Victory Arwas, *Art Deco* (London: Academy Editions, 1980), p. 169.

90. Alan G. Wilkinson, *Henry Moore's Animals* (Ontario: Art Gallery of Ontario, 1990), p. 9. W. J. Strachan, *Henry Moore: Animals* (London: Aurum Press, 1983), p. 33.

91. Baker, *Postmodern Animal,* p. 24.

92. Strachan, *Henry Moore,* p. 9.

93. Wilkinson, *Henry Moore's Animals,* p. 7.

94. Sam Hunter, *Marino Marini: The Sculpture* (New York: Abrams, 1993), p. 18. "As a child, I focused on these two objects, the man and the horse. They were for me a question mark. In the beginning there was "harmony" between them, but eventually the violent world of machines arrived to challenge this unity" (p. 22). See also A. M. Hammacher, *Marino Marini: Sculpture, Painting, Drawing* (London: Thames and Hudson, 1970).

95. Hunter, *Marini,* p. 24.

96. Martha Hill, *Bruno Liljefors: The Peerless Eye* (Hull, UK: Allen Publishing Co., 1987), p. 7.

97. Ibid., pp. 36–37.

98. For one of the few attempts to read an example of wildlife art theoretically, see Alexander Nemerov, "Haunted Supermasculinity: Strength and Death in Carl Rungius's *Wary Game,*" *American Art* 13 (1999): 2–31. Nemerov describes the animals depicted in this painting as caught between symbolizing a heroic supermasculinity yet also as automata "eerily enacting the movements of things long dead and gone."

99. Nicholas Hammond, *Modern Wildlife Painting* (Mountfield, UK: Pica Press, 1998), p. 94.

100. Ibid., p. 9.

101. Obid., p. 122.

102. Nicholas Hammond, *Twentieth Century Wildlife Artists* (London: Croom Helm, 1986), pp. 23–24.

103. Hammond, *Modern Wildlife Painting*, p. 24.

104. Arwas, *Art Deco*, pp. 135–137.

105. Ibid., p. 231. Paul Jouve, who provided the animal designs for Schmied's edition, exhibited his first lions at the age of fifteen at the Salon of the Société Nationale des Beaux-Arts in 1897. Three years later he designed the ceramic animal frieze for the Binet Gate at the 1900 Paris Exhibition. See pp. 201–202.

106. Suzanne Tennenbaum and Janet Zapata, *The Jewelled Menagerie: The World of Animals in Gems* (London: Thames and Hudson, 2001).

107. Janet Zapata, *The Jewelry and Enamels of Louis Comfort Tiffany* (London: Thames and Hudson, 1993), pp. 71, 84.

108. Tennenbaum and Zapata, *Jewelled Menagerie*, p. 100. Bulgari launched a series of Naturalia jewels in 1991 to celebrate nature. An often neglected genre of animal art is medallion art in which animals can be depicted in a variety of imaginative ways. See, for instance, Arnold Nieuwendam, "The Reliefs of Heide Dobberkan," *The Medal* 36 (2000): 70–71; Katarína Bajcurová, "Borders of Relief: The Work of Gabriela Gáspárová-Illéšová," *The Medal* 31 (1997): 105–112; Paula Jackson, "Animal Kingdoms," *The Medal* 34 (1999): 87–91.

109. Hal Foster and others, *Art since 1900: Modernism, Antimodernism, Postmodernism* (London: Thames and Hudson, 2004).

110. There are interesting side stories in this narrative such as Andy Warhol and Jamie Wyeth's taste for collecting taxidermied animals. See Joyce Hill Stoner, "Andy Warhol and Jamie Wyeth—Interactions," *American Art* 13 (1999): 58–83.

111. There have certainly been an increasing number of exhibitions devoted specifically to animals in recent years, and an increasing number of animal art objects in city biennal exhibitions. For a sample, aside from texts cited elsewhere, see for instance Christiane Schneider, ed., *Animals* (London: Haunch of Venison, 2004); Louise Lippincott and Andreas Blühm, *Fierce Friends: Artists and Animals, 1750–1900* (London: Merrell, 2005); Kim Levin, "The Lyon Biennale," *NKA—Contemporary African Art* 13–14 (2001): 96–99; *An Exhibition of Animals in Art* (Art Gallery of South Australia, 1997); Becoming Animal: Art in the Animal Kingdom, Massachussetts Museum of Contemporary Art, presented also in Nato Thompson, ed., *Becoming Animal: Art in the Animal Kingdom* (Cambridge, MA: MIT Press, 2005).

112. On the influence of African art see William Rubin, ed., *Primitivism in 20th Century Art: Affinities of the Tribal and the Modern* (New York: Museum of Modern Art, 1984). On the ambivalence of the Western recognition of that debt see Henry Louis Gates, "Europe, African Art and the Uncanny," in *Africa: The Art of a Continent*, ed. Tom Phillips (Munich: Prestel, 1996), p. 28. On the importance of exhibitions see Christopher Steiner, "Discovering African Art ... Again?" *African Arts* 29 (1996): 1, 4, 6, 8. For the debate on African aesthetics see, for instance, Frank Ugiomoh, "Photo-logos and/or Narrative Semiotics: Which Way to Rehabilitating African Art History?" *Third Text* 18 (2004): 1–11; John Peffer, "Africa's Diaspora of Images," *Third Text* 19 (2005): 339–355.

113. Ima Ebong, "Negritude: Between Mask and Flag—Senegalese Cultural Ideology and the École de Dakar," in *Reading the Contemporary: African Art Theory from*

Theory to the Marketplace, ed. Olu Oguibe and Okwui Enwezor (London: inIVA, 1999), pp. 129–143. On the history of the circulation of African art objects see Christopher B. Steiner, *African Art in Transit* (Cambridge: Cambridge University Press, 1994), pp. 4–7. See also p. 124 for an equation of the treatment of African art with the treatment of animals.

114. Sally Yerkovich, "Preface," in *Animals in Africa—From the Familiar to the Marvellous*, ed. Allen F. Roberts (New York: Museum of African Art, 1995), p. 6. For an example of the richness and manipulation of animal imagery by African artists see Dominique Zahan, "The Two Worlds of Ciwaro," *African Arts* 33 (2000): 33, 35–45, 90–91.

115. Ibid., p. 104.

116. Ibid., p. 22.

117. Ibid., pp. 98–101.

118. Donald Consentino, "Hip-hop Assemblage: The Chris Offili Affair," *African Arts* 33 (2000): 40–51, 95–96.

119. Jonathan Goodman, "Zhou Chunya: Heading Neither East nor West," in *Chinese Art at the Crossroads: Between Past and Future, between East and West*, ed. Wu Hung (London: Institute of International Visual Arts, 2001), p. 299.

120. Xiaoping Lui, "Globalism or Nationalism: Cai Guoqiang, Zhang Huan, and Xu Bing in New York," *Third Text* 18 (2004): 288–289.

121. Ibid., p. 291. See also Liu Wei's *You Like Pork* series (1995) which sets images of cuts of meat and pornography together. Dead animals are also used in Korean art. Bul Lee's *Majestic Splendour* (1995) has decorated, bejeweled fish hanging like a rack of fine clothes. See J. B. Lee, "Desire under Siege," *World Art* 3 (1995): 26–30.

122. Simon Leung and Janet Kaplan, "Pseudo-languages: A Conversation with Wendu Gu, Xu Bing, and Jonathan Hay," *Art Journal* 58 (1999): p. 93.

123. Val Wang, "Animal Games," in *Chinese Art*, pp. 195–199.

124. See Lisa Lynch, "Trans-genesis: An Interview with Eduardo Kac," *New Formations* 49 (2003): 75–90; see also the artist's Web site http://www.ekac.org.

125. Steve Baker, "Philosophy in the Wild? Kac and Derrida on Animals and Responsibility," *New Formations* 49 (2003): 97.

126. Suzanne Anker and Dorothy Nelkin, *The Molecular Gaze: Art in the Genetic Age* (Cold Spring Harbor: Cold Spring Harbor Press, 2004), p. 168. See also Renate Heidt Heller, ed., *Under the Skin: Biological Transformations in Contemporary Art* (Ostfildern-Ruit, Germany: Hatje Cantz Verlag, 2001); Erika Keil and Werner Oder, eds., *Versuchskanninchen—Bilder und andere Manipulationem* (Zurich: Museum für Gestaltung, 1997).

127. Jonathan Burt, *Rat* (London: Reaktion, 2006), pp. 94–96.

128. Laurent Mignonneau and Christa Sommerer, "Creating Artificial Life for Interactive Art and Entertainment," *Leonardo* 34 (2001): 303–307. See also Nell Tenhaaf, "Where Surfaces Meet: Interviews with Stuart Kauffman, Claus Emmeche and Arantza Etxeberria," *Leonardo* 34 (2001): 115–120.

129. http://www.fishandchips.uwa.edu.au/project.html (accessed June 1, 2007).

130. Burt, *Rat*, pp. 111–112.

131. Baker, "Philosophy in the Wild?" p. 98.

BIBLIOGRAPHY

Adams, C. *The Sexual Politics of Meat: A Feminist-Vegetarian Critical Theory.* New York: Continuum, 1990.

Adams, C. "Woman-Battering and Harm to Animals." In *Animals and Women, Feminist Theoretical Explorations,* edited by C. Adams and J. Donovan. Durham, NC: Duke University Press, 1999.

Aftandilian, D., M. Copeland, and D. Wilson. *What Are the Animals to Us? Approaches from Science, Religion, Folklore, Literature, and Art.* Knoxville: University of Tennessee Press, 2006.

Agricultural Marketing Service. "Organic Food Standards and Labels: The Facts." The National Organic Program, United States Department of Agriculture, April 2002.

Akeley, M. *Carl Akeley's Africa.* New York: Blue Ribbon, 1929.

American Pet Product Manufacturing Association. 2005–2006 National Pet Owners' Survey. http://www.appma.org/pubs_survey.asp (accessed June 1, 2007).

Andrews, T. *Animal-Speak: The Spiritual & Magical Powers of Creatures Great & Small.* St. Paul, MN: Llewellyn, 1993.

Anker, S., and D. Nelkin. *The Molecular Gaze: Art in the Genetic Age.* Cold Spring Harbor, NY: Cold Spring Harbor Press, 2004.

Apollodorus. *The Library of Greek Mythology.* Translated by R. Hard. New York: Oxford University Press, 1997.

"Are Mice Smarter Than Men?" *Popular Mechanics* 49 (1928): 519.

Arluke, A. "Sacrificial Symbolism in Animal Experimentation: Object or Pet?" *Anthrozoos* 4 (1988): 88–112.

Arluke, A. "'We Build a Better Beagle': Fantastic Creatures in Lab Animal Ads." *Qualitative Sociology* 17, no. 2 (1994): 143–158.

Arluke, A., and C. Luke. "Physical Cruelty towards Animals in Massachusetts, 1975–1996." *Society and Animals* 5 (1997): 195–204.

Arnst, C. "Building a Smarter Mouse." *Business Week* 3646 (September 13, 1999): 103.

Arwas, V. *Art Deco.* London: Academy Editions, 1980.

Ascione, F. "Battered Women's Reports of Their Partners' and Their Children's Cruelty to Animals." *Journal of Emotional Abuse* 1 (1998): 119–133.

Ascione, F. "Children Who Are Cruel to Animals: A Review of Research and Implications for Developmental Psychopathology." *Anthrozoos* 6 (1993): 226–247.

Ascione, F. "Domestic Violence and Cruelty to Animals." Paper presented at the Fourth International Conference on Family Violence, Durham, NH, July 21–24, 1995.

Ascione, F. "Enhancing Children's Attitudes about the Humane Treatment of Animals: Generalization to Human-Directed Empathy." *Anthrozoos* 5 (1992): 176–191.

Ascione, F., C. Weber, and C. Wood. "The Abuse of Animals and Domestic Violence: A National Survey of Shelters for Women Who Are Battered." *Society and Animals* 5 (1997): 205–218.

"AZA Elephant Care and Conservation Speak Louder than Extremist Hype." *U.S. News Wire,* February 2, 2006. Silver Spring, MD: American Zoo Association, 2006. http://www.elephant-news.com/index.php?id=841 (accessed June 1, 2007).

Bain, D., and B. Harris. *Mickey Mouse: Fifty Happy Years.* New York: Harmony Books, 1977.

Baker, S. "Philosophy in the Wild? Kac and Derrida on Animals and Responsibility." *New Formations* 49 (2003): 97.

Baker, S. *The Postmodern Animal.* London: Reaktion, 2000.

Baker, S. "What Does Becoming-Animal Look Like?" *Representing Animals*, edited by Nigel Rothfels. Bloomington: Indiana University Press, 2002.

Barker, P. "Setting the Stage." In *AZA Communiqué.* Silver Spring, MD: American Zoo Association, August, 2002.

Beckman, B. *Von Mäusen und Menschen: die hoch- und spätmittelalterlichen Mäusesagen mit Kommentar und Anmerkungen.* Bremgarten, Switzerland: Beckman, 1974.

Beetz, A. "Bestiality and Zoophilia: Associations with Violence and Sex Offending." In *Bestiality and Zoophilia: Sexual Relations with Animals*, edited by A. Beetz and A. Podberscek. Lafeyette, IN: Purdue University Press, 2005.

Begley, S. "The Mice That Roared." *Newsweek*, December 4, 1995, 76.

Bell, M. *Childerley: Nature and Morality in a Country Village.* Chicago: University of Chicago Press, 1994.

Benison, S., A. Barger, and E. Wolfe. *Walter B. Cannon.* Cambridge, MA: Harvard University Press, 1987.

Berger, J. *About Looking.* New York: Vintage, 1980.

Birkhead, T. *A Brand New Bird: How Two Amateur Scientists Created the First Genetically Engineered Animal.* New York: Basic Books, 2003.

Blackstock, C. "Tea Party over for PG Tips Chimps." *The Guardian*, December 1, 2001.

Bohm-Duchen, M. *Chagall.* London: Phaidon, 1998.

de Bolla, P. *Art Matters.* Cambridge, MA: Harvard University Press, 2001.

Brantl, J. "An den Grenzen des guten Geschmacks? Gedanken zum Orgien Mysterion Theater von Hermann Nitsch." *Das Munster* 4 (1997): 368–376.

Bren, L. "Cloning: Revolution of Evolution in Animal Production." *FDA Consumer*, May–June 2003. http://www.fda.gov/fdac/features/2003/303_clone.html (accessed March 18, 2006).

Breton, A. *Manifestoes of Surrealism.* Ann Arbor, MI: University of Michigan Press, 1972.

Bridges, W. *Gathering of Animals: An Unconventional History of the New York Zoological Society.* New York: Harper and Row, 1974.

Brightwell, L. *The Zoo Story.* London: Museum Press, 1952.

Broad, W. "It's Sensitive. Really. The Storied Narwhal Begins to Yield the Secrets of Its Tusk." *New York Times*, December 13, 2005, D1, D4.

Budiansky, S. *The Covenant of the Wild: Why Animals Chose Domestication.* New Haven: Yale University Press, 1992.

Bulbeck, C. "Facing the Wild: Ecotourism, Conservation & Animal Encounters." London: Earthscan, 2005.

Bulliet, R. *Hunters, Herders, and Hamburgers: The Past and Future of Human–Animal Relationships.* New York: Columbia University, 2005.

Burkert, W. *Creation of the Sacred: Tracks of Biology in Early Religion.* Cambridge, MA: Harvard University Press, 1996.

Burt, J. *Animals in Film.* London: Reaktion, 2002.

Burt, J. *Rat.* London: Reaktion, 2006.

Carlson, L. *Cattle: An Information Social History.* Chicago: Ivan R Dee, 2001.

Chipp, H. "Guernica: Love, War, and the Bullfight." *Art Journal* 33 (1973–1974): 103.

Chipp, H. *Picasso's Guernica: History, Transformations, Meanings.* Berkeley: University of California Press, 1988.

Chipp, H. *Theories of Modern Art: A Source Book by Artists and Critics.* Berkeley: University of California Press, 1968.

Choi, H. "Koreans Honor Dead Lab Animals (Who Knows—They May Return)." *Wall Street Journal*, November 10 1998, 1.

Clarke, A. "Research Materials and Reproductive Science in the United States, 1910–1940." In *Physiology in the American Context, 1850–1940*, edited by G. Geison. Bethesda, MD: American Physiological Society, 1987. pp. 323–350.

Clutton-Brock, J. *A Natural History of Domesticated Mammals.* Cambridge: Cambridge University Press, 1987.

Clutton-Brock, J. "The Unnatural World: Behavioral Aspects of Humans and Animals in the Process of Domestication." In *Animals and Human Society: Changing Perspectives*, edited by A. Manning and J. Serpell. New York: Routledge, 1994.

Coe, S., and M. Coe. *Meat: Animals and Industry*, Vancouver: Gallerie, 1991.

Colin, M. "Elite Meat." *Christian Science Monitor*, July 14, 2003.

Commoner, Barry. *The Closing Circle: Nature, Man, and Technology.* New York: Random House, 1971.

Consentino, D. "Hip-Hop Assemblage: The Chris Offili Affair." *African Arts* 33 (2000): 40–51, 95–96.

Cormack, M. *Champion Animals: Sculptures by Herbert Heseltine.* Richmond: Virginia Museum of Fine Arts, 1996.

Cox, N., and D. Povey. *A Picasso Bestiary.* Academy Editions: London, 1995.

Crowcroft, P. *The Zoo.* Milson's Point, New South Wales: Mathews/Hutchinson, 1978.

Crowther, P. *Art and Embodiment: From Aesthetics to Self-Consciousness.* Oxford: Clarendon Press, 1993.

Curl, J. *Oxford Dictionary of Architecture.* Oxford: Oxford University Press. 1999.

Daly, B., and L. Morton. "Children with Pets Do Not Show A Higher Empathy: A Challenge to Current Views." *Anthrozoos* 16, no. 4 (2003): 298–314.

Davis, S., and M. DeMello. *Stories Rabbits Tell: A Natural and Cultural History of a Misunderstood Creature.* New York: Lantern Press, 2003.

DeHaan, C., T. Van Veen, B. Brandenburg, and J. Gauthier, eds. *Livestock Development: Implications for Rural Poverty, the Environment, and Global Food Security*. Washington, DC: World Bank Publications, 2001.

Deleuze, G. *Francis Bacon: The Logic of Sensation*. New York: Continuum, 2005.

Deleuze, G., and F. Guattari. *A Thousand Plateaus*. Vol. 2, *Capitalism and Schizophrenia*, translated by B. Massumi. Minneapolis: University of Minnesota Press, 1987.

Derrida, J. "And Say the Animal Responded?" Translated by D. Wills. In *Zoontologies*, edited by C. Wolfe. Minneapolis: University of Minnesota Press, 2003.

Derrida, J. "The Animal That Therefore I Am (More to Follow)." Translated by D. Wills. In *Critical Inquiry* 28, no. 2 (Winter 2002): 373–374.

Diamond, J. *Guns, Germs and Steel: The Fate of Human Societies*. New York: W.W. Norton, 1999.

Dierking, L., K. Burtnyk, K. Buchner, and J. Falk. "Visitor Learning in Zoos and Aquariums: Executive Summary." Silver Spring, MD: American Zoo Association, 2006. http://www.aza.org/ConEd/MIRP/Documents/VisitorLearningExecutiveSummary. pdf (accessed June 1, 2007).

Dizard, J. *Mortal Stakes: Hunters and Hunting in Contemporary America*. Amherst: University of Massachusetts Press, 2003.

Donovan, J. "Animal Rights and Feminist Theory." In *Beyond Animal Rights*, edited by J. Donovan and C. Adams. New York: Continuum, 1996.

Donovan, J. "Attention to Suffering." In *Beyond Animal Rights*, edited by J. Donovan and C. Adams. New York: Continuum, 1996.

Durozoi, G. *History of the Surrealist Movement*. Chicago: University of Chicago Press, 2002.

Ebong, I. "Negritude: Between Mask and Flag—Senegalese Cultural Ideology and the École de Dakar." In *Reading the Contemporary: African Art from Theory to the Marketplace*, edited by O. Oguibe and O. Enwezor. London: IVA, 1999, pp. 129–143.

"The English Craze for Mice." *Reader's Digest* 30 (March 1937), 19.

Erickson, K. "Beef in a Box: Killing cattle on the High Plains." In *Companion Animals and Us: Exploring the Relationships between People & Pets*, edited by A. Podberscek, E. Paul, and J. Serpell. Cambridge: Cambridge University Press, 2000.

Ernst, M. *Max Ernst: Beyond Painting and Other Writings by the Artist and his Friends*. New York: Wittenborn, Schultz, 1948.

"First Pet Clone is a Cat." *BBC News Online*, February 15, 2002. http://news.bbc. co.uk/1/hi/sci/tech/1820749.stm (accessed September 9, 2003).

Fisher, J. *Zoos of the World*. London: Aldus, 1966.

de Fontenay, E. *Le silence des bêtes: La philosophie à l'épreuve de l'animalité*. Paris: Fayard, 1998.

Foreman, C. "Animal Cloning: New Issues in Public Policy." Remarks at the FDA/PIFB Workshop on Animal Cloning & Production of Food Products, Dallas, September 26, 2002.

Foster, H., R. Krauss, Y. Bois, and B. Buchloh. *Art since 1900: Modernism, Antimodernism, Postmodernism*. London: Thames and Hudson, 2004.

Franklin, A. *Animals and Modern Cultures: A Sociology of Human-Animal Relations in Modernity*. London: Sage Publications, 1999.

Franklin, A. "Neo-Darwinian Leisures, the Body and Nature: Hunting and Angling in Modernity." *Body and Society* 7, no. 4 (2001): 57–76.

Franklin, S. "Dolly Mixtures: Capitalisation of the Germplasm." In *Genetic Nature-Culture*, edited by A. Goodman, D. Heath, and S. Lindee, Berkeley: University of California Press, 2003, pp. 221–245.

Franklin, S. *Embodied Progress: A Cultural Account of Assisted Reproduction*. New York: Routledge, 1997.

Franklin, S. "Ethical Biocapital: New Strategies of Cell Culture." In *Remaking Life and Death: Towards an Anthropology of the Biosciences*, edited by S. Franklin and M. Lock. Sante Fe, NM: School of American Research Press, 2003, pp. 97–128.

Franklin, S. "Life Itself: Global Nature and the Genetics Imaginary." In *Global Nature, Global Culture*, edited by S. Franklin, C. Lury, and J. Stacey. London: Sage, 2000, pp. 188–227.

Frazer, J. *The New Golden Bough: A New Abridgement of the Classic Work*. Edited by T. Gaster. New York: Criterion, 1959.

Fromm, E. *The Anatomy of Human Destructiveness*. Harmondsworth, UK: Penguin Books, 1990.

Fukuyama, F. *Our Posthuman Future: Consequences of the Biotechnology Revolution*. New York: Picador, 2002.

Gambrell, J. "The Best and the Worst of Times." *Art in America* (November 1992): 54.

Gilligan, C. *In a Different Voice*. Cambridge, MA: Harvard University Press, 1982.

Glancey, J. "Waddling Off: Penguins Moved from Listed Pool." *The Guardian*, July 3, 2004, 10.

Goodman, J. "Zhou Chunya: Heading Neither East nor West." In *Chinese Art at the Crossroads: Between Past and Future, Between East and West*, edited by W. Hung. London: Institute of International Visual Arts, 2001.

Gorman, G. "Down on the Pharm: Agribusiness in the 21st Century." *Nutrition Health Review* (Winter 2002): http://www.encyclopedia.com/doc/1G1-99292185.html (accessed May 31, 2007).

Grier, K. "'The Eden of Home': Changing Understandings of Cruelty and Kindness to Animals in Middle-Class American Households, 1820–1900." In *Animals in Human Histories*, edited by M. Henninger-Voss. Rochester, NY: University of Rochester Press, 2002.

Grimassi, R. *The Witch's Familiar: Spiritual Partnership for Successful Magic*. St. Paul, MN: Llewellyn, 2003.

Grisham, J. "Pigs Cloned for First Time." *Nature Biotechnology* 18, no. 365 (2000): 365.

Grohmann, J. *Apollo Smintheus und die bedeutung der mause in der mythologie der Indogermanen*. Prague: J.C. Calve, 1862.

de Gubermatis, A. *Zoological Mythology, or the Legends of the Animals*. 1872. Reprint, Detroit: Singing Tree Press, 1968.

Guerrini, A. "The Ethics of Animal Experimentation in Seventeenth-Century England." *Journal of the History of Ideas* 50, no. 3 (1989): 391–407.

Guerrini, A. *Experimenting with Humans and Animals: From Galen to Animal Rights*. Baltimore: Johns Hopkins University Press, 2003.

Guillery, P. *The Buildings of London Zoo*. London: Royal Commission on the Historical Monuments of England, 1993.

Gura, S. "Losing Livestock, Losing Livelihoods." *Seedling Magazine*, January 2003, 8–12.

Hagenbeck, C. *Beasts and Men*. Translated by H. Elliott and A. Thacker. London: Longmans, Green, 1910.

Hamlyn, P. *African Mythology*. London: Geoffrey Parrinder, 1967.

Hammerton-Kelly, R., ed. *Violent Origins: Ritual Killing and Cultural Formation*. Stanford: Stanford University Press, 1987.

Hammond, N. *Modern Wildlife Painting*, Mountfield, UK: Pica Press, 1998.

Hammond, N. *Twentieth Century Wildlife Artists*. London: Croom Helm, 1986.

Hammond, P. *L'Age d'Or*. London: BFI, 1997.

Hancocks, D. *Animals and Architecture*. London: Evelyn, 1971.

Hancocks, D. *A Different Nature: The Paradoxical World of Zoos and Their Uncertain Future*. Berkeley: University of California Press, 2001.

Hancocks, D. "Zoological Gardens, Arboreta, Botanical Gardens: A Trilogy of Failure?" Paper presented at the National Conference of the American Association of Botanical Gardens and Arboreta, Pasadena, California, June 15–19, 1994.

Hansen, B. "American's First Medical Breakthrough: How Popular Excitement about a French Rabies Cure in 1885 Raised New expectations for Medical Progress." *American Historical Review*, 103 no. 2 (April 1998): 373–418.

Haraway, D. "Alpha Bitches On-Line: The Dog Genome for the Next Genderation." Lecture presented at the IV European Feminist Research Conference, *Body Gender Subjectivity. Crossing Borders of Disciplines and Institutions*. Bologna, Italy, September 28–October 1, 2000. http://www.women.it/cyberarchive/files/haraway.html (accessed March 18, 2006).

Haraway, D. "Cloning Mutts, Saving Tigers: Ethical Emergents in Technocultural Dog Worlds." In *Remaking Life and Death: Toward an Anthropology of the Biosciences*, edited by S. Franklin and M. Lock. Sante Fe: School of American Research Press, 2003, pp. 293–328.

Haraway, D. *Modest Witness @ Second_Millenium.FemaleManMeets Oncomouse*™: *Feminism and Technoscience*. New York: Routledge, 1997.

Harriman, M. *House Rabbit Handbook*. Alameda, CA: Drollery Press, 1985.

Hart, J. "Transcendental Phenomenology and the Eco-Community." In *Animal Others*, edited by H. Steeves. Albany: State University of New York Press, 1999.

Hartland, E. *The Science of Fairy Tales: An Inquiry into Fairy Mythology*. London: Scott, 1891.

Hediger, H. *Studies of the Psychology and Behaviour of Captive Animals in Zoos and Circuses*. Translated by G. Sircom. London: Butterworth, 1955.

Hediger, H. *Wild Animals in Captivity: An Outline of the Biology of Zoological Gardens*. Translated by G. Sircom. London: Butterworth, 1950.

Hendrickson, R. *More Cunning than Man: A Social History of Rats and Men*. New York: Dorset Press, 1988.

Herbert, M. "Old Dogs—New Tricks." *Art Review* (June 2000).

Hesiod. *Theogony, Works and Days*. Translated by M. L. West. New York: Oxford University Press, 1991.

de Heusch, L. *Sacrifice in Africa: A Structuralist Approach*. Manchester: Manchester University Press, 1985.

Heyer, P. *American Architecture: Ideas and Ideologies in the Late Twentieth Century*. New York: Wiley, 1993.

Hill, M. *Bruno Liljefors: The Peerless Eye*. Hull, UK: Allen Publishing Co, 1987.

Hirst, D., and G. Burn. *On the Way to Work*. London: Faber, 2001.

Holthof, M. "To the Realm of Fables: The Animal Fables from Mesopotamia to Disneyland." Translated by Milt Papatheophanes. In *Zoology on (Post) Modern Animals*, edited by B. Verschaffel and M. Vermick. Dublin: Liliput Press, 1993, pp. 37–55.

Hornaday, W. T. *The Minds and Manners of Wild Animals: A Book of Personal Observations*. New York: Kessinger, 1922.

"House Mice Indicated as Nerve Disease Carriers." *Science News Letter* 35 (1939): 329.

Humphrey, F. T. "Serious Plague of Mice in California." *Scientific American* 136 (1927): 330–331.

Hunter, S. *Marino Marini: The Sculpture*. New York: Abrams, 1993.

Huxley, A. *Brave New World: A Novel*. New York: Harpers, 1932.

Ingold, T. "From Trust to Domination: An Alternative History of Human–Animal Relations." In *Animals and Human Society: Changing Perspectives*, edited by A. Manning and J. Serpell. London: Routledge, 1994.

Irvine, L. *If You Tame Me: Understanding Our Connection with Animals*. Philadelphia: Temple University Press, 2004.

Jaschinski, B. *Wild Things*. London: powerHouse, 2003.

Jaschinski, B. *Zoo*. London: Phaidon, 1996.

Johnson, R. "White Mice." *Nature Magazine* 13 (1929): 48–50.

Johnson, S. *Emergence: The Connected Lives of Ants, Brains, Cities and Software*. New York: Simon and Schuster, 2002.

Jones & Jones. *Woodland Park Zoo: Long Range Plan, Development Guidelines and Exhibit Scenarios*. Seattle: Department of Parks and Recreation, 1976.

Keeler, C. "In Quest of Apollo's Sacred White Mice." *Scientific Monthly* 34 (January 1932): 48–53.

Keeler, C. *The Laboratory Mouse: Its Origin, Heredity and Culture*. Cambridge, MA: Harvard University Press, 1931.

Kiley, K. "Copy This: Livestock Cloning Faces an Uneasy Public." *Consumer Markets Insider*. November 14, 2005.

Klein, J. *The Biology of the Histocompatibility-2 Complex of the Mouse*. New York: Springer-Verlag, 1975.

Knight, W. "Dolly the Sheep Dies Young." *New Scientist*, 17 (February 14, 2003), p. 56.

Kohler, R. *Lords of the Fly: Drosophila Genetics and the Experimental Life*. Chicago: University of Chicago Press, 1994.

Kolata, G. "Studies on a Mouse Hormone Bear On Fatness in Humans." *New York Times*, April 2, 2004, p. 1.

Krauss, R. *The Optical Unconscious*. Cambridge, MA: MIT Press, 1993.

Kwon, M. "In Conversation with *Mark Dion*." In *Mark Dion*, edited by L. Corrin, M. Kwon, and N. Bryson. London: Phaidon, 1997.

Kwon, M. "Unnatural Tendencies: Scientific Guises of Mark Dion." In *Natural History and Other Fictions—An Exhibition by Mark Dion*. Birmingham, UK: Ikon Gallery, 1997.

Lankheit, K. *Franz Marc: Watercolours, Drawings, Writings*. London: Thames and Hudson, 1960.

Lanza, R., J. Cibelli, D. Faber, R. Sweeney, B. Henderson, W. Nevala, M. West, and P. Wettstein. "Cloned Cattle Can Be Healthy and Normal." *Science* 294, no. 5546 (November 16, 2001): 1459–1462.

Lanza, R., B. Dresser, and P. Damiani. "Cloning Noah's Ark." *Scientific American* (November 2000): 84–89.

Larson, N. *Walt Disney: An American Original*. Mankato, MN: Creative Education, 1974.

Lawrence, C. "Cinema Vérité?: The Image of William Harvey's Experiments in 1928."
    In *Vivisection in Historical Perspective*, edited by N. Rupke. London: Routledge,
    1990, pp. 295–313.

Lederer, S. "The Controversy Over Animal Experimentation in American, 1880–1914."
    In *Vivisection in Historical Perspective*, edited by N. Rupke. London: Routledge,
    1990, pp. 236–258.

Lederer, S. "Political Animals: The Shaping of Biomedical Research Literature in Twen-
    tieth Century America." *Isis* 83 (1992): 61–79.

Ledo, A. "Intimate Traces." *Lapiz* 23 (2004): 48–63.

Leepa, A. *The Challenge of Modern Art*. London: Peter Owen, 1957.

Lemonick, M. "Smart Genes?" *Time* 154, no. 11. September 13, 1999, 54–59.

Leopold, A. "Thinking Like a Mountain." *A Sand County Almanac: And Sketches Here
    and There*. New York: Oxford University Press, 1968, pp. 129–132.

Leppert, R. *Art and the Committed Eye: The Cultural Functions of Imagery*. Boulder,
    CO: Westview Press, 1996.

Leung, S., and J. Kaplan. "Pseudo-Languages: A Conversation with Wendu Gu, Xu
    Bing, and Jonathan Hay." *Art Journal* 58 (1999): 93.

Lévi-Strauss, C. *The Raw and the Cooked*. Translated by J. Weightman and D. Weight-
    man. New York: Harper and Row, 1969.

Lévi-Strauss, C. *The Savage Mind*, Translated by J. Weightman and D. Weightman.
    Chicago: University of Chicago Press, 1966.

Lévi-Strauss, C. *Totemism*. Translated by R. Needham. Boston: Beacon Press, 1963.

Levinas, E. "Interview." In *The Provocation of Levinas*, edited by R. Bernasconi and
    D. Wood. London: Routledge, 1988.

Levinas, E. "The Name of a Dog, or Natural Rights." In *Animal Philosophy: Ethics and
    Identity,* edited by P. Atterton and M. Calarco. London: Continuum, 2004.

Levine, F. *The Apocalyptic Vision: The Art of Franz Marc as German Expressionism*.
    New York: Harper and Row, 1979.

Levine, F. "The Iconography of Franz Marc's Fate of the Animals." *The Art Bulletin*
    58 (1976): 269.

Lewis, C. "A New Kind of Fish Food: The Coming of Biotech Animals." *FDA Con-
    sumer,* January–February 2001. http://www.fda.gov/fdac/features/2001/101_fish.
    html (accessed March 18, 2006).

Lisboa, M. *Paula Rego's Map of Memory: National and Sexual Politics*. Aldershot, UK:
    Ashgate, 2003.

Little, C. "A New Deal For Mice: Why Mice Are Used in Research on Human Dis-
    eases." *Scientific American* 152 (1937): 16–18.

Lombardo, P. "Eugenic Sterilization Laws." Essay for the Human Genome Project
    Eugenics Archive, 2003. http://www.eugenicsarchive.org/html/eugenics/essay8text.
    html (accessed May 31, 2007).

Lombardo, P. "Miscegenation, Eugenics and Racism: Historical Footnotes to Loving v.
    Virginia." *University of California Davis Law Review*, 21 (1988): 421–452.

Lomborg, B. *The Skeptical Environmentalist: Measuring the Real State of the World*.
    Cambridge: Cambridge University Press, 2001.

Lui, X. "Globalism or Nationalism: Cai Guoqiang, Zhang Huan, and Xu Bing in New
    York." *Third Text* 18 (2004): 288–289.

Mackay, J. *The Animaliers: The Animal Sculptors of the 19th and 20th Centuries*. Lon-
    don: Ward Lock, 1973.

Malamud, R. *Poetic Animals and Animal Souls*. New York: Palgrave, 2003.

Malamud, R. *Reading Zoos: Representations of Animals and Captivity*. New York: New York University Press, 1998.

Malriey, P. *Le Bestiare Insolite:* L'Animal *dans la Tradition, le Mythe, le Rêve*. Realmont, France: Editions la Duralie, 1987.

Mamet, D. *The Village*. London: Faber and Faber, 1994.

Maple, T. "Strategic Collection Planning and Individual Animal Welfare." *Journal of the American Veterinary Medical Association* 223, no. 7 (October 2003): 967.

Marchesini, R. *Post-human: Verso nuovi modelli di esistenza*. Turin, Italy: Bollati Boringhieri, 2002.

Marcolescou, I. "'I Am a Transmitter, I Radiate,' Joseph Beuys." *Scultpure* 24 (2005): 53–54.

Margulis, L., and D. Sagan. *Microcosmos: Four Billion Years of Microbial Evolution*. New York: Touchstone, 1991.

Marvin, G. *Bullfight*. Oxford: Blackwell, 1988.

Marvin, G. "Natural Instincts and Cultural Passions: Transformations and Performances in Foxhunting." *Performance Research* 5, no. 2 (2000): 108–115.

Marvin, G. "Wild Killing: Contesting the Animal in Hunting." In *Killing Animals*, edited by The Animal Studies Group. Urbana: University of Illinois Press, 2006.

Matilsky, B. *Fragile Ecologies: Contemporary Artists' Interpretations and Solutions*. New York: Rizzoli, 1992.

McDowell, N. "Mini-Pig Clone Raises Transplant Hope." *New Scientist* 16, no. 35 (January 13, 2003). Online only at www.newscientist.com/article.ns?id=dn3257 (accessed May 31, 2007).

McEwen, J. *Paula Rego*. London: Phaidon, 1997.

McHugh, S. "Bitches from Brazil: Cloning and Owning Dogs through The Missyplicity Project." In *Representing Animals*, edited by N. Rothfels. Bloomington: Indiana University Press, 2002, pp. 180–198.

McLeod, C. *Pondering Nature: An Ethnography of Duck Hunting in Southern New Zealand*. Ph.D. diss., University of Otaga, Dunedin, New Zealand, 2004.

Melson, G. "Studying Children's Attachment to Their Pets: A Conceptual and Methodological Review." *Anthrozoos* 4 (1991): 91–99.

"Mice Beautiful." *Time* 30, July 19, 1937, 50.

"Mice as Disease Carriers." *Science* 69, supp. 14 (1929): 1631.

"Mickey Mouse is Eight Years Old." *Literary Digest* 122 (1936): 18–19.

"Mickey Mouse's Miraculous Movie Monkey-Shines." *The Literary Digest* 6 (1930): 36–37.

Midgley, M. *Animals and Why They Matter*. Athens: University of Georgia Press, 1983.

Mighetto, L. *Wild Animals and American Environmental Ethics*. Tucson: University of Arizona Press, 1991.

Mignonneau, L., and C. Sommerer. "Creating Artificial Life for Interactive Art and Entertainment." *Leonardo* 34 (2001): 303–307.

Miller, J., and L. Kimmel. *Biomedical Communications*. San Diego: Academic Press, 2001.

Milliet, J. "A Comparative Study of Women's Activities in the Domestication of Animals." In *Animals in Human Histories*, edited by M. Henninger-Voss. Rochester, NY: University of Rochester Press, 2002.

Morse, H., ed. *The Origins of Inbred Mice: Proceedings of an NIH Workshop in Bethesda, MD*. New York: Academic Press, 1978.

Motavalli, J. "The Case Against Meat." *E Magazine* 13, no. 1, January/February, 2002.

Moulton, H. "Pestilence and Mice." *Classical Review* 15 (1901): 284.

"Mouse Show." *Newsweek* 9, January 23, 1937, 40.

Mudimbe, V. "*Reprendre*: Enunciations and Strategies in Contemporary African Arts." In *Reading the Contemporary: African Art from Theory to the Marketplace*, edited by O. Oguibe and O. Enwezor. London: IVA, 1999.

Mullan, B., and G. Marvin. *Zoo Culture*. Urbana: University of Illinois Press, 1987.

Muller, H. J. "The Measurement of Gene Mutation Rate in Drosophila, Its High Variability, and Its Dependence Upon Temperature." *Genetics* 13 (July 1928): 279–357.

Munroe, M. *The Animal Image: Contemporary Objects and the Beast*. Washington, DC: Smithsonian Institution Press, 1981.

Nagel, T. "What is it Like to Be a Bat?" *Philosophical Review* 83, no. 4 (October 1974): 435–450.

National Academy of Sciences. "Animal Biotechnology: Science-Based Concerns." Committee on Defining Science-Based Concerns Associated with Products of Animal Biotechnology, Committee on Agricultural Biotechnology, Health, and the Environment, National Research Council. Washington, DC: National Academy of Sciences Press, 2002.

Nisbet, M., and B. Lewenstein. "Biotechnology and the American Media: The Policy Process and the Elite Press, 1970 to 1999." *Science Communication* 23, no. 4 (2002): 359–391.

Noddings, N. *Caring: A Feminine Approach to Ethics and Moral Education*. Berkeley: University of California Press, 1984.

Noske, B. *Beyond Boundaries: Humans and Animals*. Montreal: Black Rose Books, 1997.

Ogden, J., C. Vernon, K. Wagner. "Measuring Our Impact." In *AZA Communiqué*. Silver Spring, MD: American Zoo Association, September 2002.

Ogonuki, N., K. Inoue, Y. Yamamoto, Y. Noguchi, K. Tanemura, O. Suzuki, H. Nakayama, K. Doi, K. Ohtomo, M. Satoh, A. Nshida, and A. Ogura. "Early Death of Mice Cloned from Somatic Cells." *Nature Genetics* 30 (February 11, 2002): 253–254.

Ojoade, J. "Nigerian Cultural Attitudes to the Dog." In *Signifying Animals: Human Meaning in the Natural World*, edited by R. Willis. London: Routledge, 1994.

Olly & Suzi. *Arctic Desert Ocean Jungle*. New York: Abrams, 2003.

Oransky, I. "First Dog Cloned." *The Scientist Daily News*, August 3, 2005, http://www.the-scientist.com/article/display/22746 (accessed May 31, 2007).

Ortega y Gasset, J. *La Caza y Los Toros*. Madrid: Revista de Occidente, 1968.

Osgood, Charles. "Dog Genome." *The Osgood File*. CBS Radio Network. August 27, 2002. http://www.acfnewsource.org/science/dog_genome.html (accessed March 18, 2006).

Otto, R. *The Idea of Holy*. New York: Oxford University Press, 1958.

Paige, K., L. Clima, M. Yaremchuk, J. Vacanti, and C. Vacanti. "Injectable Cartilage." *Plastic & Reconstructive Surgery* 96 (1995): 1390–1400.

Paul, D. "The Rockefeller Foundation and the Origins of Behavior Genetics." In *The Expansion of American Biology*, edited by K. Benson, J. Maienschein, and R. Rainger. New Brunswick, NJ: Rutgers University Press, 1991, pp. 262–283.

Paul, E. "Love of Pets and Love of People." In *Companion Animals and Us: Exploring the Relationships Between People & Pets*, edited by A. Podberscek, E. Paul, and J. Serpell. Cambridge: Cambridge University Press, 2000.

Peacock, J. "Ethnographic Notes on Sacred and Profane Performance." In *By Means of Performance*, edited by R. Schechner and W. Appel. Cambridge: Cambridge University Press, 1990, pp. 208–220.

Peffer, J. "Animal Bodies/Absent Bodies: Disfigurement in Art after Soweto." *Third Text* 17 (2003): 74.

Plumwood, V. *Environmental Culture: The Ecological Crisis of Reason*. London: Routledge, 2002.

Potter, M., and R. Lieberman. "Genetics of Immunoglobulins in the Mouse." *Advances in Immunology* 7 (1967): 91.

Powell, A. "Breaking the Mold." *Landscape Architecture*, October 1997, 120–129, 145–152.

Pratchett, T. *Men at Arms: Discworld Book 15*. New York: Harper, 1993.

Pray, L. "Missyplicity Goes Commercial." *The Scientist*, November 27, 2002. http://www.the-scientist.com/news/20021127/03 (accessed December 5, 2005).

Preece, R. *Animals and Nature: Cultural Myths, Cultural Realities*. Vancouver: University of British Columbia Press, 1999.

"Produce from Cloned Cattle 'Safe.'" *BBC News*, April 12, 2005.

Pursel, V., C. Pinkert, K. Miller, D. Bolt, R. Campbell, R. Palmiter, L. Brinster, and R. Hammer. *Genetic Engineering of Livestock*. Beltsville, MD: U.S. Department of Agriculture.

Rader, K. *Making Mice: Standardizing Animals for Biomedical Research, 1900–1955*. Princeton: Princeton University Press, 2004.

Rader, K. "Of Mice, Medicine, and Genetics: C.C. Little's Creation of the Inbred Laboratory Mouse, 1909–1918." *Studies in the History and Philosophy of Biology and the Biomedical Sciences* 30, no. 3 (Spring 1999): 319–343.

Raloff, J. "Hormones: Here's the Beef." Environmental Concerns Reemerge over Steroids Given to Livestock." *Science News Online* 161, no. 1, January 5, 2002, 10.

Reed, E. "The Affordances of the Animate Environment." In *What is an Animal?*, edited by T. Ingold. London, Routledge, 1994.

Regan, T. *The Case for Animal Rights*. Berkeley: University of California Press, 1983.

Reichenbach, H. "A Tale of Two Zoos: The Hamburg Zoological Garden and Carl Hagenebeck's Tierpark." In *New Worlds, New Animals: From Menagerie to Zoological Park in the Nineteenth Century*, edited by R. Hoage and W. Deiss. Baltimore: Johns Hopkins University Press, 1996.

Richardson, J. *A Life of Picasso*. Vol. 1, *1881–1906*. London: Pimlico, 1991.

Riehl, W. *Von deutschem Land und Volk: Eine Auswahl*. Edited by P. Zaunert. Jena, Germany: Eugen Diedrichs, 1922.

Rifkin, J. *The Biotech Century: Harnessing the Gene and Remaking the World*. New York: Jeremy P. Tarcher/Putnam, 1998.

Ritvo, H. *The Animal Estate: The English and Other Creatures in Victorian England*. Cambridge, MA: Harvard University Press, 1989.

Robbins, P. "Shrines and Butchers: Animals as Deities, Capital and Meat in Contemporary North India." In *Animal Geographies: Place, Politics, and Identity in the Nature-Culture Borderlands*, edited by J. Wolch and J. Emel. London: Verso, 1998.

Roberts, A. *Animals in African Art: From the Familiar to the Marvellous*. New York: Museum of African Art, 1995.

"Rodent Control in Food Establishments." *American Journal of Public Health* 27 (1937): 62–66.

Rosenthal, M. *Franz Marc*. Munich: Prestel, 2004.

Rosenthal, M. *Joseph Beuys: Actions, Vitrines, Environments*. Houston: Menil Collection, 2004.

Rowan, A. *Of Mice, Models, and Men*. New York: State University of New York Press, 1984.

Rupke, N., ed. *Vivisection in Historical Perspective*. London: Routledge, 1990.

Rupke, N. "Pro-vivisection in England in the Early 1880s: Arguments and Motives." In *Vivisection in Historical Perspective*. London: Routledge, 1990: 188–208.

Rybczynski, W. *The Look of Architecture*. Oxford: Oxford University Press, 2001.

"Sales of Cloned Cattle Multiply." *Houston Chronicle*, November 3, 2003. http://2 09.85.165.104/search?q=cache:ho5Vt-r5kE4J:www.ofarm.org/news/oct-dec/ 11-10_1.htm (accessed May 31, 2007).

Sax, B. *Animals in the Third Reich: Pets, Scapegoats and the Holocaust*. New York: Continuum, 2001.

Sax, B. *The Frog King: On Fables, Fairy Tales, Legends and Anecdotes of Animals*. New York: Pace University Press/University Press of America, 1990.

Sax, B. "Medievalism, Paganism, and the Tower Ravens." *The Pomegranate: The International Journal of Pagan Studies*. 9, no. 1 (2007): 62–77.

Sax, B. *The Mythical Zoo: An Encyclopedia of Animals in World Myth, Legend, and Literature*. Santa Barbara, CA: ABC-CLIO, 2002.

Sax, B. *The Serpent and the Swan: Animal Brides in Literature and Folklore*. Austin: McDonald and Woodward/University of Tennessee Press, 1998.

Schechner, R. *Performance Theory*. London: Routledge, 1988.

Schieffelin, E. "Problematizing Performance." In *Ritual, Performance and Media*, edited by F. Hughes-Freeland. London: Routledge, 1998, pp. 194–207.

Schlosser, E. *Fast Food Nation: The Dark Side of the All American Meal*. New York: Harper Perennial, 2002.

Schochet, E. *Animal Life in Jewish Tradition: Attitudes and Relationships*. New York: Ktav, 1984.

Schweitzer, A. *The Animal World of Albert Schweitzer: Jungle Insights into Reverence for Life*. Translated by C. Joy. Hopewell, NJ: Ecco, 1996.

Schweitzer, A. "Man and Creature." In *The Teaching of Reverence for Life*, translated by R. Winston and C. Winston. New York: Holt, Rinehart and Winston, 1965.

Scott, J., and J. Fuller. *Genetics and the Social Behavior of the Dog*. Chicago: University of Chicago Press, 1965.

Secord, J. "Nature's Fancy: Charles Darwin and the Breeding of Pigeons." *Isis* 72 (June 2, 1991): 163–186.

Seidensticker, J., and J. Doherty. "Integrating Animal Behavior and Exhibit Design." In *Wild Mammals in Captivity: Principles and Techniques*, edited by D. Kleiman, M. Allen, K. Thompson, and S. Lumpkin. Chicago: University of Chicago Press, 1996.

Serpell, J. *In the Company of Animals: A Study of Human-Animal Relationships*. Cambridge: Cambridge University Press, 1986.

Serpell, J., and E. Paul. "Pets and the Development of Positive Attitudes to Animals." In *Animals and Human Society: Changing Perspectives*, edited by A. Manning and J. Serpell. London: Routledge, 1994.

Shepard, P. *The Others: How Animals Made Us Human*. Washington, DC: Shearwater, 1996.

Sherwin, A. "Single Birds End the Tea Party for PG Chimps." *The Sunday Times* (London), December 1, 2001.

Silver, L. "Thinking Twice, or Thrice, About Cloning." In *The Cloning Sourcebook*, edited by A. Klotzko. Oxford: Oxford University, 2001, pp. 60–63.

Silverstein, H. *Unleashing Rights: Law, Meaning, and the Animal Rights Movement.* Ann Arbor: University of Michigan Press, 1996.

Singer, P. *Animal Liberation,.* St. Paul: Ecco Books, 2001.

Slater, D. "Humouse™." *Legal Affairs*, November/December 2002, p. 1.

Slicer, D. "Your Daughter or Your Dog?" In *Ecological Feminist Philosophies*, edited by K. Warren. Bloomington, IN: Indiana University Press, 1996.

Smith, Z. *White Teeth.* New York: Random House, 2000.

Solans, P. "Horror and Animality." *Lapiz* 23 (2004): 38–40.

Spies, W. *Max Ernst Loplop: The Artist's Other Self.* London: Thames and Hudson, 1983.

The Staff of the Jackson Laboratory. *The Biology of the Laboratory Mouse.* New York: McGraw Hill, 1966.

Stokvis, W. *Cobra: An International Movement in Art after the Second World War.* New York Rizzoli, 1988.

Strachan, W. *Henry Moore: Animals.* London: Aurum Press, 1983.

Streatfield, D. "Regionalism in Landscape Design." In *Jones & Jones: Ideas Migrate, Places Resonate*, edited by K. Kobayashi. Tokyo: Process Architecture, 1995, p. 20.

Strehlow, H. "Zoos and Aquariums of Berlin." In *New Worlds, New Animals: From Menagerie to Zoological Park in the Nineteenth Century,* edited by R. Hoage and W. Deiss. Baltimore: Johns Hopkins University Press, 1996.

Sunstein, C., and M. Nussbaum, eds. *Animal Rights: Current Debates and New Directions.* Oxford: Oxford University Press, 2004.

Sylvester, D. *Interviews with Francis Bacon 1962–1979.* London: Thames and Hudson, 1980.

Tennenbaum, S., and J. Zapata. *The Jewelled Menagerie: The World of Animals in Gems.* London: Thames and Hudson, 2001.

Tisdall, C. *Joseph Beuys Coyote.* Munich: Schirmer Mosel, 1976.

Todes, D. "Pavlov's Physiology Factory." *Isis* 88 (1997): 205–246.

Todes, D. *Pavlov's Physiology Factory: Experiment, Interpretation, Laboratory Enterprise.* Baltimore: Johns Hopkins University Press, 2002.

Thompson, C. "Strategic Naturalizing: Kinship in an Infertility Clinic." In *Relative Values: Reconfiguring Kinship Studies*, edited by S. Franklin and S. McKinnon. Durham, NC: Duke University Press, 2001, pp. 175–202.

Thurston, M. *The Lost History of the Canine Race.* New York: Andrews McMeel Publishing, 1996.

Travis, J. "Cloning Hearing Creates Media Frenzy." *Science News* 160, no. 7 (August 18, 2001): 105.

Tuan, Y. *Dominance and Affection: The Making of Pets.* New Haven: Yale University Press, 1984.

Tudge, C. *The Day Before Yesterday: Five Million Years of Human History.* London: Cape, 1995.

Turkle, S. *Life on the Screen: Identity in the Age of the Internet.* New York: Touchstone, 1995.

Tylor, W. *The Origins of Culture.* New York: Harper and Row, 1958.

Uexküll, J. *Instinctive Behavior: The Development of a Modern Concept.* Translated by C. Schiller. New York: International Universities Press, 1957.

Ufkes, F. "Building a Better Pig: Fat Profits in Lean Meat." In *Animal Geographies: Place, Politics, and Identity in the Nature-Culture Borderlands*, edited by J. Wolch and J. Emel. London: Verso, 1998.

USDA Agricultural Research Service. National Program Annual Report, 1998.

Vegetarian Resource Group, Roper Poll. "How Many Vegetarians Are There?" *Vegetarian Journal* 16, no. 5 (September/October 1997): 21–22.

Vetlesen, A. *Perception, Empathy, and Judgment*. State College, PA: Pennsylvania State University Press, 1994.

Vischer, T., ed. *Mark Wallinger: Lost Horizon*. Basel, Switzerland: Museum für Gegenwartskunst, 2000.

Wade, N. "Of Smart Mice and an Even Smarter Man." *New York Times*, Science Times, September 7, 1999.

Wadman, M. "U.S. Lab Animals May Win in Lawsuit." *Nature* 407 (2000): 549.

Walter, N. "What Sort of Man Designs a Penguin House That Children Can't Even See Into?" *The Observer* (London), September 22, 1996, 9.

Wang, V. "Animal Games." In *Chinese Art at the Crossroads: Between Past and Future, Between East and West*, edited by W. Hung. London: Institute of International Visual Arts, 2001: 195–199.

Wansborough, R. "Cosmetic Tail Docking of Dogs' Tails." *Australian Veterinary Journal* 74, no. 1 (July 1996): 59–63.

Weise, E. "Organic Chicken May Not Be All It's Cut Out To Be." *USA Today*, February 26, 2003.

Weiss, R. "Cloned Cows' Milk, Beef Up to Standard: Researchers Find No Significant Differences with Products of Conventionally Raised Cattle." *Washington Post*, April 12, 2005, A3.

Wheen, F. *How Mumbo-Jumbo Conquered the World: A Short History of Modern Delusions*. London: Fourth Estate, 2004.

Wilkinson, A. *Henry Moore's Animals*. Toronto: Art Gallery of Ontario, 1990.

Wilmut, I., A. E. Schnieke, J. McWhir, A. J. Kind, and K. H. S. Campbell. "Viable Offspring Derived from Fetal and Adult Mammalian Cells." *Nature* 385 (February 27, 1997): 810.

Wilmut, I. K. Campbell, and C. Tudge. *Second Creation: Dolly and the Age of Biological Control*. New York: Farrar, Strauss, and Giroux, 2000, pp. 20–21, 30–32.

Wilson, E. and C. Michener. "Alfred Edwards Emerson." In *Biographical Memoirs*. Washington, DC: National Academy of Sciences, 1982, p. 164.

Winstead, E. "Endangered Wild Sheep Clone Reported to be Healthy." *Genome News Network* 12 (October 2001), http://www.genomenewsnetwork.org/articles/10_01/cloned_sheep.shtml (accessed March 18, 2006).

Wischnitzer, R. "Picasso's *Guernica*: A Matter of Metaphor." *Artibus et Historiae* 6 (1985): 153–172.

Wolfe, C. *Animal Rites: American Culture, the Discourse of Species, and Posthumanist Theory*. Chicago: University of Chicago Press, 2003.

Woods, G. L., K. White, D. Vanderwall, G. Li, K. Aston, T. Bunch, L. Meerdo, and B. Pate. "A Mule Cloned from Fetal Cells by Nuclear Transfer." *Science* 301, no. 5636 (August 22, 2003): 1063.

Worster, D. *Nature's Economy: A History of Ecological Ideas*. New York: Cambridge University Press, 1994.

Wyschogrod, E. "Does Continental Ethics Have a Future?" In *Ethics and Danger*, edited by A. Dallery, C. Scott, and P. Roberts. Albany, NY: State University of New York Press, 1992.

Zapata, J. *The Jewelry and Enamels of Louis Comfort Tiffany*. London: Thames and Hudson, 1993.

Zeuner, F. *A History of Domesticated Animals*. New York: Harper and Row, 1963.

Zhou, Q., J.-P. Renard, G. Friec, V. Brochard, N. Beaujean, Y. Cherifi, A. Fraichard, and J. Cozzi. "Generation of fertile cloned rats using controlled timing of oocyte activation." *Science* 302, no. 1179 (2003).

Zitner, A. "Patently Provoking a Debate." *Los Angeles Times*, May 12, 2002, A1.

Zuckerman, S. *The Social Life of Monkeys and Apes*. London: Routledge and Kegan Paul, 1932.

NOTES ON CONTRIBUTORS

Ralph R. Acampora, associate professor of philosophy at Hofstra University, teaches in the areas of applied ethics and history of (especially modern) philosophy. He conducts research in the fields of environmental philosophy, bioethics, and animal studies. He has authored *Corporal Compassion: Animal Ethics and Philosophy of Body* (University of Pittsburgh Press, 2006), coedited *A Nietzschean Bestiary* (Rowman and Littlefield, 2004), and is an associate editor of the "Animal Theory" section of *Society and Animals.*

Jonathan Burt is a freelance writer who lives in Cambridge, England. He is the author of *Animals in Film* (Reaktion, 2002) and *Rat* (Reaktion, 2006), as well as general editor of the Reaktion Animal series that features detailed cultural and historical monographs on individual animals. He works with the Animal Studies Group (UK) promoting the study of animals in the humanities. His current book project is on animals and the environment in the First World War.

Margo DeMello holds a Ph.D. in cultural anthropology and currently lectures at Central New Mexico Community College, teaching sociology, cultural studies, and anthropology. Her publications include *Bodies of Inscription: A Cultural History of the Modern Tattoo Community* (Duke University Press, 2000), *Stories Rabbits Tell: A Natural and Cultural History of a Misunderstood Beast* (Lantern, 2003), *Why Animals Matter: The Case for Animal Protection* (Prometheus, 2007), and *Encyclopedia of Body Adornment* (Greenwood, 2007). She is also active in animal protection, volunteering primarily for House Rabbit Society, a rabbit advocacy organization.

David Hancocks is a registered member of the Royal Institute of British Architects, and is involved in various natural-history based planning projects around the world. Although he never visited a zoo as a child, he became involved with them after graduating from the University of Bath to improve the living conditions for the animals and the learning environment for zoo visitors. He has written *A Different Nature: The Paradoxical World of Zoos and Their Uncertain Future* (University of California Press, 2001) and *Animals and Architecture* (H. Evelyn, 1971).

Britta Jaschinski, whose work appears on the cover of this volume, is a photographer based in London. Her books are *Zoo* (Phaidon, 1996) and *Wild Things* (powerHouse, 2003).

Randy Malamud is professor of English at Georgia State University. He has written *Reading Zoos: Representations of Animals and Captivity* (Macmillan/ New York University Press, 1998) and *Poetic Animals and Animal Souls* (Palgrave, 2003). He is on the editorial boards of *Society & Animals* and Brill's Human-Animal Studies book series, and he is a patron of The Captive Animals' Protection Society (UK). He is a frequent collaborator with Britta Jaschinski.

Garry Marvin has lectured in anthropology at the Universities of East Anglia, St. Andrews and Swansea. He joined Roehampton University in 1996. He has worked as a researcher and producer for television documentary programs and has made films on religious movements in India, American football, Chinese exercise systems, social and cultural change in Spain, and suicides in the River Thames. The main focus of his research is human–animal relationships; he has written on bullfighting, cockfighting, and zoos. He is the author of *Bullfight* (University of Illinois Press, 1994) and, with Bob Mullan, *Zoo Culture* (Weidenfeld and Nicolson, 1987).

Karen A. Rader is the director of the Science, Technology, and Society (STS) Initiative and associate professor in the Department of History at Virginia Commonwealth University. She is the author of *Making Mice: Standardizing Animals for American Biomedical Research* (Princeton University Press, 2004), and is currently working on a history of life science displays in American science museums.

Boria Sax has published many books including *Animals in the Third Reich* (Continuum, 2000), *Mythical Zoo* (ABC-Clio, 2002), *Crow* (Reaktion, 2003), and, most recently, *Stealing Fire* (Ad Infinitum, 2007). He lives with his wife in White Plains, New York, and teaches a course, "Animals and Human Civilization," online for the State University of Illinois at Springfield. He is founder of the organization Nature in Legend and Story (NILAS).

INDEX